THE LAST ADVENTURE

THE LAST ADVENTURE

FOREWORD

To celebrate the turn of the century and the new millennium, **THE EVENTFUL CENTURY** series presents the vast panorama of the last hundred years – a century which has witnessed the transition from horse-drawn transport to space travel, and from the first telephones to the information superhighway.

THE EVENTFUL CENTURY chronicles epoch-making events like the outbreak of the two world wars, the Russian Revolution and the rise and fall of communism. But major events are only part of this glittering kaleidoscope. It also describes the everyday background – the way people lived, how they worked, what they ate and drank, how much they earned, the way they spent their leisure time, the books they read, and the crimes, scandals and unsolved mysteries that set them talking. Here are fads and crazes like the Hula-Hoop and Rubik's Cube . . . fashions like the New Look and the miniskirt . . . breakthroughs in entertainment, such as the birth of the movies . . . medical milestones such as the discovery of penicillin . . . and marvels of modern architecture and engineering.

THE LAST ADVENTURE describes a century of journeys of exploration, made by those with the inappeasable ambition to find out what lies beyond the horizon. In 1900, many parts of the world, including the desert wastes of North Africa, the rain forests of the Amazon and the icy expanse of the Antarctic, remained unexplored and unmapped. One by one, the secrets of these unknown places and many more were revealed, from the Mountains of the Moon in Africa to the wastes of Outer Mongolia, from the North Pole to the jungles of Papua New Guinea. Captain Robert Scott and Roald Amundsen raced to the South Pole. Edmund Hillary and Tenzing Norgay climbed Mount Everest. Charles Lindbergh made the first non-stop solo flight across the Atlantic. And Jacques Cousteau explored the secrets of the seabed. Throughout the century, intrepid men and women have set off on foot, on camels, in the early motor cars or flimsy planes, braving a host of risks from head-hunters to frostbite, in search of knowledge, fame or the ultimate adventure.

THE LAST ADVENTURE

PUBLISHED BY
THE READER'S DIGEST ASSOCIATION LIMITED
LONDON NEW YORK SYDNEY MONTREAL

THE LAST ADVENTURE

Edited and designed by Toucan Books Limited
Written by Tim Healey
Edited by Helen Douglas-Cooper and
Robert Sackville West
Designed by Bradbury and Williams
Picture research by Julie McMahon & Wendy Brown

FOR READER'S DIGEST

Series Editor Christine Noble
Editorial Assistant Caroline Boucher
Production Controller Byron Johnson

READER'S DIGEST GENERAL BOOKS

Editorial Director Cortina Butler
Art Director Nick Clark

First English edition copyright © 1999
The Reader's Digest Association Limited,
11 Westferry Circus, Canary Wharf,
London E14 4HE
www.readersdigest.co.uk

We are committed to both the quality of our
products and the service we provide to our
customers. We value your comments, so please feel
free to contact us on 08705 113366, or by email at
cust_service@readersdigest.co.uk

If you have any comments about the content
of our books, you can contact us at
gbeditorial@readersdigest.co.uk

Reprinted 2001

Copyright © 1999
Reader's Digest Association Far East Limited
Philippines copyright © 1999
Reader's Digest Association Far East Limited
All rights reserved

Printing and binding: Printer Industria Gráfica S.A.,
Barcelona
Separations: Litho Origination, London
Paper: Perigord-Condat, France

ISBN 0 276 42383 6

FRONT COVER
Background picture: Crewmen in the rigging of
Captain Scott's *Terra Nova*, top; sherpas preparing
for the 1953 Everest expedition, bottom.
From left to right: Isabelle Eberhardt; Alberto
Santos-Dumont flies around the Eiffel Tower;
Edmund Colson on his camel; Ernest Shackleton.

BACK COVER
Clockwise from top left: Amy Johnson; Sno-cat stuck
in Antarctic snow; Prince Borghese on his Peking-
Paris journey; exploring the wreck of the *Titanic*.

Page 3 (from left to right): Embroidered Buddha
from China; Jack Fawcett on horseback; Professor
Bebbe in his bathysphere; Borg Ousland on his way
to the North Pole.

Background pictures:
Page 15: The desert of Arabia's Empty Quarter
Page 31: The lily *Lilium regale*
Page 69: Sun temple at Machu Picchu
Page 89: Arctic mountains
Page 111: Underwater exploration
Page 131: Hot-air balloon

CONTENTS

JOURNEYS TO THE UNKNOWN

EXPLORERS VENTURED TO EVER REMOTER PLACES, IN EVER HARDER WAYS, IN THE QUEST TO DO WHAT NO ONE HAD DONE BEFORE

In February 1996 newspapers announced that the South Pole's marker was in the wrong place: a much-photographed post in Antarctica, used to indicate the spot, was about 18 in (45 cm) from where the latest calculations placed it. The pole's new position was plotted by satellite mapping at the United States Geological Survey in Reston, Virginia. And Gordon Shupe, a scientist with the organisation, flew to the Antarctic to make sure that the marking post was relocated in the right place.

The report illustrates the pinpoint accuracy of modern satellite mapping – just one of the hi-tech aids available to present-day scientists exploring planet Earth. From the bleak heart of Antarctica where Captain Scott's frostbitten party once trudged, expeditions can today file reports and digitised pictures on the Internet, to be downloaded almost instantly by computer users around the world. And no longer is human vision confined to what the human eye can see; seismic probes disclose Earth's subterranean

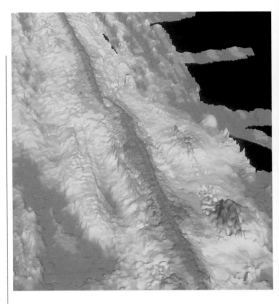

HIGH-TECH EXPLORATION The mid-ocean ridge on the Pacific floor, as revealed by sonar and echo-sounding. The colours show the depth from blue (deepest) to red (shallowest).

topography while sonar scanning has helped map submerged ridges and canyons miles below the surface of the ocean.

Yet in 1900, vast tracts of the Earth were still unknown; the world's highest mountains and ocean depths remained to be conquered; powered flight was no more than a dream. Explorers were still hacking their way through unknown jungle in leather knee boots and solar topis, encumbered with heavy box cameras, telescopes, theodolites and brass sextants. At night in their canvas tents, they wrote up their reports by the light of a candle or hurricane lamp.

The age of empires was at its height in 1900, and armies of native porters bore luggage for the Europeans; equipment included big game guns and rifles, as well as crate-loads of ammunition in case of conflict with hostile tribes. Many explorers at the beginning of the 20th century were army officers who routinely took with them a huge armoury of weapons. In Papua New Guinea, mothers warned: 'Be a good boy now. If you are naughty, look out – for the white man will get you.'

The mountainous interior of Papua New Guinea was just one of the Earth's last frontiers, a place where many villagers had never yet seen or heard of white men, and the scene of many startling 20th-century encounters between Western and Stone Age native cultures. In the interwar period, Jack Gordon Hides, an Australian administrative official, came upon a number of unsuspected villages whose inhabitants offered violent resistance. Once in 1935, in the Wen country between the Strickland and Purari rivers, his expedition was attacked amid 'a terrific din of yodelling' by a mass of natives armed with bows, arrows and short, stabbing spears. After the attackers had been repulsed they came out of the jungle again, this time bearing bunches of bananas and bundles of spinach as gifts. A feast was proposed; fires were built; two pigs killed and potatoes dug from the ground.

From unknown tribes to astonishing landscapes, the story of 20th-century exploration has been a tale of unfolding wonders. The fabulously decorated Caves of the 1000 Buddhas in China, with their frescoes and sculptures, were first explored by Sir Mark Aurel Stein in 1907. Venezuela's Angel Falls, the world's highest cataract, had not been seen by Western eyes before airman Jimmy Angel discovered them in 1935. It was only in 1956 that

VINTAGE EQUIPMENT The wireless belonged to Dr Hamilton Rice, scientific explorer of the Amazon. The medical kit belonged to Lord Curzon who travelled widely in Asia.

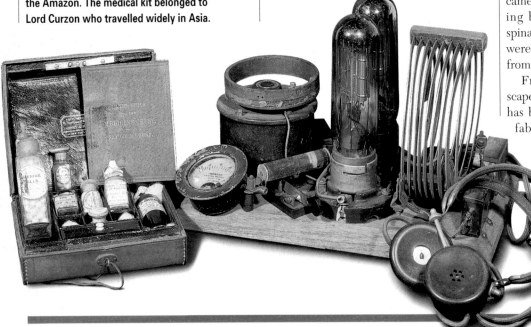

a Perth historian, Harry Turner, revealed the marvels of the Pinnacles Desert, a weird forest of limestone rock stacks that rise like hooded Druids from a corner of south-west Australia. The Gunung Mulu Caves in the Malaysian state of Sarawak, which incorporate the largest cave chamber in the world, were unknown to modern geographers before 1980.

Why go exploring?

In the 20th century much of the unexplored Earth has been wilderness: the bleak interior of Antarctica; creeper-tangled Amazonian rain forests; bare Mongolian plains; the arid desert wastes of Arabia. None offered much promise of material reward. What prompted 20th-century explorers to penetrate these hostile zones?

Any answer must begin with humanity's pure, questing drive – an instinct which transcends the ages. In the 18th century, Captain Cook wrote of 'the pleasure which naturally results to a man from being the first discoverer, even was it of nothing more than sands or shoals'. The same spirit animated the men who conquered space. John Glenn, the first American in orbit, said: 'I suppose the one quality in an astronaut more powerful than any other is curiosity. They have to get some place nobody's ever been before.'

To Wilfred Thesiger, a traveller in Arabia, the desolate Empty Quarter amounted to more than a blank on the map. It was a spiritual thirst, and in that wilderness of rock and sand 'I had found all that I asked; I knew that I should never find it again.'

More recently, Robert D. Ballard, the American scientist who located the *Titanic* more than 2 miles (3.2 km) below the surface of the Atlantic, has likened his work to the quest undertaken by Jason, hero of the Greek legend of the Argonauts in his search for the Golden Fleece. 'Exploration is still the epic journey,' he has said, 'to dream, to prepare yourself, to assemble your team of argonauts, to go forth to be tested mentally and physically by the gods. To pass the test, be given the truth, and then come back and share the new wisdom.' For Ballard the exploring instinct is fundamental to human nature. 'Everyone is an explorer. How could you possibly live your life looking at a door and not go open it?'

Press sensations

Scott, Amundsen, Hillary, Heyerdahl, Rondon ...the names of the great adventurers have indeed taken on a mythic quality; and it has been enhanced by the reportage of a sensation-hungry press. In 1909, when Dr Frederick

LOST CITY The spectacular Inca citadel of Machu Picchu was unknown to geographers until July 24, 1911, when it was discovered by American explorer Hiram Bingham.

Cook reported that he had reached the North Pole, the *New York Herald* blazoned the story across the whole of its front page. The reason was that, as Cook's sponsors, they had exclusive rights to his story – or thought they had. In fact, their arch-rivals *The New York Times* published the same report on the same day, having stolen the copy from the Paris edition (which had been released nine hours earlier).

As it happens, doubts were soon expressed as to whether Cook had reached the North Pole at all. But the *Herald* continued to celebrate his supposed achievement long after his claims were called into question. The paper's editor was James Gordon Bennett Jr (1841-1918), the man chiefly responsible for intoxicating the newspaper-reading public with tales of exploration. Himself a tigerish, larger-than-life figure who was said to have 'robbed fiction of an almost incredible character', Bennett defined a great editor as someone who knows where hell is going to break loose next – and how to get a reporter first on the scene. It was he who had financed H.M. Stanley, a *Herald* reporter, in his celebrated quest for David Livingstone. Bennett funded several other expeditions, creating national heroes through sensational journalistic techniques, always stressing the conquest of nature, the race to fill in blanks on the map.

ANTARCTIC DEN Ernest Shackleton's hut at Cape Royds, Ross Island. 'The Boss', as his men dubbed him, set up his base there on February 3, 1908.

It was an arrangement that did no harm to the generally under-funded adventurers themselves. Not only did the press help to finance expeditions, but media exposure generated other sources of income such as lecture tours and book sales. Robert E. Peary, the man who supplanted Cook as conqueror of the North Pole, was able to charge a minimum of $1000 a lecture, and sometimes received as much as $7500. As Ernest Shackleton once explained to a Canadian anthropologist, lectures sold books, books sold lectures, and newspapers sold both, 'particularly when you come home from an expedition with a big hurrah'.

The sensational tradition endured long after the death of James Gordon Bennett Jr and, during the interwar years, the spotlight turned especially on the men and women conquering the skies. In May 1927, when the quiet farmboy Charles Lindbergh touched down at Le Bourget airport after his historic

MEN ON THE MASTS Crewmen high in the rigging of Captain Scott's *Terra Nova*, the vessel which took the explorer on his last Antarctic Expedition of 1910-12.

solo Atlantic flight, he was astonished to find himself greeted by a crowd of 100 000 people. His very shyness contributed to his mythic status. 'This boy is not our usual type of hero,' Will Rogers wrote in his syndicated column. 'He is all the others rolled into one and multiplied by ten.'

Popular adulation of woman aviator Amelia Earhart also owed much to press attention – and even more to the shrewd media manipulations of her publicist husband, George Putnam. Meanwhile, British pilot Amy Johnson was among the first to know the pressures of superstardom for celebrity explorers. After her 1930 flight from Britain to Australia, she returned to England by sea to be greeted by an estimated 1 million people when she arrived in London. The *Daily Mail* then sent her on a nationwide tour, but she had to give it up after only a week when her health and nerves gave out.

In the years after the Second World War, just when it seemed that the Earth's land

STARS OF THE SKY Female aviators were the focus of intense media attention during the interwar years. Above: Amy Johnson greeted by cheering crowds in Sydney. Right: Amelia Earhart after crossing the Pacific.

surface and airways could offer the public no more surprises, the aqualung opened up the blue-green world of the oceans to human gaze.

Underwater Eden

Using film and the new medium of television, French aquanaut Jacques Cousteau reminded a global audience that the silent world under the sea covers nearly three-quarters of our planet and is almost entirely unexplored. To Cousteau it was like a Garden of Eden before the Fall: '*Il faut aller voir*' – 'we must go and see', was his motto.

UNDERWATER EXPLORER **UNDERWATER EXPLORER** French oceanologist Jacques Cousteau perceived the submarine world as an undersea paradise, and brought its marvels to millions worldwide.

Meanwhile, development of submarines and deep-sea submersibles allowed humans to explore even the blackest abyssal depths. Fascinating new achievements were notched up. In 1958 the nuclear-powered submarine USS *Nautilus* made an historic first voyage under the Arctic ice cap to the North Pole. This was a difficult feat of navigation, and in two early attempts, the submariners were forced back by concealed tongues of ice which threatened disaster. On the successful attempt, the *Nautilus* crossed a 9000 ft (2750 m) submerged mountain range which had never before been reported. The submarine reached the North Pole at 11.15 pm on August 3 and, as part of the celebrations, the crew deposited mail in the shipboard post office to be stamped 'North Pole'.

No big send-off had been organised for the benefit of the press. On the contrary, the mission of the *Nautilus* was secret – families of the crew were told beforehand that they were on a routine training run to Panama.

In the years that followed, the Swiss-built US Navy submersible *Trieste* made the deepest ocean descent, reaching the Challenger Deep of the Marianas Trench in the Pacific Ocean, just seven years after Edmund Hillary and Tenzing Norgay had reached the highest point on land, the summit of Mount Everest. Later, scientists brought back pictures of the weird life forms that have evolved around the submerged volcanoes of the Mid-Atlantic Rift. In 1985, when the *Titanic* wreck was found, video footage was greeted by the public with more fascination than the latest images from outer space.

Twentieth-century technology helped to unlock these wonders, and transformed the world map in the process. While the pioneer explorers surveyed the Earth at ground level, modern man has gained orbital perspectives. The revolution began in the 1920s when, working with custom-designed cameras and aircraft, the Fairchild company started to produce aerial surveys in the United States. In the postwar period, satellite photography was developed while computers were also adapted to the needs of cartographers. The first computer-generated map was published in 1950, showing weather conditions in Europe and North America. In 1972 NASA launched the first Landsat satellite with a multispectral scanner which could make out several visible colours and invisible infrared radiation reflected from the Earth.

Increasingly sophisticated computer-based geographic information systems (GIS) allowed map-makers to manipulate the masses of incoming data to create maps that, for example, overlay radar relief images with infrared ones which display vegetation, and thermal infrared maps revealing heat. So researchers are able to chart the variety and health of trees in a forest or crops in farm fields; to discern pollution in streams or the spread of plankton in the oceans. It was

NUCLEAR SUBMARINE The USS *Nautilus* makes a landfall off southern England's Dorset coast in August 1958, after completing her historic voyage under the North Pole.

through such technology that scientists of the British Antarctic Survey were able to detect the ozone hole over the South Pole. Antarctica, it is now known, is the main 'heat switch' for the Earth's weather and it is becoming more important for humanity to understand the behaviour of the ice sheet, and its possible role in world sea-level change.

There are new priorities for explorers. Where the pioneers in past centuries may have gone to build empires, to augment trade or convert the heathen to Christianity, there is today a worldwide recognition of the need to care for planet Earth. The new challenges are understanding desertification, acid rain, global warming and other problems besetting the biosphere.

To aid research, satellite cameras with ever finer resolution have brought minute details of the Earth's topography into focus.

Terra incognita

Today, surveyors at ground level rarely go into the field without handheld electronic instruments connecting them to one or

OZONE HOLE Data from a spectrometer on the Russian Meteor-3 satellite reveals the 'ozone hole' (blue, pink and white) over Antarctica in 1993.

another of the four or five navigation satellites of the Global Positioning System (GPS). 'Not that GPS has the solution to every question of location', veteran science correspondent John Noble Wilford has written, describing a palaeontological expedition in Mongolia's Gobi desert. 'Thanks to our GPS receiver, we always knew the coordinates of our fossil beds and the distance and direction to the next destination. Still we got lost. In a land without roads or good maps, we could never be sure whether the best way forward, to avoid uncharted obstacles like ravines, was to the south, north, or straight ahead. We could only head for the nearest ger [tent], engage the Mongol herder in palaver about his horses and sheep, and finally get to the point. Though the herder could only shake his head in wonderment over the peculiar device in our hands, he alone could tell us the surest way to get where we were going.'

SATELLITE NAVIGATION A walker checking his location with handheld satellite navigation apparatus, receiving signals from the Global Positioning System (GPS).

There is still a role for the footslogging explorer, and still a few blanks left on the map. Writer Redmond O'Hanlon in his *Into the Heart of Borneo* has described how, trying to find his way through the twisting ravines and gulleys of the foothills of Bukit Batu Tiban, he found the map covered with warnings such as AREA UNSURVEYED, and RELIEF DATA INCOMPLETE. He also read RELIABILITY WARNING: OWING TO INADEQUATE SOURCE MATERIAL THERE MAY BE SIGNIFICANT POSITIONAL DISCREPANCIES IN DETAIL OVER AREAS OF THIS CHART. For the average visitor these might be disquieting words; but for O'Hanlon, the avid explorer, they were 'the most enticing legends that can be inscribed on any map'.

Only a few places are still sufficiently remote to retain that exhilarating aura of *terra incognita*, among them pockets of central African rain forest, corners of the Arctic and Antarctic, and remote escarpments in Tibet and Sichuan. In 1994, newspapers announced that a Franco-British expedition had discovered the long-sought source of the Mekong River at an altitude of 16 400 ft (5000 m) in north Tibet, well to the west of the officially designated site.

The Amazon jungle still guards some of its secrets, too, and the source of the mighty river which nourishes the rain forest has puzzled the experts. Though the source of the Amazon was identified some time ago as the headwaters of the Apurimac River in the southern Peruvian Andes, the details were only brought into sharp focus in July 1996. In that month, an international team led by Polish explorer Jacek Palkiewicz identified the source as an underground glacier – an icy creek called Apachita in a crevice 16 958 ft (5169 m) above sea level.

Accidental adventures

Every once in a while, ordinary citizens of the modern world find themselves plunged into the role of explorers, forced by accident to survive in remote and hostile terrain. One such case occurred in the Andes in 1972: 16 people, mainly members of a Uruguayan rugby team, survived an aeroplane crash high in the Andes, even though they were

RIVER QUEST A member of the 1994 Franco-British expedition to find the source of the Mekong River. It was discovered in the Tibetan highlands, west of its presumed location.

abandoned for dead by the search parties. They owed their survival to two of the party who made an amazing ten-day forced march out of the mountains to find help.

In 1992 Tabwai Mikaie and Arenta Tebeitabu, two fishermen from the Pacific island of Nikunau, were found alive after surviving for a record 177 days in an open dinghy. Caught up by a cyclone, their boat had capsized, and although they managed to right it, the vessel drifted some 1100 miles (1770 km) across the immense ocean before being washed ashore on the island of Upolu in Western Samoa. Skeletal in appearance the men had survived by collecting and drinking rainwater, spearing the occasional fish, and sometimes catching a coconut as it drifted past their boat.

Another dramatic episode came to an end on Friday, March 25, 1994, when searchers at last located a five-man team of army officers missing in a Borneo jungle hell after climbing 13 000 ft (3962 m) Mount Kinabalu, the highest mountain in South-east Asia, on an adventure training exercise. The men – two British officers and three NCOs from Hong Kong – had been part of a ten-man expedition which had set out on February 22 and conquered the summit without difficulty. But they chose a descent that involved

abseiling down through an exceptionally treacherous rift called Low's Gully, known as the Place of Death in local lore. Dark overhangs, monstrous boulders, violent cataracts and deep plunge pools made the going so slow that the 46-year-old team leader Lieutenant Colonel Robert Neill, decided that the five younger men should 'crack on and clear a path' ahead of the older men.

'Trapped like spiders'

A nightmare ensued for both parties. The advance group, pressing on ahead, found themselves spending much of their time on all fours, cutting their way through such dense vegetation that it sometimes took four days to complete a mile. On March 6, Lance Corporal Shearer, last man on an abseil, crashed 60 ft (18 m) onto rocks when his rope gave way and was left with a badly gashed head and leg injuries which slowed the group's pace even more. For natural food sources in the jungle they

RESCUE MISSION Malaysian jungle police move into the valley below Mount Kinabalu to search for the five British soldiers lost there for over two weeks in 1994. The Malaysian-British search and rescue operation deployed more than 400 personnel.

found little more than a couple of pencil-thin snakes and three raspberries. One of the men also ate some anonymous seeded fruit and suffered severe dysentery as a result. Then, while swimming after their kit, they were suddenly dragged below the surface of the river by an undertow and emerged in a cavern half-drowned. On March 10, the already ailing Shearer awoke to discover that a giant leech had attached itself to his eye overnight and sucked out a lot of blood.

By March 13, however, all five of the advance group had staggered out of the jungle and called for search parties to set out after their companions. But the rainiest monsoon in years was now setting in, and despite more than 400 Malaysian searchers and RAF mountain rescue teams flown in from Britain, the teeming rain and swollen cataracts thwarted repeated attempts to find the missing men.

At last, on Thursday, March 24, the pilot of a small Alouette helicopter thought he saw something flash from the dark recesses of Low's Gully and returned the following day to lower his small craft down the narrow, wind-lashed rift where he saw the letters SOS picked out in white pebbles. Three men were jumping up and down weakly, flailing their arms and reflecting sunlight off their mirrors. Two more lay on the ground, waving feebly. All were terribly emaciated and seized on the emergency rations thrown to them

with the desperation of starving men. They had been trapped in their gully, in the words of a British officer, 'like spiders in a bath'. Yet they survived, and were winched at last to safety.

The Adventurers' Grand Slam

There is plenty of hostile terrain left on Earth. Nonetheless, as the 20th century draws to its close, the planet's true geographic mysteries get fewer and fewer and bold spirits have had to come up with ever more rarefied proposals. Explorers have climbed Everest without oxygen equipment; they have rowed the Atlantic; they have reached the Poles solo, on foot.

Another trend has been to aim for multiple conquests where, in the past, a single triumph sufficed. In 1998 the British adventurer David Hempleman-Adams made headlines worldwide as the first person to complete the Adventurers' Grand Slam. This is a Herculean series of 11 mountaineering and polar exploration tasks which it took him 18 years to complete. The feat involved climbing the highest peaks on each of the seven continents, as well as attaining the four main poles: the magnetic North Pole in the Arctic Archipelago, the magnetic South Pole off the coast of Antarctica, and the geographic North and South Poles at the top and bottom of the world.

Hempleman-Adams began his quest in August 1980 as a 23-year-old holiday mountaineer in North America, where he climbed Alaska's Mount McKinley during a break from his postgraduate university studies. He then conquered Africa's highest peak, Kilimanjaro, the following summer. A decade later, when he had a lot more mountaineering experience under his belt, he realised that the seven summits were attainable. Hempleman-Adams climbed Everest in October 1993, breaking his ribs early on just through violent coughing. Then, in ten months from August 1994 until May 1995, he ascended the four remaining mountains needed to complete the seven summits. After Mount Elbrus, the highest peak in European Russia, he conquered the Vinson Massif in Antarctica, Aconcagua in Chile, and Australia's Cartensz Pyramid.

The poles, however, provided him with his sternest tests. And the geographic North Pole proved the toughest challenge of all. In 1997 he was forced to abandon one unsupported attempt after saving the life of Alan Bywaters, a fellow British polar explorer who had fallen through the ice and was suffering severe hypothermia and frostbite.

On March 5 the following year, the 41-year-old Hempleman-Adams set out again, from Ward Hunt Island on the edge of the polar ice cap, in company with the Norwegian Rune Gjeldnes. Despite every hi-tech development in polar exploration, their journey remained at core a primitive human ordeal of the most testing kind.

The first third of the trek was especially dangerous. While the explorers tried to sleep in their tent the world beneath them erupted in ice quakes. 'Throughout the night, as we lie in our sleeping bags, there is constant crashing, rumbling, scraping sounds,' said Hempleman-Adams. 'You hear the ice rubble falling from the pressure ridges and suddenly a noise like a rifle shot shoots through the ice as it breaks up.'

The most dispiriting fact was that even after surviving such a night, they would wake up to find that they had floated perhaps 2 miles (3.2 km) back south over the area they had toiled to haul their sledges the day before. Then came the ordeal of the leads – breaks in the ice which leave stretches of open water and require detours of several days. For Hempleman-Adams, perhaps the worst experience of his exploring career came when, while attempting to cross a lead, he plunged through the ice into the Arctic Ocean. Luckily Gjeldnes heard his desperate cries and managed to pull him out. It took over two hours, though, for the Briton's knees to stop shaking.

On they pressed, as the going got easier, playing rock music on their personal stereos, until at last, 56 days after their departure, the frostbitten Hempleman-Adams and his Norwegian partner reached their goal. The final assault came on April 28, 1998, and after attaining the North Pole the two men spent the rest of the day and the day after that walking around the Pole to be sure of registering a reading of 89.9999° north on their satellite beacon. This supplied irrefutable proof that they had hit their target and that, for Hempleman-Adams, an 18-year quest to achieve the Grand Slam was over.

DYNAMIC DUO David Hempleman-Adams (left) and his partner Rune Gjeldnes, photographed in Canada while preparing for their North Pole attempt of 1998.

UNDER A BURNING SUN

DESPITE ALL THE HEROIC EFFORTS OF THE VICTORIAN EXPLORERS, AFRICA AND THE MIDDLE EAST AT THE BEGINNING OF THE 20TH CENTURY STILL BOASTED THEIR MYSTERY ZONES. THE DESERT FASTNESS OF THE SAHARA AND ARABIA'S EMPTY QUARTER, EGYPT'S VALLEY OF THE KINGS, THE UNTRODDEN PEAKS OF THE MOUNTAINS OF THE MOON . . . THESE WERE JUST A FEW OF THE AREAS THAT CHALLENGED AND INSPIRED ADVENTURERS BOTH MALE AND FEMALE.

ON THE MOUNTAINS OF THE MOON

THE ITALIAN DUKE OF THE ABRUZZI IS FIRST TO ASCEND THE SNOW MOUNTAINS IN AFRICA

Writing over 2000 years ago, Greek authors referred to mysterious snowy mountains in the African interior. The geographer Ptolemy had no doubt about these white-clad peaks, calling them the Mountains of the Moon. He believed the range to be the source of the Nile, and although this is an error, his map does show the mountains standing in their correct place in East Africa. How this knowledge was gained remains a riddle, however, and it was centuries before Europeans dreamt of locating them again.

In 1875, the explorer Henry Morton Stanley camped for some days on the eastern slopes of the Mountains of the Moon without realising how immense were the heights above him. Impenetrable mist concealed the peaks, as it does for about 300 days of the year. The mountains' African name is Ruwenzori, meaning 'rain-maker', a reference to the great freight of moisture that usually hangs about the summits and hides their sparkling grandeur. Stanley returned to the area in 1888 and was granted a clearer vision of the snowy range from the shore of Lake Albert. 'While looking to the south-east . . . my eyes were directed by a boy to a mountain said to be covered with salt, and I saw a peculiar-shaped cloud of a most beautiful silver colour, which assumed the proportions and appearance of a vast mountain covered with snow . . . what I gazed upon was not the image or semblance of a vast mountain, but the solid substance of a real one, with its summit covered with snow.'

Bizarre vegetation

Though generally regarded as the first modern European discoverer of the Ruwenzori, Stanley himself was not equipped for mountaineering. The peaks that run along the borders of present-day Uganda and Zaire, barely 30 miles (48 km) north of the Equator, remained unconquered until

ARISTOCRATIC ADVENTURER Italian explorer the Duke of the Abruzzi was the first person to reach the summits of the Ruwenzori. The mist-covered mountains harbour a lush landscape (below).

early in the 20th century, when an expedition was mounted by the Italian duke of the Abruzzi, Luigi de Savoia. A polar explorer, the Duke in his day was considered perhaps the greatest living mountaineer. He had made his reputation as a rock climber in the Alps and in North America, and in the summer of 1906, with 250 native porters to carry supplies and equipment, he mounted a major scientific assault on Africa's mystery mountains. The aim was not just to plant a flag on the topmost summit, but to scale every peak and chart every slope, valley and glacier of what was one of the Earth's last great geographical enigmas.

Setting out from Entebbe, the party had to cut their way through miles of dense jungle at the approaches to the Ruwenzori. As it turned out, the mountains' conquest would not require exceptional climbing talents; but all of the Duke's organisational skills were required to get the scientific apparatus moved up through the tangles of weird vegetation clothing the Ruwenzori's lower slopes.

Accompanied by a party of distinguished scientists, a mountain photographer, four seasoned Alpine guides and the porters, the Duke approached the range from the southeast, struggling up through the Mobuku Valley sometimes knee-deep in black mud. Threaded by a torrent fed by a glacier at the top, the valley rises in stages with cliff faces and waterfalls at every level, and different vegetation in the different zones.

At the base, the explorers made their way through forest thick with giant conifers, tree

AFRICA'S LAST CHALLENGES

At the start of the 20th century, the great era of exploration in Africa was drawing to a close, but to Europeans much of the continent was still wild frontier country. While building the East African Railway from Mombasa to Lake Victoria, completed in 1901, surveying parties were raided by Nandi tribes and the construction of one bridge was held up by man-eating lions who killed and ate 28 workmen. There were areas of mystery in Africa, too. It was only in 1903 that France's Captain Lenfant ascended the River Niger and its tributary the Benue, and demonstrated that it connected with the Chad basin.

Northwards, between 1912 and 1917, another French soldier, Commandant Jean Tilho, mapped the cliffs and ravines of the Tibesti mountains in the Sahara and the adjoining Ennedi plateau.

The Sahara contained many of the last great areas of uncertainty for Europeans. Covering more than 3.5 million sq miles (9 million km2) of rock and sand, the world's largest desert receives only 6-7 in (150-180 mm) of rain a year and the most desolate places, such as the Tanezrouft, are virtually devoid of life. The desert also sheltered many nomadic tribes who were opposed to foreign penetration. In the early years of the 20th century, France ruled the Sahara and General François Laperrine did much to secure desert routes against Tuareg raids. The Sahara, however, remained far from stable. In 1916 the French explorer Charles de Foucauld, living as a hermit in the southern Sahara, was murdered by Senussi.

WATERY HIGHWAY French explorer Eugene Armand Lenfant on his mission to the banks of Lake Chad in 1903.

ferns, tangled creepers and flaming orchids. At the second level, they reached a heath forest where trees were grotesquely contorted by thick layers of moss. The third level of the Ruwenzori was the most extraordinary: a weird Alpine meadow sprawling from the rim of a glacier and stacked with freakish plants – gaunt candelabra of groundsels and lobelia looming like gigantic funeral torches to three times the height of a man. The incredibly humid climate, rich soil and lack of competition have combined to give these normally modest-sized garden plants their colossal size. And lack of competition above the tree line has given them space to expand.

Above the clammy, equatorial otherworld lay the untrodden summits of the Ruwenzori – half a dozen snow-capped peaks rising to 16 765 ft (5110 m) at Mount Stanley. Licked by the glistening tongues of glaciers, stalactites and ice cornices much like those of their sister Alps in Europe, they offered no great mountaineering problems. But though the massif may not be Himalayan in scale, the highest points are still 1000 ft (305 m) higher than Mont Blanc and provided the explorers with breathtaking panoramas,

especially at dusk when the sun set in crimson and gold over the broad sweep of the Congo Forest.

The conquest of Mount Stanley was the climax of the expedition. As they burst through the mist around the lower part of the mountain into splendid clear sunlight, they saw two peaks. These, Mount Stanley's twin peaks, the Duke of the Abruzzi named Margherita (the taller) after the queen of Savoy and Alexandra (the lesser) after the queen of England.

There remained the patient, prosaic business of charting the mountains and cataloguing their flora and fauna. Some peaks were scaled more than once to verify observations, and the whole job was done with such thoroughness that by the time the explorers left the Ruwenzori they had built up a more accurate picture of them than was available for many habitable parts of Africa. The expedition was a solid scientific achievement. John Buchan, that most patriotic of writers, conceded: 'No Englishman will grudge that the honours of the pioneer fell to so brilliant a climber and so unwearied a traveller as the Duke of the Abruzzi.'

WOMAN OF THE DESERT

TRAVELLER, SCHOLAR AND DIPLOMAT, GERTRUDE BELL FINDS LONELINESS AND FAME IN ARABIA

In 1913, before embarking on her first journey into the heart of Arabia, Gertrude Bell wrote, 'I want to cut all links with the world'. Wealthy and brilliant, this remarkable Englishwoman nonetheless abandoned the comforts of home in favour of what she described as 'the road and the dawn, the sun, the wind and the rain, the camp fire under the stars, and sleep, and the road again...'

Gertrude had spent her girlhood in the Yorkshire home of her father, Sir Hugh Bell, and stepmother, Florence, with both of whom she later kept in close and affectionate contact. Following a dazzling career at Oxford, where she took a first-class degree in history in 1887, she succumbed to the lure of the East during a visit to Tehran where her uncle, Sir Frank Lascelles, was British Minister. To Horace Marshall, an old friend, she wrote: 'Oh the desert around Tehran! miles and miles of it with nothing, nothing growing; ringed in with bleak bare mountains snow crowned and furrowed with the deep courses of torrents. I never knew what desert was till I came here...'

'Like the Arabian Nights'

For the Tehran trip, Gertrude took a course in Persian in which she quickly became fluent. Then in November 1899, she visited Jerusalem where, immediately on her arrival, she hired a horse and an Arab teacher.

SCHOLARLY TRAVELLER A courageous explorer, Gertrude Lowthian Bell was also a brilliant linguist, known for her translations of the medieval Persian poet, Hafiz.

Languages were never a problem to her – she would master Hindustani for a trip to India – and she acquired an archaeological expertise that won her a reputation as an authority, following expeditions to sites in Syria and Mesopotamia. But the wild interior of central Arabia became the magnet that attracted her thoughts more and more. In 1913, spurred perhaps partly by unrequited love for a dashing but married soldier named Major Charles Doughty Wylie, Gertrude set out from Damascus with 20 camels, hired cameleers and a guide, for Hail, an ancient market town and oasis that lay on the old caravan and pilgrim route from Iraq to Medina and Mecca.

The going in winter was rough. Gertrude wrote of Arctic cold one night in the desert, where her companions' tent was frozen hard and they had to light fires under it to unfreeze the canvas. Then they were attacked by Druse horsemen who stripped her men of their revolvers, cartridge belts and cloaks. Only the intervention of some Druse sheikhs permitted their escape. Through cold rains and stony hills, by ancient ruined fortresses and the orange-red sand dunes of the Great Nafud, the party journeyed on. Gertrude wrote of experiencing true loneliness for the first time and of 'how to bear pain without crying out'.

At last they reached Hail: a walled city rising from palm groves in the shining mirage of a plain. This important desert centre had already been explored by Westerners, though only one European woman, Lady Anne Blunt, had ever penetrated the place before – and that was 30 years earlier. Encircled by its zigzag ornamented mud battlements, Hail was dominated by the round towers of the palace of the Amir or governor. Gertrude found it eerily quiet: 'Though it is a town like any other, of streets and houses, Hail retains something of the wilderness. There is no clatter of civic life. Silent ways are paved with desert dust . . . the creak of wheels is not heard. The noiseless slow footfall of the camel is all the traffic here.'

The city she entered was capital of the Ibn Rashid family – one of the two rival seats of power in central Arabia. Their opponents were the Sauds, who in 1921 would win victory over them and later create the state of Saudi Arabia. But the Rashids were also their own worst enemies, forever involved in blood strife among themselves. At the time of Gertrude's visit, the Amir, or governor, was away from Hail and involved in a murderous intrigue against an uncle. The Amir's deputy, named Ibrahim, placed Gertrude in virtual captivity in a guest house in the city, and amid the rich divans and Bedouin carpets, the slaves and the eunuchs, she was obliged to offer bribes – from revolvers to

THE ROAD TO HAIL Gertrude Bell travelled to the desert capital by way of the Great Nafud. She continued from Hail to Baghdad before returning across the desert to Damascus.

Damascus

Baghdad

Hail

Zeiss binoculars – to members of the royal household in order to keep on good terms.

With no idea of what was in her hosts' minds concerning her fate, Gertrude felt that 'it was all like a story in the Arabian Nights', adding that 'I did not find it particularly enjoyable to be one of the dramatis personae.' A nonchalant remark, maybe, but she faced real danger. Hail's princely house had been thinned by a succession of murders in the preceding decades. It took real courage to enter the city – a woman alone – and courage to make her exit, too.

After drinking tea endlessly, wandering the garden and making repeated appeals for permission to depart, she eventually delivered the bold declaration that she intended to leave tomorrow. It is a tribute to her courage and her purposeful air that she was – quite suddenly – granted permission to go. Gertrude Bell travelled to Baghdad and then back across country to Damascus.

A phial of barbiturates

Gertrude's expedition to Hail became famous. And her knowledge was put to good use in the years that followed, for soon after her return the First World War broke out, and she worked with military intelligence, collecting information about the Arab tribes. From 1917 she was political secretary in Baghdad and played an important role in shaping the postwar administration of Mesopotamia, supporting the regime of King Feisal of Iraq.

In 1923, when a new High Commissioner was appointed, she accepted the post of Honorary Director of Antiquities at the National Museum in Iraq and won further renown as custodian of the archaeological treasures of Babylon and Assyria.

By now the most famous English figure in Arabia, Gertrude Bell died an enigmatic death. On the night of July 11, 1926, she attended a dinner party in the large ballroom of the Baghdad High Commission. Following this, she took her customary evening swim and then retired to bed. During the night she took a fatal dose from the phial of barbiturates known as Dial, which she kept beside her bed.

The official view was that it was an accidental death brought on by exhaustion following her many years of strenuous work. However, in his autobiography published in 1977, archaeologist Sir Max Mallowan – a close companion of Gertrude in her last years – suggested that she took the overdose deliberately, depressed by her gradual exclusion from political affairs.

It is known that an official inquiry was held at the time of Gertrude's death, at which the doctors involved gave evidence. However, the report was destroyed 25 years later, along with her personal file. The final verdict on the death of this remarkable woman must remain open.

WAS IT SUICIDE?

Gertrude Bell's death from an overdose of barbiturates prompted widespread conjecture. Was it an accident, or suicide? Archaeologist Sir Max Mallowan favoured the latter theory in his autobiography:

'She was discredited politically, for she had swept aside the warnings of the High Commissioner, Sir Arnold Wilson, that there would be serious trouble in Iraq, and serious trouble there was, involving the loss of many lives…Whitburn and I called on her in Baghdad, in her little house, on our way home in 1926, in order to pay our respects. She was glad to see us, for she was lonely and mortified that she was no longer a power in the land. Three months after this visit she died through an overdose of a sleeping draught which was thought to have been taken deliberately.'

DESERT MEETING The Arab leader Ibn Saud (left) meets with Gertrude Bell and British political officers in March 1917, during negotiations between the two countries.

WOMEN EXPLORERS

WHILE FEMALE ADVENTURERS BRAVED JUNGLE AND DESERT WASTE, OTHER BOLD SPIRITS CARRIED 'VOTES FOR WOMEN' SLOGANS TO THE HIGHEST HIMALAYAN PEAKS

Though Mary Kingsley, Florence Baker and other intrepid travellers journeyed deep into Africa during the Victorian Age, convention denied most women the opportunities as explorers. Attitudes changed around the turn of the century with the campaign for women's suffrage. In 1908, wearing an Eskimo suit borrowed from the Museum of Natural History, 58-year-old Annie Smith Peck became the first person to conquer the north peak of Huascarán, at 22 132 ft (6746 m) the highest mountain in the Peruvian Andes. Soon afterwards, she planted a Votes for Women banner on Peru's Mount Coropuna (21 079 ft/6425 m).

WILD ROMANTIC
Swiss-born Isabelle Eberhardt, photographed at the age of 18, roamed the Algerian desert dressed in male attire.

Peck's great rival was a fellow American named Fanny Bullock Workman, who in 1906 had set a world altitude record for women by climbing to 22 815 ft (6954 m) on Pinnacle Peak in the Nun Kun range of the Himalayas. When Annie Peck claimed to have bettered that record with her Huascarán ascent, Fanny hired scientists to measure the Peruvian peak and proved that it was not quite as high as the Himalayan mountain she had climbed. If the two agreed on nothing else, however, they shared a commitment to suffrage. On one of her Himalayan peaks, Fanny was photographed reading a paper titled 'Votes for Women'.

Not all female pioneers of exploration and adventure supported the suffragettes. Gertrude Bell – the first woman to obtain a first-class honours degree in history at Oxford – was totally opposed to votes for women. She campaigned actively against the feminists, and was a founder-member of the Anti-Suffrage League in England. Gertrude was a paradox. She might travel alone in the fastness of the desert, but she never went out in London without a chaperone. While pursuing a liberated existence herself, she distrusted others of her sex, and more than once remarked on their unfitness to engage in activities normally entrusted to men.

The truth is that women explorers conform to no easy stereotype. While Gertrude Bell was a careful and scholarly desert traveller, Isabelle Eberhardt was a wild vagabond. Born in 1877 in Geneva of Russian stock, Isabelle moved with her mother to North Africa at the age of 20. Her mother's death from a heart attack left her distracted, and from July 1900 she began an intense nomadic life. Dressed in Arab men's clothes, and taking the name of Si Mahmoud, she ranged on horseback across Algeria's deserts, plateaus and oases, intoxicated by the country's limitless spaces. Now moving with the camel caravans, now sleeping on the mud floors of village huts, she was as voracious for drugs and alcohol as she was for Arab lovers. Scandalous, debauched, wildly romantic, she died a death as bizarre as her brief life had been: she drowned in the desert. On the thunderous morning of October 21, 1904, a flash flood burst from the mountains and surged through a narrow ravine to the little clay-hut town of Ain-Sefra at the Sahara's edge. Isabelle perished – along with many Arab inhabitants – in the foaming yellow waters.

Whilst pure wanderlust animated Isabelle Eberhardt, American explorer Delia Akeley was moved to set out on her greatest adventure by the collapse of her marriage to zoologist and taxidermist Carl Akeley. The Wisconsin-born daughter of Irish immigrants, Delia was divorced in 1923 and set out the following year on an African expedition commissioned by Brooklyn Museum to collect specimens. 'Woman to Forget Marital Woe by Fighting African Jungle Beasts' was how one newspaper headlined the departure. Delia first travelled to the remote forests of the Ituri River, now in north-eastern Zaire, where she visited Pygmy villages never before visited by white explorers. Following a severe bout of fever, she then travelled to Kisangani, and thence by riverboat down the Congo River to Kinshasa. Reaching the Atlantic Ocean in September 1925, she became the first woman known to have crossed Africa.

The Swiss-born traveller Ella Maillart was a mystic at heart. In the 1930s, Ella lived among Kirghiz and Kazakh tribesmen, and in her book *Forbidden Journey* she describes a trip across the Gobi and Taklimakan deserts. Exploration was for Maillart always an inner journey, and she later spent five years practising meditation with a guru in southern India. The Parisienne Alexandra David-Néel was also attracted by Eastern mysticism. A student of Oriental religions, she spent the winter of 1914-15 meditating in a remote cave in Sikkim. In 1924, disguised as a Buddhist nun and accompanied by a young Sikkimese lama, Yongden, Alexandra became the first European woman to enter Lhasa, capital of Tibet. She reached the Forbidden City during the Buddhist New Year, and was able to roam (still in disguise) throughout the city, as well as tour the Potala, the great palace of the Dalai Lama.

In contrast, Dame Freya Stark candidly acknowledged that when she set out on a life of adventure she did so 'single-mindedly for fun'. Freya had suffered long years of ill health in her youth, and decided that she would rather die than continue to live as an invalid. One of her most celebrated exploits, in 1930, was to penetrate the Valley of the Assassins – an ancient Persian sect of murderous hashish-eaters (our word assassin derives from Hashishin). The ruins of their fortress of Alamut loomed from a rockstack in the remote Elburz mountains of Iran, an area that at the time was scarcely known to European eyes, and virtually unmapped. Racked by dysentery and malaria, Freya Stark almost died on this trip but recovered to continue her witty, acerbic travel writing – and to live to the age of 100.

TWO TRAVELLERS Witty, commonsensical Freya Stark (left) went exploring for pure enjoyment, as an observer of the world and human nature. She wrote vividly and entertainingly about her experiences. For Parisienne Alexandra David-Néel (right), however, travel was a mystic quest. The first European woman to enter the Forbidden City of Lhasa, she was a noted authority on Buddhism.

IN THE VALLEY OF THE KINGS

HOWARD CARTER'S FABULOUS DISCOVERY TAKES THE WORLD OVER 3000 YEARS BACK IN TIME

A telegram sent by archaeologist Howard Carter to his patron, Lord Carnarvon, in November, 1922, marked the end of a six-year quest, and heralded the greatest archaeological finds ever made. 'AT LAST HAVE MADE WONDERFUL DISCOVERY IN VALLEY. A MAGNIFICENT TOMB WITH SEALS INTACT. RECOVERED SAME FOR YOUR ARRIVAL. CONGRATULATIONS.' No discovery before or since has equalled the splendour and magnificence of Tutankhamun's tomb. Its excavation made Howard Carter's name famous – and it also familiarised the whole world with a dusty, rubble-strewn notch in the west bank of the Nile known as the Valley of the Kings.

HIDDEN SPLENDOUR When archaeologists Howard Carter and Lord Carnarvon opened the pharaoh's sarcophagus, they found a nest of three coffins.

Traditionally, Egypt's kings had been laid to rest in the pyramids, but despite the ingenuity of the builders they proved such a magnet to thieves that the Pharaoh Thutmose decided about 3500 years ago on a new, more secret location. He created an underground tomb for himself in the Valley of the Kings, lying to the west of the Nile across the river from the country's capital, Thebes. From then on, throughout the period of the New Kingdom (1567-1085 BC), virtually all pharaohs and several queens were buried in the valley.

Tombs were tunnelled into the limestone cliffs, with winding passages, false chambers and hidden doors to thwart intruders. Into the burial chambers with the mummified body came fantastically rich furnishings, intended to provide the pharaoh in the afterlife with all the comforts and accoutrements of palace existence: not just food and drink but fine linen, gilded chariots, treasure chests crammed with jewels, ivory gaming boards, beds, thrones, statues of the gods, and magical

WORLDLY GOODS The antechamber to Tutankhamun's tomb was packed with disorderly stacks of artefacts, including gilded couches, chairs, boxes and chariots.

servant figures to do their masters' bidding in the afterlife.

Almost before the tombs were sealed, however, robbers began to penetrate the burial places. The offenders included light-fingered tomb workmen, artisans from the local villages, scribes, and even priests from nearby temples. Punishments ranged from mutilation to impalement on a stake and being buried alive. But neither the ferocious sentences nor the armies of guards and watchmen employed to safeguard the royal cemetery succeeded in lessening the menace of theft. By 1000 BC, every sepulchre except one in the valley had been robbed. The sole exception was the tomb of the boy king Tutankhamun (c.1372-1352 BC). Coming to the throne at the age of 11, he ruled for only nine years and was relatively insignificant as a historical figure. This very lack of importance may have helped to keep his grave intact when other, more glamorous subjects were targeted.

Finding Tutankhamun's tomb became an obsession to the English archaeologist, Howard Carter. First arriving in Egypt in 1891 at the age of 17, he was engaged to help with the drawings of an archaeological survey. In 1907, he began working in partnership with his benefactor, George Herbert, 5th Earl of Carnarvon. The Earl was a keen Egyptologist, and one of the few people who shared Carter's faith that an intact tomb might yet be discovered in the much-plundered Valley of the Kings. By the turn of the 20th century, the valley had already been scoured by dozens of archaeologists and explorers, and although ancient antiquities still turned up from time to time, the consensus was that all the royal tombs had already been found.

Carter pinned his hopes on some relatively minor discoveries made in the valley by an excavator named Theodore Davis; these included a faience cup bearing the name of Tutankhamun, and fragments of mourning wear possibly used at the boy king's funeral. The young pharaoh must have been buried somewhere – where else, if not the Valley of the Kings?

'Mountains of rubbish'

Carnarvon acquired the concession to dig in the valley, and Carter's assault on it began in 1917. 'The difficulty was,' he wrote, 'to know where to begin, for mountains of rubbish

DIGGING UP THE PAST Under Carter's direction, a chain of workmen bring rubble up from Tutankhamun's tomb. **Right:** One of a pair, this 'black guard' stood beside the sealed entrance to the burial chamber.

thrown out by previous excavators encumbered the ground in all directions.' Nothing came of excavations that year, and the following year was equally barren. In 1919, Carter came on a cache of 13 alabaster jars bearing signs of Ramses II, and as this was the nearest he and his patron had come to a real find 'we were naturally somewhat excited'. But the digging seasons of 1920-1 proved fruitless again. Toiling in the appalling heat of the valley was exhausting, and the whole enterprise proved terribly costly. Carnarvon had spent some £50 000 on the excavations by the summer of 1922, when he informed

SEARCH FOR THE PAST

Some of the richest insights into human origins and early civilisation have come from Africa and the Middle East. Besides the discovery of Tutankhamun's tomb, the Sumerian city of Ur, in Mesopotamia, also provided a grand archaeological surprise. Lying at the edge of the Arabian desert, Ur of the Chaldees, as it is called in the Book of Genesis, was excavated by Sir Leonard Woolley in 1922-34, and its royal cemetery yielded fabulous gold and silver artefacts which stimulated huge interest in the archaeology of the Biblical lands.

That interest was enhanced when researchers explored a series of limestone caves in the barren cliffs near Qumran, north-west of the Dead Sea in Israel. A huge cache of scrolls, wrapped in linen cloth, had been deposited in clay jars there in ancient times. In 1952, a French and American team recovered about 600 documents, in Hebrew and Aramaic, from the site. The Dead Sea Scrolls turned out to be the library of a

ANCIENT PROCESSION A detail from the Royal Standard of Ur, which is dated around 2500 BC. The figures are composed of shell set in lapis lazuli with engraved details.

Jewish community that existed at the time of Christ, and to include prayers, psalms and texts of many Old Testament books that were immensely valuable to Biblical scholars.

The thirst for knowledge about man's past has led deeper into prehistory. From a cave near Shanidar in the remote Zagros mountains of north-eastern Iraq, a team led by Ralph S. Solecki of the Smithsonian Institution discovered the 60 000-year-old grave of a crippled Neanderthal man. Microscopic pollen grains indicated that he had been laid to rest with tributes of picked flowers – remarkable evidence of ceremonial rites among the supposedly brutish Neanderthals.

From the Olduvai Gorge in Tanzania, between 1959 and 1961, British palaeontologist Louis Leakey and his family recovered fossil skulls of proto-humans much older than the Neanderthals. The australopithecines, as they have been called, lived between about 5 million and 1.5 million years ago. They had a small brain, but their skull and skeletal features were more like those of modern man than of the apes, and they walked erect. Fossilised footprints found at Laetoli, Tanzania, are thought to have been made by these ancient hominids.

DISTANT COUSINS Louis Leakey compares a chimpanzee skull (left) with that of a hominid from Olduvai Gorge.

soil and dug deeper as step followed step. A dozen stairs in all led to a sealed doorway. Brushing away the debris, Carter recognised the seal of the royal cemetery, the jackal and nine prostrate captives, hinting at the importance of the find. He could not resist making a hole large enough to shine a torch through and peering into the passage beyond, which was filled with rubble as protection against robbers. Was the tomb intact? This was the moment when he sent his historic telegram announcing the wonderful discovery to Lord Carnarvon in England. And it is to Carter's credit that he then contained his excitement, filled in the excavation, and waited 18 days for his benefactor to arrive.

'The day of days'

What followed is one of the great stories of archaeology. Having re-cleared the stairwell and the corridor, Carter and Carnarvon discovered some worrying evidence of intrusion by grave robbers in ancient times. Then the explorers pushed on to a second sealed door. Beyond, Carter glimpsed details of an inner chamber choked with 'strange animals, statues, and gold – everywhere the glint of gold'.

ALL SMILES Howard Carter (on the left) and Lord Carnarvon (right) standing outside Tutankhamun's burial place a few days after the tomb was discovered.

Carter that the search must be called off. The Earl was 56 years old and in poor health. He had at last lost faith that new tombs remained to be found there. Even if one was unearthed, it would probably have been robbed like the others.

Howard Carter, though, would not admit defeat. He craved just one more season to explore the only spot in the whole valley that had not yet been excavated – a patch just to the side of the entrance to the tomb of Ramses VI. He said that he was prepared to pay for the dig himself if Carnarvon would just grant him permission under the concession. Should he find anything it would be

credited to the Earl, Carter said – and confronted with such a generous offer, Lord Carnarvon agreed to fund one last attempt.

The target area lay beneath a group of 20th Dynasty huts built to house the workmen who worked on the tomb of Ramses VI. On November 3, 1922, Carter told his assembled labourers to dig a trench straight through the middle of the dwellings. Next morning, not long after dawn, he arrived at the site to find his workmen standing in silence, looking down into the trench where a clean white step could be seen, cut into the limestone bedrock. Excitedly, but with a care born of years of systematic toil, they cleared

LUCKY CHARM Two baboons with moon discs worship the Sun god, represented in scarab beetle form, on this pendant found in Tutankhamun's tomb.

Certainly, thieves in ancient days had carried off some of the jewellery buried with the king. But a fantastic haul of treasures had survived: gilt couches, their sides in the form of weird animals, life-sized statues of the pharaoh in black bitumenised wood with golden kilts and headdresses, a golden throne inlaid with semiprecious stones,

inlaid caskets, alabaster vessels and much more. Carter wrote that November 26, 1922, was 'the day of days, the most wonderful that I have ever lived through, and certainly one whose like I can never hope to see again'. The ultimate discovery was that of Tutankhamun's sarcophagus, which contained a nest of three coffins set inside one another. The innermost coffin was made of solid gold and contained the mummified body of the young king. His head was hidden by a gold mask, and in the wrappings of the body Carter found a total of 143 precious objects of gold and jewellery.

The Tutankhamun discovery transformed our understanding of Egyptian history – and it caught the public imagination as no other archaeological find has done. While visitors

AN UNPROMISING START

Howard Carter, who made the find of the century, worked as a young man under the celebrated archaeologist Sir Flinders Petrie. He failed to impress the great man. 'Mr Carter is a good natured lad whose interest is entirely in painting and natural history,' wrote Petrie. 'It is of no use to me to work him up as an excavator.'

on donkeys or in sandcarts flocked to the newly discovered tomb, the fashion houses of London, Paris and New York were swept by an Egyptian vogue for heavy kohl eyeshadow, turbans and pencil dresses. Patents for Tutankhamun umbrellas and bathing suits were taken out. Meanwhile, Lord Carnarvon's death in April 1923, from an infected mosquito bite, spawned long-lasting press reports that a curse befell those who had profaned the pharaoh's resting place.

TREASURE CHEST Among the pharaoh's possessions was this chest decorated with an image of Tutankhamun as a charioteer.

LOST IN THE SAHARA

A FRENCHMAN, HENRI LHOTE, JOURNEYS ON FOOT ACROSS THE HEART OF THE WESTERN SAHARA

At the turn of the 20th century, the western Sahara remained one of the world's regions most hostile to European exploration. Pitiless sunshine and sandstorms accounted only in part for its inaccessibility; the harsh terrain was also home to raiding parties of Tuareg, who brutally killed more than one Victorian explorer. The Tuareg are camel nomads, known as 'the people of the veil' because the menfolk all wear a *litham*, or black face-covering, which they raise only when they eat. Famed for the speed

WHEN THE SAHARA WAS GREEN

During the 1950s, French explorer Henri Lhote revealed to the world the splendours of ancient Saharan rock art. Thousands of paintings can be seen on the cliffs and in the caves of Tassili N'Ajjer, a sandstone massif in the central Sahara about 1240 miles (2000 km) south-east of Algiers. Though this eroded region of canyons and gorges is now surrounded by parched desert, investigators have learnt that Tassili was once green and fertile enough to support human settlements and a wealth of animal life, both wild and domestic.

The earliest images are hunting scenes that date from 6000 to 4000 BC, and show dark-skinned men chasing gazelles, elephants, buffaloes and hippopotamuses; even ostriches are depicted. Later scenes portray herdsmen with huge herds of long-horned cattle, as well as women and children working by village huts: evidently the Tassili people had by now adopted a pastoral life.

At the time when the paintings were made, the climate was much damper than it is today. However, the Sahara started to dry out during the phase when the inhabitants were farming, and by the time of Christ was as arid in the interior as it is now.

THE LIVING DESERT Cave paintings from Tassili N'Ajjer in the central Sahara recall a time when the area was green and fertile, and vibrant with human and animal life.

and endurance of their racing camels, or *mehari*, the Tuareg are also highly renowned for their skills as warriors.

The land of fear

Lying in Tuareg country, the Tanezrouft region of the Sahara is a rock-strewn desert sprawling over some 58 000 sq miles (150 000 km²). Dubbed the 'land of fear' by white explorers, this is perhaps the most extreme region in the whole Sahara – a wind-scoured inferno virtually devoid of plant life. And in July 1931, a young French explorer and ethnologist named Henri Lhote made crossing this parched fastness his goal.

FRENCH EXPLORER
The young Henri Lhote, already a noted expert on the Sahara, displays a Tuareg sword, its blade dating from the Middle Ages.

Lhote set off on camel-back from Gao on the Niger for Tamanrasset in the Hoggar mountains, with a Tuareg guide, a camel-driver and two mounted tribesmen. But not long after they had left camp, the guide fell victim to an eye infection that caused both eyes to swell so badly they closed up, and he had to force them open with his fingers to find the way.

One day, as Lhote returned to camp from an early morning surveying trip, he was startled to find the guide dead, and his three weeping companions digging a grave. The problem was serious, since none of the others knew the way forward. The two tribesmen refused to continue, and the depleted caravan went without them.

Surviving the sandstorm

That night a blinding sandstorm erupted, lashing Lhote and his camel-driver with such ferocity that they could only make progress by crawling. Taking refuge by a rocky hillock, they unloaded the beasts, took shelter among the baggage and fell asleep. When they awoke, they found that the camels had vanished.

After a search, Lhote managed to recover his own racing camel, and he lent it to the driver so that he could go off and find the other beasts. Even as he did so, however, Lhote had a presentiment that his companion would desert him. And whether the hunch was right or the camel-driver simply got lost in the desert, he never returned. The young Frenchman was left alone, on foot, in the heart of the Tanezrouft.

His worries were eased a little by the playful antics of Boubou, a small monkey that he had been given by a woman on the Niger. Deciding to make the best of his situation, Lhote gathered dried dates, rice, coffee and a skin holding two gallons of water from the baggage rations. Other necessities included compass, binoculars, map, notebook and automatic pistol. Lhote's shoes were worn out, and he made a pair of sandals from an antelope skin, packing some strips of leather in case repairs should be needed. Lastly, the explorer took a long rope, in case he found the opportunity to draw water from a well.

Surprise encounter

Laden with this equipment, Lhote trudged off, his burden increased by the weight of Boubou perched on the haversack. He trekked by night and day, using a long antelope horn for a walking stick, resting during the annihilating heat of midday, and then moving on as the shadows lengthened. In 24 hours he had reached the foothills of the Akarot mountains, where he slept in a wadi, or dried-out riverbed, and was woken by Boubou's shrieks at an approaching hyena. The creature slunk back into the night.

Continuing into the mountains, Lhote was soon lost in a maze of granite walls and gullies with no clear memory of how he had got in. Briefly he was able to follow some old camel tracks that appeared to lead west. Then he lost them again and, with his sandalled feet lacerated by rock spurs, his shoulders rubbed raw from the weight of his load, he had to scale the rocky inclines in search of an exit from the labyrinth.

Eventually, in the basin-shaped hollow of a wadi, Lhote detected a dampness in the ground and began to dig with an oryx horn. Two feet down he found water – and from the muddy hole he was able to extract enough liquid to fill a waterskin. Not long afterwards, Boubou suddenly gripped his leg. Silently, under the killing sun, a man was watching them from a distance. Instinctively, Lhote grabbed his revolver calling out in Tuareg: 'Who are you?'

The stranger – who was bare-chested and wore no veil – seemed as astonished by the encounter as Lhote. He made no reply at first, but eventually identified himself as 'a man of the mountains'. He was not a Tuareg but one of the Ifôghas people, and his camp was pitched about half a day's journey away.

The harshness of desert life has made one law universal among Sahara people – that of hospitality to the exhausted traveller. Lhote was taken to the safety of the stranger's camp and became a cause of great astonishment among the tribesmen. Allah was indeed great, people said, to permit an infidel to survive such an ordeal. Later, Lhote learnt that a patrol had been sent out for him and that the commandant had told the troops to take some canvas with them with which to make a shroud for the missing explorer.

DESERT WARRIORS

Feared by all explorers in the Sahara, the Tuareg provided serious opposition to European intruders. Led by a warrior aristocracy, they fought on racing camels famous for their grace and speed, with a barbed lance, a double-edged sword and a bracelet dagger attached by a band to the left wrist. Four confederations of the tribes partitioned the desert among themselves: the Hoggars in the central Sahara; the Ajjers to the north; the Ifôghas in the south-west; and Kelouis in the Air mountains.

MEN OF THE VEIL Tuareg riders struck fear into the hearts of European travellers.

ACROSS THE EMPTY QUARTER

BERTRAM THOMAS AND HARRY PHILBY VIE TO BE FIRST TO CROSS THE DESERT OF THE RUB'AL KHALI

One of the world's most dry and hostile terrains is the Rub'al Khali desert, which extends for some 251 000 sq miles (650 000 km²) from southern Saudi Arabia into Yemen and Oman. Known as 'The Empty Quarter', this waterless region of rock and wind-blown sand dunes has yet to be fully charted. In the early years of the 20th

FATHER OF THE FAMOUS KIM

Desert explorer Harry St John Philby was the father of the notorious double agent, Kim Philby. His own record of service was impeccable, however, and he died in Beirut in 1960, three years before his son's defection to the Soviet Union.

century, it was probably the world's largest totally unexplored area outside the polar wastes. Largely shunned even by the Bedouin, it provided one of the last great

PILGRIM IN ARABIA Philby with an Arab escort near Hejaz, Arabia. He learnt to speak perfect Arabic and acquired a love of Arab customs.

challenges for desert explorers, and an object of particular fascination for the Englishman, Harry St John Philby.

Born in Sri Lanka to parents who formed part of the British colonial administration there, Philby served as a political officer in Iraq during the First World War and in 1917 was sent to Riyadh in central Arabia. Philby became associated with Lawrence of Arabia in supporting Arab independence. He also travelled; on a political mission to the Red Sea port of Jeddah, he became only the second European to cross Arabia from east to west (the first was an English soldier in 1819). For this achievement, the Royal Geographical Society awarded him a medal.

A seaward dash

In 1918 Philby went on a journey of exploration into the relatively well-settled central plateau region of Arabia known as the Nejd. He got as far south as the oasis of As-Sulayyil on the edge of the Empty Quarter, and it was while looking out over its vast, desolate spaces that he was seized by the desire to cross the desert – a feat no Westerner had accomplished before. For years after the war, Philby dreamed of the trip. He took up a post as adviser to Ibn Saud, the Arab nationalist leader who was soon to become the first king of Saudi Arabia. In 1930, Philby converted to Islam, and as a result Ibn Saud gave him

THE EXPERT Known as 'Sheikh Abdallah', Englishman Harry St John Philby reputedly 'knew the desert better than any Arab'.

permission to make his long-planned expedition across the Rub'al Khali.

Philby hoped to make the journey in the winter of 1930-1, but was forced to cancel his plans, and thereby missed out on being the first European to cross the Empty Quarter. He was beaten in this by Bertram Thomas, another former British political officer, who was adviser to the ruler of Muscat.

Thomas crossed the desert from south to north that winter, following the only well-watered route used by

DESERT QUEST

TODAY, SATELLITES AND MICROLIGHT AIRCRAFT SCAN THE FORBIDDING ARABIAN WASTES THAT ONCE CHALLENGED THE HARDIEST EXPLORERS

The challenge of desert travel is the challenge of confronting extremes: of heat and cold and privation. Explorer Wilfred Thesiger, who twice crossed the Arabian Empty Quarter between 1946 and 1949, wrote that 'to others my journey would have little importance. It would produce nothing except a rather inaccurate map which no one was ever likely to use. It was a personal experience, and the reward had been a drink of clean, nearly tasteless water. I was content with that.'

During the First World War, the northern deserts of Arabia were little known, and in roaming across great swathes of the Hejaz at the head of the Arab revolt, T.E. Lawrence was as much an explorer as a guerrilla fighter. But by the 1930s the last great unexplored area was the Rub'al Khali, the Empty Quarter, which drew Bertram Thomas and Harry St John Philby like a magnet. No further attempt was made on this vast wilderness until Wilfred Thesiger's first expedition. An English soldier, writer and photographer, Thesiger was assigned after the Second World War to the Middle East Anti-Locust Unit, which had been created to destroy the hordes of pests then threatening agricultural production. His *Arabian Sands* survives as a notable record of a Bedouin society already threatened by 20th-century values – before long, the petroleum wealth of the Arabian peninsula would transform traditional life. 'I shall always remember,' he wrote, 'how often I was humbled by those illiterate herdsmen who possessed, in so much greater measure than I, generosity and courage, endurance, patience, and light-hearted gallantry. Among no

FACE OF EXPERIENCE This photograph of Wilfred Thesiger was taken after one of his crossings of Arabia's Empty Quarter.

other people have I felt the same sense of personal inferiority.'

The heroic tradition of the individual explorers is now fading, but new expeditions are continually mounted in the name of scientific research. It became clear during the 1970s that the world's deserts were expanding due to deforestation, over-grazing and other practices. Since then, multinational teams supported by computers, satellite imagery, microlights and radio-controlled ATVs (All-Terrain Vehicles) have all played their part in the study of dune formation, erosion, ecosystems and so on. The problem of desertification needs urgent international action, and one major project, undertaken in 1985-6, was a study of the Wahiba Sands, in the eastern region of the Sultanate of Oman. Organised by the British Royal Geographical Society and the Sultanate, the 43-strong team studied the desert as a complete ecosystem – looking at the relationships between people, biological resources and the sands themselves.

OLD MEETS NEW A traditional desert traveller passes a vehicle of the Wahiba Sands Project which made full use of modern technology.

LIVING LEGEND British soldier T.E. Lawrence, known as 'Lawrence of Arabia', won fame through his First World War desert exploits, recounted in his book *The Seven Pillars of Wisdom*.

SEA OF SAND The Empty Quarter is the world's largest expanse of continuous sand.

the Bedouin. Thomas travelled with a large party of Bedouin, camels and pack animals, and from the water hole of Shanna made a final seaward dash across the fearsome sands with 12 picked men. On the morning of February 5, 1931, the Bedouin 'moved forward at a sharp pace, chanting the water chants. Our thirsty camels pricked up their ears with eager knowingness . . . Half an hour later we entered the walls of the fort. The Rub'al Khali had been crossed.'

Undeterred by his rival's success, Philby began his own expedition a year later, taking a much more arduous route. On January 7,

RECORD ACHIEVEMENT In 1931, Bertram Thomas emerged from the sands at Doha as the first European to have crossed the Empty Quarter. 'Damn and blast Thomas', wrote his rival, Harry Philby.

1932, he set out from the wells of Dulaiqiya near the town of Al-Hufuf, due west of Qatar. With a party of 19 Bedouins and 32 camels, he crossed the al Jafurah desert in weather so bitterly cold that their water skins had to be unfrozen every morning.

From the oasis of Jabrin they entered unknown country where, it was said, lay the ruins of the legendary city of Wabar. Arab lore told how this sinful metropolis had been destroyed by fire from heaven, and reduced by divine wrath to an iron block no bigger than a camel. Suddenly one day, from a hill in the heart of the sands, Philby found himself gazing down on the site. But it was not the ruins of a city that lay before him – it was the site of two meteoric craters 100 yd (91.5 m) wide. 'Wabar', evidently, was the place of impact of a meteorite shower. Philby even came upon a lump of rusted meteoric iron, which must have been the iron block of the heavenly fire legend.

Philby pressed on to Shanna, the water hole where Thomas had begun his crossing. His first attempt to trek on across the desert to the oasis of As-Sulayyil met with failure – the exhausted camels could not go on. On a second attempt, Philby's party travelled light

INTERPRETING CAMEL TRACKS

The explorer Bertram Thomas learnt from his Bedouin companions how much could be read into tracks in the sand:

'As we went we crossed many recent camel tracks which showed Farajja to be a popular water-hole. The grouped tracks of four camels walking in line arrested my companion's attention, and he turned to me and asked me in play which camel I saw in the sands to be best. I pointed – pardonably, I persuaded myself – to the wrong one. "There," he said, "do you see that cuffing up of the toes? It is a good sign: but not that skidding (pointing to mine) between the footmarks. That," he said of the third, "is an animal that has recently been in the steppe. Do you see the rugged impressions of her feet? Camels that have been long in the sands leave smooth impressions, and that (pointing to the fourth) is her baby. Your camel is big with young – see the deep impressions of her small hind feet." And thus and thus. It was not the least important piece of Hamad's lore – a lore shared by nearly every dweller of the sands in varying degree – to read the condition of the strange camel, as yet unseen, from her marks, and hence to know whether to flee or to pursue.'

and pushed themselves to the limit. Travelling 1800 miles (2880 km) through parched desert in 90 days, they reached As-Sulayyil on March 11. Philby was the first European to make an east-west crossing of the Rub'al Khali. It says much for the rigours of the trip that no further attempts were made on the Empty Quarter until after the Second World War.

THE LURE OF THE EAST

ASIA'S WILD PLACES YIELDED MANY TREASURES TO SPIRITS BOLD ENOUGH TO TACKLE HER MOUNTAINS AND PLAINS. EXPLORERS FOUND DINOSAUR EGGS IN OUTER MONGOLIA . . . A BLUE POPPY AND A FORBIDDEN CITY IN THE HIMALAYAS . . . A SECRET HAUL OF ANCIENT MANUSCRIPTS IN CHINA'S CAVE OF THE THOUSAND BUDDHAS. THE JUNGLES OF BORNEO AND NEW GUINEA, MEANWHILE, SHELTERED HEADHUNTING TRIBES WHOSE LIFESTYLE WAS UNCHANGED SINCE THE STONE AGE.

THE YOUNGHUSBAND EXPEDITION

A BRITISH OFFICER LEADS OVER **1000** SOLDIERS INTO LHASA, THE FORBIDDEN CITY OF TIBET

Guarded from the south by the mighty Himalayas and from the north by the rugged wilderness of the Tibetan plateau, Lhasa, the Forbidden City and the capital of Tibet, is among the most remote cities in the world. Site of the terraced palace of the Dalai Lama, known as the Potala, and a wealth of ancient temples and monasteries, it was closed to foreigners in the 19th century, and came to hold a peculiar fascination as a mystic realm and a supposed storehouse of Asian riches. In 1879, the great Russian explorer Nikolai Przhevalsky was forced to turn back by Tibetan soldiers when he was 170 miles (272 km) from Lhasa. In 1901, the Swedish explorer Sven Hedin disguised as a Mongol, did not get much closer and was repulsed by officials.

However, the Forbidden City was by no means a complete mystery to Europeans. Catholic priests in earlier times had reached Lhasa and, even when the ban on foreigners was in operation, British officials in India

THE SOLDIER EXPLORERS Sir Francis Younghusband's military party was ostensibly engaged on a diplomatic mission.

routinely sent in native secret agents to gather information. Tibet occupied a strategic position at the northern margin of Britain's Indian Empire, and its politics were therefore of great interest to the British. The situation came to a head when it was learned that a Russian agent named Dorjieff, a Mongolian and former Buddhist monk, had taken up residence in Lhasa and won influence over the Dalai Lama. This might have been dangerous to British interests.

Bands of desperate swordsmen

In the summer of 1903, Sir Francis Younghusband, an English soldier who had explored the Karakoram and Pamir mountains, was chosen to lead a mission to Tibet to counter the growing Russian influence in Lhasa. Over 1000 soldiers and 300 sepoys were involved. The troops assembled that winter on the icy plateau of Tuna and, in March 1904, the force headed north for the Tibetan capital. It was ostensibly a diplomatic mission, but one aimed at forcing a treaty on the Dalai Lama that would give Britain effective dominion over his realm. Not surprisingly, it met resistance.

Before dawn on May 5, a force of 800 Tibetans attacked a British post at Chang Lo

ROUTE TO LHASA The British troops assembled at Tuna and headed north by way of the Giangtse region.

manned by barely 120 riflemen. Yelling war cries, the Tibetans thrust their antique muskets through the slits in the building's walls usually used by defenders for firing outwards, and fired into the British position. For some minutes confusion reigned, but the garrison suffered no losses and quickly turned their own weapons on the attackers

OVERTAKEN BY A BLIZZARD

Edmund Candler, a *Daily Mail* correspondent, described a British supply column's difficulties in stockpiling at the little town of Tuna, chosen as winter quarters for Younghusband's advance:

'In mid-March a convoy of the 12th Mule Corps, escorted by two companies of the 23rd Pioneers, were overtaken by a blizzard on their march between Phari and Tuna, and camped in two feet [60 cm] of snow with the thermometer 18 degrees below zero. A driving hurricane made it impossible to light a fire or cook food. The officers were reduced to frozen bully beef and neat spirits, while the sepoys went without food for thirty-six hours...The drivers arrived at Tuna frozen to the waist. Twenty men of the 12th Mule Corps were frost-bitten, and thirty men of the 23rd Pioneers were so incapacitated that they had to be carried in on mules. On the same day there were seventy cases of snow-blindness among the 8th Gurkhas.'

with devastating results. After two hours, the Tibetans had been repulsed and were fleeing over the plain with the garrison in pursuit. Tibetan casualties were put at 250 killed or seriously wounded. The British had just two sepoys wounded.

Further clashes took place in the Giangtse region south-west of Lhasa. At the

fortified monastery of Naini, British troops met a kind of fighting hardly known since the sackings of the Thirty Years' War: medieval street fighting in the endless monastic labyrinths where, said *The Times* correspondent, Perceval Landon, 'bands of desperate swordsmen were found in knots under trapdoors and behind sharp turnings. They would not surrender, and had to be killed by rifle shots fired at a distance of a few feet.' At the fortress of Giangtse, Tibetan walls were breached by heavy British gunfire and troops stormed up a steep ravine while masses of rubble poured down on the invading redcoats.

In the end, the defenders' muskets were no match for British machine guns, and Younghusband himself conceded that the slaughter of Tibetans was 'a terrible and ghastly business'. By July 14, the serious fighting was over, and the British officer led his men out of Giangtse along the road to Lhasa. The route climbed to the 16 500 ft (5029 m) Karo La Pass, and beyond to visions of the Yam-dok or Turquoise Lake – a fantastic natural feature of the Lhasa region. The pale

HOLY CITADEL Buddhist prayer flags festoon the approach to Lhasa, perched high amid the Himalayan peaks.

blue waters, rimmed with white curving sandspits, are edged with spangles of dog rose and forget-me-not, while the ice fields of the high Himalayas form a distant backdrop. On the shore lay the convent of Samding, home of the Dorje Phagmo, or pig goddess.

Eventually, in a state of growing excitement, the soldiers caught their first glimpse of the golden temple roofs and white walls of the

A CITY OF WOMEN

The vast number of celibate monks in Llasa at the time of the Younghusband Expedition led to a very unbalanced population in the rest of the city. Excluding the monks, the population numbered about 10 000 people, of whom at least two-thirds were women.

many-storeyed houses of Lhasa itself, rising above a green plain threaded with dykes and canals. One of the discoveries of the Younghusband expedition was that the Tibetan plateau is not wholly an arid waste; about one-third is nearly as fertile and well watered as Kashmir. The Tibetans were very fond of parks and gardens, which flourished all about; and with the immense, golden-roofed citadel of the Potala rising high over all, ringed by dark mountains, the scene was spectacular.

At closer quarters, though, the troops saw another side of Lhasa. When Younghusband rode at the head of his mission through the city gates, he found a squalid slum. The crooked streets were extremely narrow and filled with beggars. Rain transformed the streets into muddy pools in which the British saw, here and there, the corpse of a yak or other pack animal, while pigs and ravens scavenged in the open sewers.

Holy of Holies

Looming from its rocky eminence, the great Potala palace, taller than St Paul's Cathedral in London, lost some of its original enchantment when it was revealed, on closer inspection, to consist of a warren of small rooms and broken stairways. The Potala's central building comprised the crimson-painted private quarters of the Dalai Lama, and the sanctuaries around were impressive enough, curtained by yak-hair draperies 80 ft (24 m) long. But the Dalai Lama was not there to greet them. The spiritual head of the Buddhist church, and temporal ruler of 6 million people, had fled his palace by night and was borne away in a palanquin before the British arrival.

More impressive than the Potala was Lhasa's great cathedral, three storeys high

BOOBY TRAP Using an old ambush technique, Tibetan troops unleash rocks from a tilting-table onto the British Expeditionary Force.

and capped by gilded roofs. Certain members of the British mission were invited to enter this Holy of Holies and were the first white men to approach the inner sanctuary of the Buddhist faith. Amid the many candle-lit chambers, in the central shrine, sat the great golden Buddha, roped with jewels and crowned with turquoise and pearl. The face of the statue was decorated with burnished gold, applied in the form of a powder; it flickered continually in the light of the golden lamps fed with animal fat that had been placed before it by worshippers. The British visitors were stoned by local people on leaving the building, but the sight was reckoned risking much to see. Otherwise the invaders met little resistance. Younghusband noted in a telegram that everyone seemed in fear, not so much of the British, but of each other: 'General attitude of Tibetans, though exasperating, is probably more futile and inept than intentionally hostile.'

Eventually, the Tibetan authorities agreed to a British ultimatum, and on September 7 the Regent, acting for the Dalai Lama, conceded to the invaders' demands to bar non-British foreigners from entering the country. After seven weeks in Lhasa, with the Treaty

PALACE IN THE SKY The golden-roofed Potala palace crowns the summit of Lhasa. In 1905, its terraces swarmed with British soldiers and journalists.

END OF A DREAM British troops march into Lhasa, where they met little resistance and found slum-like conditions.

in their baggage, the redcoats began their homeward march. The mission had been a triumph, and there were substantial geographical benefits, too. A party of four British officers and six Gurkhas diverged from the main group and explored the Tsangpo River and the Sutlej valley, adding much to Western knowledge of the Himalayas. They established that the rumoured northern rivals to Mount Everest did not exist. Above all, the Younghusband Expedition dispelled the dream of a mysterious sacred city glimpsed through travellers' tales and steeped in the fairytale lore of Kublai Khan and the Arabian Nights. Mapped and photographed, Lhasa, the Forbidden City, entered the guidebooks as just another place on the 20th-century map of Asia.

ZEALOUS PILGRIMS

In 1904, the year of the Younghusband Expedition, the *Strand Magazine* reported on a visit to Lhasa made in 1900 by a Mongolian Russian named G.T. Tsybikov. He went with a pilgrim caravan, and described how worshippers would abase themselves on the road that ran for 8 miles (13 km) around the Forbidden City:

'The devout are in the habit of making the circuit, prostrating themselves continually. A zealous pilgrim can complete the journey in two days, making three thousand prostrations a day. They travel, in fact, on their stomachs, drawing up their legs as far as possible, and pushing themselves forward a body's length at a time, standing erect, however, between the movements and falling flat again. Sometimes the pilgrims protect their hands with boards, though these are not the most fervent devotees. Thus they traverse not only the circuit of the city, but often pass three times and even seven times round it. The last feat takes about a fortnight, and requires about forty-two thousand prostrations!'

FORBIDDEN CITY

BEFORE THE COMING OF THE YOUNGHUSBAND MILITARY EXPEDITION, FEW WESTERN EYES HAD SEEN LHASA AND ITS ARCHITECTURAL SPLENDOURS

As early as 1661, two Jesuit priests, fathers Grueber and d'Orville, passed through Lhasa on their way back from China. On their return to Europe they described the Himalayan sacred city as comparable to Rome in the number of its priests, monasteries and convents. More European visits followed, but during the 19th century, entry was barred to Europeans. Lhasa is accessible only by a few mountain passes, which are easily patrolled, and which, in any case, are closed by snows in winter.

The last Englishman to penetrate the Forbidden City in the 19th century was an eccentric called Thomas Manning who went in 1811, perfunctorily disguised as 'a Chinese gentleman'. In January 1846, two French missionaries named Evarist Huc and Joseph Gabet managed to enter the city disguised as Buddhist monks, in a Chinese caravan of 2000 men. Their foreign origin was betrayed by their long noses, but the pair were allowed to stay in Lhasa for nearly two months before being expelled.

In May 1900, a Mongolian Russian named G.T. Tsybikov entered Lhasa with a pilgrim caravan and spent over a year in the Forbidden City, afterwards writing of the people and their customs. Food, he noted, consisted chiefly of the flour of roasted barley, which was mixed with tea, or mashed into a porridge with chopped radishes – the main vegetable. Meat was eaten raw, or underdone, yak-meat, mutton and pork being prized more highly than beef. Both men and women drank great quantities of a cheap but not very intoxicating barley wine, and the men smoked leaf tobacco in pipes, the monks crushing it into snuff.

Tsybikov observed that women were especially active in society; Tibet was 'the land of women and of women's rights' and nowhere in the world were female citizens more involved in business. But in other respects, the society was medieval. Suspected criminals were interrogated with whips, and tortures included cauterisation with blazing sealing wax. Punishments included exile into slavery, blinding, amputation of the fingers and perpetual fetters or stocks.

The inefficiency of Tibet's blue-clad soldiers also attracted Tsybikov's attention. Tibetan troops went armed with swords, muzzle-loading firearms, and bows and arrows; armour amounted to little more than a feathered helmet and a small shield. Discipline was poor, the soldiers living in their villages, and assembling only periodically for drill in archery and in the use of firearms. 'The Central Tibetan is averse to war and military service,' wrote Tsybikov. 'One often sees a soldier on the way to the drill-ground placidly spinning wool or sewing on a boot-sole or perhaps employing the time which would otherwise be wasted in telling a rosary or turning a prayer-cylinder.' Men like these would be no match for the disciplined British soldiers who marched on Lhasa in 1904.

ROOFTOP ADORNMENTS Gilded bell-pillars and a tantra-wheel on the roof of Lhasa's great cathedral. To the invading troops, this was the most impressive of the city's buildings.

O THE CAVE OF THE 000 BUDDHAS

PLORER MARK AUREL STEIN RECOVERS A STORE MANUSCRIPTS FROM ANCIENT CAVES IN CHINA

Marco Polo, the medieval Venetian, was the first traveller to reveal the wonders of the Silk Road to Western eyes. Along the trade route connecting China with the Mediterranean, exotic silks and spices had been carried since ancient times. But until the 19th century, Polo's narrative remained a rare source of information about

SACRED GROTTOES Mark Aurel Stein (inset) was the first European to see China's Dunhuang caves. Today, walkways provide access to caves on several levels.

the arduous caravan road that led over the mountains and desert plains of central Asia. It was left to Victorian explorers to begin charting the route, and even in the early 20th century mystery still lingered about it.

One name associated with 20th-century exploration of the Silk Road is that of the archaeologist Sir Mark Aurel Stein. In a 30-year career, he trekked some 25 000 miles (40 000 km), seeking the tombs and temples of a long-lost Buddhist civilisation. Stein crisscrossed the lonely wastes of western China so thoroughly that a map of his journeys looks, in the words of travel writer Eric Newby, like the footprints of a demented centipede.

Born in Budapest, Hungary, Stein won a place at Oxford University as a postgraduate

and thereafter thought of England as his home. He later accepted a post at Punjab University in India, where he remained for some years before realising his main ambition of investigating archaeological sites in

STEPPE-DWELLERS Kirghiz herdsmen of central Asia photographed outside their felt tents by Mark Aurel Stein.

PAINTED FACADE The decorated porch of one of the Dunhuang sacred caves, long venerated by Chinese Buddhists.

central Asia. Supported by the Indian government, Stein embarked on his first expedition in March 1900. He took a small fox terrier called Dash, who became an indispensable travelling companion; Stein wrote affectionately in his letters of how the dog enlivened many hours of solitude with his antics. When Dash died, Stein replaced him with another fox terrier, Dash II, and by the time of his death at the age of 80, he had Dash VII.

NIGHT-TIME REMOVALS

In 1907, archaeologist Sir Mark Aurel Stein furtively removed an astonishing quantity of ancient manuscripts over a period of days from the Caves of the 1000 Buddhas, with assistance from his Chinese secretary, Chiang-ssu-yeh:

'It was late at night when I heard cautious footsteps. It was Chiang who had come to make sure that nobody was stirring about my tent. A little later he returned with a big bundle over his shoulders. It contained everything I had picked out during the day's work...For seven nights more he thus came to my tent, when everybody had gone to sleep, with the same precautions, his slight figure panting under loads which grew each time heavier, and ultimately required carriage by instalments. For hands accustomed to wield only pen and paper it was a trying task, and never shall I forget the good-natured ease and cheerful devotion with which it was performed by that most willing of helpmates...

'But my time for feeling true relief came when all the twenty-four cases, heavy with manuscript treasures rescued from that strange place of hiding, and the five more filled with paintings and other art relics from the same cave, had been deposited safely in the British Museum.'

Stein's first expedition was prompted by Sven Hedin's discovery of the ruins of an ancient city in western China's fearsome Taklimakan desert, the 'desert of death', whose towering sand dunes both dwarf and devour travellers. The Silk Road had skirted the margins of the desert, following a string of isolated oasis towns along the foothills of the mighty Tien Shan and Kun Lun mountain ranges. Even in the heyday of the route, however, many caravans of merchants, pilgrims and soldiers lost their way between the stations, never to be heard of again. In Stein's day, the ancient route had long since decayed, shifting sands had covered several lost towns, and the people – without written records of their own history – could offer no information.

The race to the caves

During his first trip, Stein excavated 14 temples and houses in the buried city of Dandan-Uiliq, recovering 8th-century copper coins and revealing stucco reliefs of many Buddhas and Bodhisattvas. He also discovered quantities of ancient documents at other sites near the city of Khotan. But his most celebrated find came during his second expedition, begun in April 1906, when he travelled to the oasis town of Dunhuang (Tun-huang) on the border of Kansu, China's north-west frontier province.

On the outskirts of Dunhuang there were reported to be cliffs honeycombed with hundreds of grottoes that had long been venerated by Chinese Buddhists as sacred temples. Decorated with frescoes and sculptures, the caves were no secret, and it would not be long before other European archaeologists made them their target. In seeking out the treasures of ancient China, Stein had many competitors – German, French, Swedish, American and Japanese. Though often spoken of as the man who discovered the 'Caves of the 1000

Buddhas', Stein was, more properly, the first to reach them.

With camels and 15 mule-loads of supplies, Stein approached by way of the forbidding Lop desert, a wasteland of rutted clay

FOOTSTEPS IN THE DESERT

Explorer Mark Aurel Stein crossed and recrossed the remote region between the Hindu Kush and the Gobi desert so frequently that he once came upon his own footprints from three years earlier. In 1908, while exploring the Kun Lun mountains, Stein became so badly frostbitten that he had to have all the toes of one foot amputated.

banks sandblasted by the Mongolian winds. A Buddhist monk named Fa-hsien (Faxian) had crossed this desert in AD 399 and written of it: 'Though you look all round most earnestly to find where you can cross, you know not where to make your choice, the only mark and indication being the dry bones of the dead left upon the sand.' The broken ground caused Stein's camels to

ANCIENT ARTISTRY The Bodhisattva Kuan-Yin, a painting on silk, was found by Stein in the Dunhuang caves.

days on end they saw no sight of another human being. And then, on March 12, after a trek over a plain stacked with ruined watch-towers, they reached Dunhuang.

The sacred caves lay about 12 miles (19 km) south-east of the town. Rock-cut steps had once connected many of the smaller caves, but these had long since decayed so that the dark apertures were accessible only by ropes or ladders. Decorated porches had collapsed, and sand had drifted into the lower shrines. But the ruin of the monuments could not disguise their former grandeur. Here were carved-out halls with frescoes and stucco sculptures of the Buddha as much as 90 ft (27 m) high, the bright colours on the plastered walls preserved by the dry atmosphere.

In a typical cave temple, the antechapel led into a passageway

SAVED OR STOLEN? The silk painting (left) and embroidered banner (below) were among several cartloads of items taken by Stein to the British Museum.

groan in pain, and the driver had to sew oxhide to their cracked feet. Fourteen miles (22 km) a day was the best they could manage over such terrain.

After a week-long trek across the desert, they came upon the gale-torn ruins of Loulan, a Chinese outpost from the 2nd century that had been discovered by Sven Hedin. Stein made important excavations there before pressing on in increasingly vicious winter weather. In February 1907, three of their donkeys died of exhaustion and they reached a region so desolate that for 17

and an inner cell, carved from the living rock where a huge stucco figure of a Buddha sat flanked by Bodhisattvas. The images betrayed strong Indian influence – and indeed it was clear that the style of the grottoes was derived from the rock-temples of India. This valley had been a place of pilgrimage since the 4th century AD, and at its height in the 7th-10th centuries Dunhuang was a bustling oasis to which visitors came from far afield.

Removal of the manuscripts

The caves were not only richly decorated, they had also served as a storehouse for sacred manuscripts, books and paintings. Stein heard a rumour that a secret hoard had been discovered in one of the grottoes, and learnt that they were locked up in a side chapel. He persuaded a priest named Wang to let him look at a bundle of papers, which turned out to be versions of the Buddhist texts brought from India and translated by the 7th-century Chinese Buddhist pilgrim Hiuen Tsiang (Xuanzang). This semi-legendary figure had made a

SECRET STOREHOUSE A stairway leads into the grottoes at Dunhuang, which in Stein's day had been walled off since the 11th century.

SVEN HEDIN – SWEDISH ADVENTURER

As an explorer of the Asian desert wastes, Mark Aurel Stein had a celebrated precursor in the Swedish adventurer Sven Hedin. In 1895, on his first major expedition, Hedin crossed the dreaded Taklimakan desert from south to north, a venture that nearly cost him his life. The water ran out and, mad with thirst, the party resorted with disastrous consequences to drinking camel's urine and spirits from the Primus stove. Sheep's blood was tried too.

Immensely tough and determined, however, Hedin survived and later returned to the Taklimakan to discover the sand-buried ruins of ancient Silk Road cities. 'There stood I like the prince in an enchanted wood, having awakened to new life the city which had slumbered for over a thousand years.' Hedin was not himself an archaeologist, but his reports spurred others to investigate the sites. In 1906-8, Hedin travelled extensively in Tibet, and in 1928-34 he did important work as head of a major Sino-Swedish scientific expedition in China. Unfortunately, his reputation has been tarnished by his later association with Nazism. In 1936, Hedin spoke at the Berlin Olympic Games, and during the Second World War he had meetings with Adolf Hitler. However, his contacts allowed him to save the lives of 13 Norwegian Resistance fighters and a Jewish colleague at a German university.

VETERAN EXPLORER Sven Hedin was leader of the 1928-34 Sino-Swedish expedition that discovered many important archaeological sites in western China.

celebrated journey to the country in which his faith had originated, and collected Sanskrit texts. As Stein investigated further, he discovered an incredible manuscript haul: 'Heaped up in layers, but without any order,' he wrote, 'there appeared in the dim light of the priest's little lamp a solid mass of manuscript bundles rising to a height of nearly ten feet (3 m), and filling, as subsequent measurement showed, close on 500 cubic feet (14 m³).'

Altogether, Stein's discovery was regarded as the greatest archaeological find ever made in Asia. But what followed has met with mixed approval. After a cursory examination of the secret library's contents, Stein handed Wang a modest sum in silver ingots towards renovation in the caves, and discreetly filled up 29 packing cases with manuscripts, paintings, embroideries and other antiquities. On June 14, the expedition left the valley with their fantastic haul – destined for the British Museum – in horse-drawn carts.

Stein made many further expeditions and contributed immensely to Western knowledge of central Asia. But his location of the caves is regarded as his most remarkable achievement. Stein believed that the treasures were suffering from dire neglect at the time that he removed them, and that he had rescued them from possible destruction. In Chinese eyes, however, he was a 'foreign devil' – a typical imperialist brigand. Just as the Greeks want to see the return of the famous Elgin Marbles to Athens, so the Chinese have called for the return of all Dunhuang relics to the caves. Certainly, it is an irony that only a fraction of Stein's haul is on display at the British Museum. The bulk are stored away in the museum basements, hidden from public view.

DINOSAUR EGGS IN OUTER MONGOLIA

FLAMBOYANT YOUNG AMERICAN HEADS EXPEDITIONS INTO THE GOBI DESERT

Looking out from the black-and-white photographs of his Mongolian expeditions, American explorer Roy Chapman Andrews appears the very picture of a *Boy's Own* hero. Clean-jawed beneath his bush hat, with a 6.5 mm Mannlicher rifle and revolver tucked into his cartridge belt, he is ready for any eventuality. Shoot-outs with brigands, 100 mph (160 km/h) sandstorms and face-offs with secret agents, all were the staple fare of

leaf by a whirling sandstorm. I have fought with Chinese bandits. But these things are all a part of the day's work.'

Yet his career began modestly enough, sweeping floors in the taxidermy department of the American Museum of Natural History. Andrews started there in 1906, at the age of 22. While studying marine mammals for a masters degree from Columbia University, he became seized by an idea of his boss, palaeontologist Henry Fairfield Osborn, that

central Asia would prove to have cradled the world's first mammals. More particularly, Osborn had predicted that it would furnish the Missing Link – the hypothetical animal connecting man with the anthropoid apes. This was because the oldest known human fossil, the so-called 'Java Ape-man', had been found at the edge of Asia, and it seemed reasonable to surmise that older remnants might still be found deeper in the continent.

To test the theory, Andrews planned an assault on the Gobi desert, in the

> ## THE FLAMING CLIFFS
>
> During his first expedition to Mongolia in 1922, Roy Chapman Andrews came upon a treasure trove of dinosaur fossils in a sandstone depression close to the Bogd ranges:
>
> 'This was one of the most picturesque spots that I have ever seen. From our tents, we looked down into a vast pink basin, studded with giant buttes like strange beasts carved from sandstone. One of them we named the "dinosaur", for it resembles a strange Brontosaurus sitting on its haunches. There appear to be mediaeval castles with spires and turrets, brick-red in the evening light, colossal gateways, walls and ramparts. Caverns run deep into the rock and a labyrinth of ravines and gorges studded with fossil bones make a paradise for the palaeontologist. One great sculptured wall we named the "Flaming Cliffs", for when seen in early morning or late afternoon sunlight it seemed to be a mass of glowing fire.'

this larger-than-life character on whom the screen hero Indiana Jones of *Raiders of the Lost Ark* is said to have been based.

'I have been so thirsty that my tongue swelled out of my mouth,' Andrews once wrote. 'I have ploughed my way through a blizzard at fifty below zero, against wind that cut like a white-hot brand. I have seen my whole camp swept from the face of the desert like a dry

EGG INSPECTION Roy Chapman Andrews examines 10-million-year-old fossil dinosaur eggs, some containing skeletons of embryo dinosaurs.

Asian heartland. After two preliminary trips examining the feasibility of motor travel on the high, dusty plains, he proposed a larger expedition with a team of specialists. It would, of course, take money. In addition to winning support from the museum, he embarked on a series of fund-raising dinners and lectures. The Press picked up on the story, and before he left he received hundreds of letters from admirers. A St Louis lady telegraphed offering him assistance in finding the Missing Link from her Ouija board. Another lady, enclosing a photograph, offered herself as a female companion: 'I could create the home atmosphere for you in those drear wastes.'

An unruly land

Preparations were completed in the winter of 1921-2, when scores of camels were assembled in China to carry equipment, in addition to Dodge automobiles and trucks from Fulton, Long Island. The Gobi begins at Kalgán, just beyond the Great Wall. 'Below us lay that stupendous relief map of ravines and gorges; in front was a limitless stretch of undulating plain. I knew then that I really stood upon the edge of the greatest plateau in the world and that it could only be Mongolia', wrote Andrews.

The team was entering an unruly land where ambush by bandits or soldiers was an ever-present threat. In the vast Gobi, the only other people were scattered families of herdsmen, who were terrified of all strangers. Andrews himself had to fight off armed bandits as well as wild dogs, which on one occasion mistook the explorers for corpses and attacked them in their sleeping bags. Then there were obstructive local authorities. The expedition's route led them to Urga, where Mongolian officials were reluctant to grant permission to proceed. They were only won over by Andrews's

promise to capture a legendary 'worm' said to live in the Gobi, a long, sausage-shaped creature so poisonous that merely to touch it meant instant death. Andrews promised that if he saw one, he would capture it with his long, steel collecting forceps, wearing dark glasses as a further precaution.

FOLLOW THAT CAR!

While trying to get permission from Mongolian officials at Urga to continue his work in the Gobi, Roy Chapman Andrews was tailed by a security man. The agent was on foot, however, and became exhausted trying to keep pace with the American's rapid sorties in his motor car. Relenting, Andrews invited him to ride with him in the car – an offer that the spy gratefully accepted.

From Urga the expedition headed southwest towards the three Bogd ranges and an obscure site called Ulan Usu 3000 miles (4800 km) from their starting point, which Andrews dubbed Flaming Red Cliffs after the effect of the setting sun on the pink rock. Almost as soon as they entered Mongolia, they had obtained valuable fossils, including relics of the first dinosaurs ever found north of the Himalayas. But Flaming Red Cliffs was 'a paradise for the palaeontologist'. Sedimentary strata in the ravines and gorges yielded immense troves of fossils, which were packed off in crates to America. The following year, when the expedition returned to the site, they discovered the remains of duck-billed dinosaurs and predatory Velociraptors and – most astonishing of all – dinosaur eggs.

The $5000 egg

Until the Andrews expedition, it was by no means certain that dinosaurs laid eggs at all. The discovery began with a cluster of five fossilised ovals about 8 in (20 cm) long, whose pebbled surface was as perfect as if they had been laid the day before. Two were broken in half and, inside, the investigators could make out the delicate vestige of the embryonic dinosaurs. While they were digging out the cluster, they even found the skeleton of a small, toothless dinosaur preserved in the soil underneath; it appeared to have been overtaken by a sandstorm in the very act of robbing the dinosaur nest and was christened *Oviraptor*, 'the egg-seizer'.

Bucketfuls of dinosaur eggs were found in the weeks that followed. One Mongolian woman turned up daily with examples which she cheerfully swapped for tin cans. It appeared that the site had offered a perfect habitat for laying eggs over many thousands of years. Though lakes and forests had covered some of the region in prehistoric times, this area seemed to have offered a dry place where female dinosaurs could cover their nests with sandy soil to keep them warm

EXTRAORDINARY FIND Dinosaur eggs discovered by Andrews in the desert astonished scientists and delighted the public.

prior to hatching. Back in America the public went wild, and when Andrews came home he was mobbed everywhere. A single egg was sold at auction for $5000, and the actor John Barrymore successfully begged Andrews to give him just a few fragments of broken shell.

In five expeditions between 1922 and 1930, Andrews never did find the Missing Link. But apart from discovering several new species of dinosaur, he transformed the public perception of the creatures themselves. Dinosaurs became more than mere monsters; they were family creatures with babies and nesting instincts. And Andrews found more. The skull of one tiny animal found at Flaming Red Cliffs turned out to belong to one of the first mammals, a small, shrew-like creature, and it proved that mammals coexisted with the dinosaurs as far back as the middle of the Cretaceous Period. Andrews proved himself an outstanding discoverer whose talent for self-promotion concealed the qualities of a real and patient scientist.

WHEELS ACROSS ASIA

A FANTASTIC MOTORCADE ATTEMPTS TO FOLLOW THE OLD SILK ROAD FROM EUROPE TO CHINA

LAND CRUISER Georges-Marie Haardt (right) led Citroën's African and Asian expedition. For the Asia crossing, he used vehicles with caterpillar tracks like the one modelled below.

The explorers Aurel Stein and Sven Hedin tackled the old Silk Road as heroic individuals. But if anything brought modernity to the ancient, romantic thoroughfare, it was an extraordinary motor expedition mounted in 1931 by the French automobile magnate André Citroën. In the 1920s, Citroën had already sponsored two great African motor journeys – across the Sahara from north to south and from Algeria to Madagascar – in order to explore the problems faced by heavy vehicles travelling over rough terrain. For his third journey, Citroën looked eastwards, employing a special type of car, rigged up with caterpillar tracks and a steel roller to lift the front of the car over soft sand and similar obstacles.

The expedition was led by Georges-Marie Haardt, the man who had headed the two previous 'cruises', as the journeys were called. And the aim this time was to cross the whole continent of Asia, from Beirut to Peking, following the road of the ancient caravans. A second party, led by Lieutenant Victor Point, was to move westwards from the Chinese end and rendezvous with Haardt's party at Kashgar in the Sinkiang province of China. Both parties carried powerful short-wave radio sets in the hope that they would be able to keep in contact.

Haardt's caravan comprised 14 specially built caterpillar cars, with a wealth of equipment, such as winches, derricks, steel cables and girders, so that the team could improvise bridges and tracks if necessary. Passing through Afghanistan, they found an early use for the winches, which were needed to haul the tracked cars through swollen torrents.

It took the expedition three months to reach Srinagar in the foothills of the Himalayas, where the road dwindled to a narrow pack-trail that snaked up steep mountainsides that plunged into frightening chasms and overhung precipices. Often the cars had to be unloaded and hauled by hand over rickety bridges or around alarming hairpin bends. Elsewhere, cars had to be let down ravines by means of cables; or dismantled and carried – in manageable loads – by coolies negotiating a landslide.

It was exhilarating when the vehicles at last dropped to the flat Indus Valley and could bowl along more briskly. But disquieting news now arrived that Lieutenant Point's group had been imprisoned in China, and needed assistance from Haardt. At the town of Gilgit, a decision was made to abandon the motor

MODERN CARAVAN Citroën's *Croisière Jeune*, or Yellow Cruise, stops on the banks of a river on the Chinese leg of the journey.

UPHILL STRUGGLE   One of the new-fangled Citroën vehicles crawls up a rugged mountain slope in the Pamirs.

vehicles and continue by speedier means. Yaks carried the adventurers across the Pamirs, the mountainous land of the tent-dwelling, sheepskin-clad Kirghiz tribesmen, and down onto the level plains of China. When they reached Kashgar, the appointed meeting place, they discovered that Point's group was being held at the town of Aksu, 300 miles (480 km) away.

The adventures of Lieutenant Point

The Chinese press had been hostile to Lieutenant Point's team from the outset, and on the Mongol plains beyond the Great Wall, the adventurers had run into a party of 100 armed bandits. Then they found themselves driving into a full-scale battle between 1000 Chinese soldiers and the troops of a Muhammadan warlord bent on the conquest of Sinkiang province. Cautiously, Point's party pushed on through the rebel lines – only to come under suspicion of being Muhammadan sympathisers.

At Urumchi, the capital of Sinkiang, the Chinese authorities placed Point under arrest and threatened to requisition the cars. Held prisoner for ten days, he managed to get a Morse code message describing his

INTREPID ADVENTURERS   Haardt (right) and fellow explorer L. Audouin-Dubreuil. The expedition took machine guns as a precaution against China's warring factions.

situation secretly transmitted by wireless to the outside world. It was picked up by Haardt on his short-wave radio, as well as by a number of radio stations in the Far East. Responding to the distress call, the French Legation took immediate action to protect the beleaguered party, and the Chinese government at last gave permission for Point to continue.

Through bandit country

After many further difficulties had been overcome, Haardt and Point were at last reunited, and with access to Point's nine motor vehicles, Haardt's eastward cruise continued, striking out across a large unmapped region at the edge of the Mongolian plateau. It was winter now, and they were in the frozen heart of Asia, where temperatures dropped to -29°C (-20°F) at night, and even boiling water froze when poured into the ice-gripped engines.

Later, pressing on through bandit country not far from Wu Yuen, they were ambushed one night, and met the gunfire with hails of bullets from their machine guns. Suddenly a Chinese soldier emerged from the shadows bearing a flag of truce; Haardt's party had themselves been mistaken for bandits by a group of government troops.

Two weeks later, after travelling 7219 miles (11 618 km), the ramshackle motorcade at last made its entrance into Peking, where it was fêted by the French Legation. The journey had taken 315 days.

PIONEER MOTORISTS

WITH GRINDING GEARS AND SCREAMING ENGINES, MOTOR CARS MET THE CHALLENGES OF TRAVEL OVER MOUNTAIN, MARSH AND DESERT WASTE

By the turn of the 20th century, there were some 8000 motor vehicles on American roads alone, and over the next few decades production increased until, by 1929, US registration of motor vehicles had risen to more than 26 million. This popularity of the motor car was mirrored in Europe.

During this early period, pioneer motorists tested the potential of the new vehicles over long distances. In August 1907, Prince Borghese of Italy won a gruelling 8000 mile (12 870 km) Peking to Paris motor race in 62 days, overcoming everything from a brush fire to a Belgian policeman who stopped him for speeding. In 1908, the French newspaper *Le Matin* staged a round-the-world car race, won by an American Thomas vehicle that took 170 days to cover the 13 500 mile (21 700 km) course. The steepest gradients presented no problems to the pioneers. In 1911, a car was first driven to the summit of Ben Nevis – Britain's highest mountain – which rises to 4406 ft (1343 m) in the Scottish Highlands.

The First World War stimulated development in the use of motor vehicles for rugged terrain, and it was with the approval of the French war secretary that automobile magnate André Citroën mounted his 1924 long-distance run across the Sahara. Dubbed the *Croisière Noire*, or Black Cruise, the expedition employed eight teams of vehicles

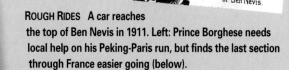

ROUGH RIDES A car reaches the top of Ben Nevis in 1911. Left: Prince Borghese needs local help on his Peking-Paris run, but finds the last section through France easier going (below).

mounted on caterpillar tracks to open up a road between Algeria and the French colonies of West Africa. Thereafter, the teams split up, each following prescribed routes for Djibouti and Dar es Salaam in East Africa, and for the Cape of Good Hope at the southern extremity of the continent. Citroën's vehicles braved the rigours of desert, marsh and savannah to complete their historic cruise, and were encouraged by their success to tackle the heartland of central Asia.

This was territory already known to the trailblazing American Roy Chapman Andrews, a keen motorist who not only went questing for dinosaur fossils in his Dodge sedan, but also charged bandits in it. Once, attacked by three mounted brigands, he slammed his foot hard on the accelerator and drove headlong at the enemy, gun in hand. The horsemen's steeds reared in terror, having probably never seen a motor car before. 'In a second the situation had changed. The only thing the brigands wanted to do was to get away, and they fled in panic. When I last saw them they were breaking all speed records on the other side of the valley', wrote Andrews.

IN THE LANDS OF THE BLUE POPPY

FRANK KINGDON-WARD JOURNEYS THROUGH WILD MOUNTAIN COUNTRY IN SEARCH OF EXOTIC PLANTS

THE SEARCHER Frank Kingdon-Ward devoted half a century to finding rare plants. From the remote valleys of the Himalayas he brought back a wealth of primulas, rhododendrons, lilies and gentians.

Gardening books describe the Himalayan blue poppy as a summer-flowering plant that flourishes in moist, peaty soil and is easily raised from seed pans in the greenhouse. What most of these books fail to tell readers, however, is the hardship endured by adventurers who journeyed to the ends of the Earth to obtain seeds of this and other unusual flowers. The collector George Forrest, for example, narrowly escaped a massacre in Tibet, and Reginald Farrer died of pneumonia while plant-hunting in the Burmese mountains.

Seeds of the Himalayan blue poppy (*Meconopsis betonicifolia*) were first collected by Frank Kingdon-Ward, who found sky-blue clumps growing in a remote valley of the Assam Himalayas. Years later, he came upon some examples growing in London's Hyde Park. 'I found it growing on the roof of the world and now I saw it growing in the hub of the world', he wrote.

The mystery river

Born in Manchester, the son of a botanist, Kingdon-Ward started his career as a teacher in Shanghai. In 1910 he was hired by Bees Nurseries to look for new varieties of alpines in Yunnan, and for half a century afterwards he explored China, Tibet, Upper Assam and Burma in search of rare plants. The maple *Acer wardii*, the gentian *Gentiana wardii*, the fine yellow *Rhododendron wardii*, and the purplish lily *Lilium wardii* are just a few of the plants that today bear his name.

But Kingdon-Ward returned with more than his seeds and specimens. He also brought back knowledge of much previously uncharted land in the maze of snowcapped Himalayan mountains where China borders eastern Tibet. Primarily a botanist, Frank Kingdon-Ward was also known as one of the foremost explorers of his day.

On a 1913-14 expedition, the collector crossed the ranges dividing the Mekong and Salween rivers, and explored the latter's granite gorges. His only guide on this occasion was a murderous local named Atung, who vanished after

FLOWER OF THE MOUNTAINS
The Himalayan blue poppy was collected by Kingdon-Ward in the mountains of Assam.

mugging their interpreter on a narrow precipice. The explorer struggled on, nonetheless, into the gorge, where he had to climb soaring cliffs with only notched tree trunks for ladders, and crawl on hands and knees across the raging river on a perilously sloping log bridge.

During his 1926 expedition, Kingdon-Ward explored 50 miles (80 km) of Tibet's

GETTING TO THE SOURCE

In Ward's 1930 expedition, he helped to establish the source of the Irrawaddy, the great river that runs the length of Myanmar (formerly Burma). Plant-hunting in the river's upper reaches, he found a secret valley thick with gold saxifrage and gentian. This led him to the Kalaw tributary, the Irrawaddy's farthest headwater, which rises in a range of massive Tibetan snow mountains.

Tsangpo gorge, a region which had for many years defied all other efforts by Europeans. This was a mysterious country where the river known in Tibet as the Tsangpo disappears into a tangle of mountains, to re-emerge in the Assam area of India under the name Brahmaputra. In past times, it had not been known for certain that the two rivers were the same. During the 1880s, however, a pundit, or learned man, named Kintup decided that he would try to prove their shared identity by dropping 50 marked logs into the Tsangpo and having a colleague in Assam watch out for the re-emergence of the logs on the Brahmaputra. Unhappily, Kintup was sold into servitude to Tibetan lamas while trying to prove his theory. When he finally won his freedom and tipped his logs into the river, his message to Assam failed to get through – with the result that there were no observers on the Brahmaputra to watch for their emergence.

In Kingdon-Ward's day the mystery gorge was still uncharted, though people had calculated that the Tsangpo must make a hairpin bend and drop 8000 ft (2440 m) into Assam's Abor foothills. The great question was: how did the water descend? Would the explorers find some immense

RARE SPECIMENS Frank Kingdon-Ward (right) examines a plant specimen with a colleague, E.J.H. Corner.

Niagara in the gorge? The journey began in the Tsangpo valley where, on flowery terraces, villagers tended crab apple, walnut and peach trees. Pressing onwards into wilder country, the explorers used oxen and sturdy little ponies to carry their supplies, eating local goat meat and yak milk eked out with luxurious cocoa and Quaker Oats. Sometimes small, strong Tibetan girls acted as porters too, but the make-up of the expedition changed continually, for the explorers had to get new transport at each village and sometimes they encountered a new village four times a day. To speed up the changeover,

the party sent a messenger on ahead, with an arrow letter requesting transport and supplies. The letter was wrapped around a bamboo cane and decorated with two white feathers, which signified 'express'.

Rope bridges

The expedition's ponies sometimes bolted, strewing the track with the wreckage of boxes and packing cases. And river crossings presented recurring difficulties. 'Rope bridges supply one of the more doubtful joys of the traveller's life in the gorge country', Kingdon-Ward wrote. A common type of bridge consisted of two cables of twisted bamboo. These were tied to trees above the river on either bank, and on them rode a wooden carrier. 'The ordinary mortal attaches himself to this carrier, with his arms free for hauling, and courageously but ungracefully pulls himself across. Superior persons (we, thank heaven, were superior persons) are literally tied hand and foot to two carriers, and pulled across by slow jerks which shake

IN SEARCH OF RARE FLOWERS

IN THE EARLY YEARS OF THE 20TH CENTURY, PLANT HUNTERS TRAVELLED IN SEARCH OF EXOTIC SPECIES IN EQUALLY EXOTIC LANDS

Several 20th-century plant hunters have investigated the remote, botanically rich regions of Asia. One of these was the Scotsman George Forrest, who from 1903 collected for the horticulturalist Arthur Kilpin Bulley. At the time of Forrest's first expedition to Yunnan in China, the area was racked by anti-British feeling prompted by the recent Younghusband Expedition. Forrest was hunted day and night, and 16 of his native collectors were caught, tortured and slaughtered. He himself made a desperate lone journey chased by armed Tibetans before he finally escaped. Undeterred by this fraught beginning, Forrest went on to send back some 30 000 botanical specimens in half a dozen expeditions before his death in 1932. He is particularly remembered for the introduction of the spectacular *Pieris forrestii*, which bears snowy flowers amid leaves of molten red, as well as for several rhododendrons.

Yorkshire-born collector Reginald Farrer became a convert to Buddhism during his travels in the Far East. In 1914, with fellow plant-hunter William Purdom, he explored the rugged Kansu region of northern China, then in a state of turmoil and banditry. Despite difficulties, Farrer brought back a wealth of plants including *Buddleia alternifolia*, *Viburnum fragrans* and *Gentiana farreri*, a new gentian whose exciting discovery on August 30, 1915, he later described: 'Hardly had I started when, in the fine turf that crowned the top of a sloping boulder, there stared at me a new Gentian, a Gentian that instantly obliterates all others of its race...

RARE COLOUR New growth and clusters of white flowers festoon *Pieris forrestii* in spring.

Not the faintest hope possessed me that this glaring miracle could be a new species. Had not Przewalsky crossed this range? How then could he possibly have missed a splendour so assaulting as this?' Farrer's next journey was in 1920, to Upper Burma where the cold, damp climate proved fatal. Aged only 40, he died of pneumonia and was buried near the village of Konglu.

Ernest Henry Wilson knew hardships too. Dubbed 'Chinese' Wilson, this indefatigable plant-hunter started his career in the service of the firm of Veitch for whom, in 1902, he brought back the handkerchief tree *Davidia involucrata* from the mountains of south-western China. Wilson proved extremely popular among the Chinese, despite the fact that his first expedition had been made at the time of the Boxer Rebellion when anti-European feelings ran high. In 1910 Wilson made his most famous discovery of all, the lily *Lilium regale*. This splendid flower, whose long-stemmed white trumpets now grace many a suburban garden, was discovered in a remote valley on the Chinese-Tibetan border, where it could only be reached by crossing a narrow gorge. A falling rock smashed Wilson's leg, and he lay without moving as each one of his 50 mules carefully stepped over the injured limb without touching it. English surgical practice would have called for amputation, but a missionary doctor saved the leg and Wilson went on to send back 7000 bulbs. It is a sad irony that this intrepid collector, who survived so much in far-flung corners of the world, should have succumbed to the streets of Massachusetts. In October 1930, his car skidded and crashed on a wet highway and both Wilson and his wife were killed.

ROYAL SPLENDOUR *Lilium regale* flourishes in Western gardens.

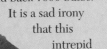

HIGHLY PRIZED ORNAMENT The handkerchief tree is a native of south-west China.

THE GLORIOUS FIFTH OF JUNE

On June 5, 1948, a day he called the Glorious Fifth of June, Frank Kingdon-Ward and his wife Jean discovered specimens of *Primula sherriffae* growing near the summit of Sirhoi Kashong in Manipur:

'"What is it?" Jean whispered in an awe-struck voice.

'"By God, it's a *primula*," I whispered back (as though it might overhear us and run away)...

'We rushed up the slope and knelt down in front of the little rock as though before a shrine. Growing out of a crack was a rosette of soft, crinkled green leaves glistening with silky hairs, and from the centre rose a short mealy white scape bearing three flowers. It was a primula all right – one I had never seen before in my life, wild or in cultivation – and of almost unearthly beauty... The whole plant was only about four inches [10 cm] high, and each corolla about an inch across, of a pale lilac mauve shade with a white star of powdery meal in the centre. But what most astonished us was the extraordinary length of the slender tube, which was fully two inches [5 cm] long! One would have thought that a primula... whose slender tube reached a length of two inches, would have an almost giraffe-like ungainliness; to stick one's neck out like that... is asking for laughter. But there was nothing ridiculous about this... flower – it was as near perfection as a rock primula could be.'

every tooth in the head and rack every nerve in the body.'

Consolation for Kingdon-Ward came in the fantastic varieties of plants found in the rhododendron moorlands, the alpine meadows and the primula-studded bogs. Among the species of primula, Kingdon-Ward's own favourite was the giant cowslip *Primula florindae*, which he named after his first wife and which sent up flower stalks 4 ft (1.2 m) high, bearing hundreds of blooms in a cluster. He noted with satisfaction how well it later took to English gardens, 'especially when wet and shady'.

The explorers never found their Niagara, however. Time and again they heard the roar of surging waters round cliffs up ahead, and saw clouds of spray with dancing rainbows, only to discover a cascade of modest size. It transpired that the Tsangpo falls fairly

THE IMMIGRANTS *Primula florindae*, brought back by Kingdon-Ward from the Himalayas, grace the edge of a garden pond in Yorkshire.

steeply along the course of its mystery gorges but there are many small cataracts rather than one solitary titan.

Eventually the expedition reached the Abor foothills, where they met the Lopa people, whom Kingdon-Ward called the most savage of the Assam jungle tribes. 'They were unfriendly, spoke no Tibetan, and wore next to no clothes; but they carried 80 lb (36 kg) loads over tracks that would kill a white man, and crossed the Doshong La almost naked in deep snow, and in the teeth of the awful, interstellar wind which eternally scours the Tibetan upland.'

In January 1927, frostbitten and exhausted, the explorers at last left the windswept heights behind them and made their way into the dark, welcoming forest that led to the flowery plains of Hindustan. Theirs had been an historic journey from which they brought back new geographical knowledge – as well as the seeds of 250 plant species, many sealed in thermos flasks to protect them against violent temperature changes.

RED CENTRE

UNTIL THE 1930S, THE SANDSTONE RIDGES OF
AUSTRALIA'S SIMPSON DESERT DEFIED EXPLORATION

In his 1845 attempt to reach the heart of the Australian continent, explorer Charles Sturt was forced to halt at the southern edge of the Simpson Desert. Before him lay a forbidding landscape of red sandstone ridges where no one lived. Even the Aborigines shunned this land as a place of death haunted by evil spirits. Sweltering in the pitiless heat, this strange terrain was corrugated by dunes that extended northwards in parallel lines beyond the horizon. Eastwards and westwards, the ridges succeeded each other 'like the waves of the sea'. The explorers could hardly believe their eyes: 'My companion,' wrote Sturt, 'involuntarily uttered an exclamation of amazement when he first glanced his eye over it. "Good Heavens," said he, "did ever man see such a country!"'

The Simpson Desert sprawls over 50 000 sq miles (130 000 km²) of Australia's arid heart, on the borders of the Northern Territory, South Australia and Queensland. Its distinguishing features are its long straight dunes, as much as 100 ft (30 m) high, which are quite unlike the shifting dunes of the Sahara and other deserts. In the Simpson, dunes run parallel as tramlines,

IN THE OUTBACK C.T. Madigan (right) and his 1939 expedition as they descend a sand ridge near the Queensland border.

aligned with the prevailing south-easterly wind. Red is the colour of this bizarre terrain – for here, as elsewhere in the central Australian outback, the soil is rusted by iron oxides produced by weathering in the parched climate. Annual rainfall over the desert is barely 4 in (100 mm). The ridges have been shaped over aeons by constant longitudinal winds, with loose sand drifting above a consolidated core. There are more than 1000 of these stationary dunes, extending unbroken for as much as 75 miles (120 km).

A gigantic gridiron

Sturt and his party were forced to turn back from the desert, and the fiery land remained unexplored during the early decades of the 20th century. History does not record how many settlers and prospectors perished in the arid waste, but plenty of grim events have been reported. In 1900, for example, three stockmen who lost their way in the Simpson were so maddened by thirst that they slashed their horses' throats and drank the blood – dying nevertheless.

In 1929, Australian geologist Dr Cecil Thomas Madigan made the first survey flights over the Simpson Desert. The

THE HOMESTEADER In 1936, on camelback, farmer Edmund Colson became the first man to cross the Simpson Desert.

ribbed expanse below he likened to 'a pink and gigantic, circular gridiron'. Though Madigan's report seemed to confirm that the desert was uncrossable by land, a homesteader named Edmund A. Colson, of Bloods Creek, was inspired by the survey flights to attempt the feat. Living at the desert's edge, west of the Outback township of Oodnadatta, Colson declared that year that he could achieve the unthinkable crossing, given camels, an Aborigine guide and 'a good season'. By this he meant one of the region's rare wet seasons, when rain would cause the seeds dormant in the sand to germinate and upholster the desert with moisture and plant life.

Colson had to wait seven years for his good season, but in 1936 an exceptional downpour offered hope of success, and the 55-year-old farmer set out from Bloods Creek, heading for Birdsville 200 miles (320 km) to the north-east. With him he took five camels, a month's supply of food and water, and an Aborigine named Peter. Colson's route led across the southern extremity of the Simpson Desert, and the going was tough from the outset. By day, temperatures soared to 37.8°C (100°F), and by night they dropped below freezing. As the party progressed into the waste, the ridges got higher and higher, and the thirsty camels were sometimes forced to struggle over them on their knees. Cresting a dune on the third day, Colson knew that he had guessed right. There, in the middle of the supposedly life-less waste, was a swathe of purple plants known to the Aborigines as 'parakeelya'. These succulent herbs of the *Calandrinia* genus retain water in their fleshy fronds, and provided such a feast for Colson's camels that they afterwards frisked like lambs. In the days that followed, Colson's party came upon several more pockets of luxury, which provided vital refreshment on their trek.

After 16 days, they trudged into Birdsville and stopped outside the hotel. The aston-ished townsfolk at first refused to believe that the dusty travellers had crossed the

ARID HEART A dry waste of dunes and spinifex, the great Simpson Desert was the last major challenge for explorers in Australia.

Simpson Desert, and it was only when Colson's photographs were developed that his historic conquest was properly acknowl-edged. The homesteader was not looking for adulation, however. Content to have proved his point, he nonchalantly saddled up his camels, and made his way back across the dunes to his homestead on the other side of the simmering desert.

The living desert

Conquest of the northern end of the Simpson Desert was achieved by Dr C.T. Madigan – the man whose aerial surveys had prompted Colson's expedition. It was Madigan who named the desert after the

STARTING FOR HOME Madigan and his party begin their return journey after crossing the northern Simpson Desert in 1939.

Australian geographer A.A. Simpson. In 1939, Madigan filled in this last significant blank on the Australian map with a party of seven companions, 19 camels and a two-way radio. They travelled, like Colson, during a wet season, and sometimes had to wade knee-deep through water. Madigan's expedition completed the 300 mile (480 km) journey in a month, and brought back a wealth of informa-tion, not only about the geography of the desert but also about the flora and fauna that bursts into life when nourished by rainfall.

WELL-ADAPTED WILDLIFE

Though apparently lifeless, the Simpson Desert supports a number of creatures that are adapted to its intense heat and prolonged droughts. C.T. Madigan found lizards to be the most abundant animals. Most lizards live on a diet of insects, which supply moisture as well as nourishment, and many species survive long periods of drought by storing moisture in their skins or body tissue.

Many desert creatures avoid the heat of daytime, hiding in their burrows and emerging with the cool of dusk. One such is the hopping mouse. A seed-eating creature, it finds all the moisture it needs in the seeds, and may never drink water in its life. Another shy inhabitant is the marsupial mole – a small, pale yellow, burrowing marsupial *Notoryctes typhlops*. The creature's eyes are wholly non-functional and it 'swims' blindly through the sands with a breaststroke action, in search of the desert insects and larvae on which it feeds. The marsupial mole gorges itself in the times of plenty that follow the wet season. But in the hottest and driest months, its metabolism drops very low and the creature lies dormant, waiting for the rains to trigger another upsurge of life.

Spinifex grasses grow on the sand dunes and help to stabilise them with their long, underground stems, or rhizomes. The tussocks offer cover to birds such as the elusive grass-wren which, when threatened, runs into the spinifex rather than flying away. Birds, like mammals, are well adapted to the Simpson's irregular rainfall patterns. Nesting is best done with the profusion of plants and insects that come with the downpour, and some bird species have the ability to start their breeding cycle with it. The black-faced wood swallow is legendary among Australian bird-watchers for beginning to court frantically with the first drop of rain, or even – it has been joked – on sighting a cloud.

OPPORTUNIST IN LOVE The black-faced wood swallow starts courting the instant it senses the onset of rain.

SEED-EATER The hopping mouse can survive in the desert without drinking any water at all.

AMONG HEAD-HUNTERS

A SWISS COLONEL PENETRATES THE MOUNTAIN DOMAIN OF BURMESE HEAD-HUNTERS

A giant horseshoe of mountains isolates Myanmar (formerly Burma) from her neighbours. The dense upland jungle sheltered hill tribes who went necklaced with wild boars' tusks and still made fire in the Stone-Age manner, with firesticks. Well into the 20th century, the North Burmese hill tribes followed their ancestral custom of head-hunting. In 1936, a tribe called the Kalyo Kengyu, from the Naga Hills, wiped out two villages, taking 150 heads and carrying off most of the children from the district.

Episodes like this prompted the governments of China and British India to send punitive expeditions into the jungle to bring the violent tribes under the rule of law. But though the primary aim of the expeditions was to stop the raids and release captives, they also offered opportunities to map unknown country and to explore the culture of its inhabitants – for with the armed platoons went surveyors and anthropologists.

One international expedition to enter the territory of the Wa tribes was mounted in March 1937. These notorious head-hunting tribes occupied a remote no-man's-land between Burma and Yunnan, where no international boundary had ever been drawn. The purpose of the expedition was to establish a frontier so that responsibility for maintaining law and order in the area could be allocated. Accompanied by a troop of Chinese infantry, the party was headed by a Swiss artillery officer, Colonel Iselin, who was chosen as a neutral and a specialist in frontier problems. They set out from Meng Tung, a small Chinese frontier town whose desecrated temple and burned-out huts bore evidence of recent pillaging by bandits. Even before entering Wa country, the party first had to travel through the bandit lands,

FEARSOME REPUTATIONS People of the Wa tribe pose in traditional dress. By the mid 1930s governments were trying to curb the practice of head-hunting.

where their route was barred by an enemy stockade. It took a three-day siege to force the bandits' submission, and the explorers continued their route with their wounded soldiers borne on litters.

Entering Wa country, they pitched camp on the River Dung Ding and doubled their sentries, conscious that an ambush might

EUROPEAN HEAD-HUNTERS

Head-hunting was still practised in Europe in the early 20th century. In the Balkans, taking an enemy's head implied taking possession of his soul, and episodes were reported from Montenegro as late as 1912.

occur at any time. But contact with the head-hunters – when it came – was peaceful. Just as Iselin and the Chinese commissioner were sitting down to a meal of barking deer, news came that two native chiefs had entered the camp. Conducted to the leaders' tent, the men entered bowing in submission, with their hands folded on their foreheads. One of the Wa then reached into a sack and placed a gift on the

20TH-CENTURY HEAD-HUNTERS

THE MACABRE PRACTICE OF SEVERING AND PRESERVING ENEMY HEADS LONG REMAINED CURRENT IN BORNEO, NEW GUINEA, BURMA AND ELSEWHERE

The practice of cutting off human heads and preserving them as trophies has ancient origins. It seems to have been known in Stone-Age Europe, for some Late Palaeolithic graves in Bavaria have revealed decapitated heads that had been given ritualistic burials separate from the bodies. Head-hunting has been known around the world, and often arose from a belief that the head was the home of the soul. To seize another's head was to take possession of his spirit and so augment one's own powers.

Head-hunters have kept their trophies in a variety of forms. In New Zealand, for example, Maoris carefully dried and preserved the heads of their enemies so that tattoo marks and facial features were recognisable. In Papua New Guinea, severed heads were smoked to preserve them. The famous 'shrunken heads' produced by South American peoples such as the Jivaro were made by removing the skull and filling the skin with hot sand to shrink it to the size of a fist, while preserving facial features intact.

Head-hunting survived well into the mid 20th century among certain tribes of Borneo. Among the Iban and other people, the taking of a head was regarded by women as an essential masculine virtue, and no maiden would accept the advances of a youth who had not supplied his grisly token.

For decades the British authorities in Borneo tried to stamp out the macabre practice, but when, during the Second World War, Japan invaded the country, they suddenly changed their minds. It was not inconsistent with British war aims for the inhabitants to cut off Japanese heads, and so, armed with traditional blowpipe and parang (a large-bladed knife), tribesmen enjoyed an Indian summer of unrestricted head-hunting.

Old habits died hard. In the 1960s British troops fought a secret war to defend the new-born Federation of Malaysia (Malaya, Singapore

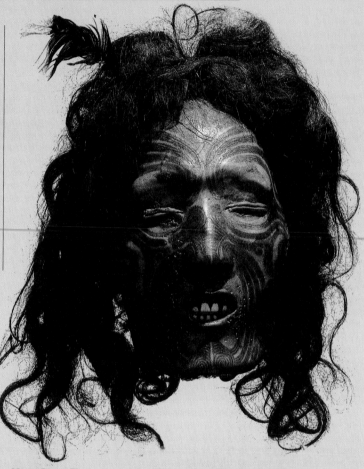

MAORI RELIC The native peoples of New Zealand became avid head-hunters to supply a European market for the curios.

and northern Borneo) against incursions from Indonesia. To help defend Borneo's 900 mile (1450 km) jungle frontier, tribesmen were employed as scouts. Writer Peter Dickens recorded an occasion when Captain Malcolm McGillivray told two Iban scouts to collect the weapons from some enemy bodies. The scouts returned not only with the men's rifles, but with their heads in plastic bags – and were greeted with cheers by their fellow tribesmen. The heads had been removed with such precision that the men must have been practised at it. 'Those plastic bags too, new and of exactly the right size; for what other purpose might they have been brought?' asked Dickens. It was clear that head-hunting had not died out when the Japanese left Borneo 20 years earlier.

IBAN WARRIOR In the Second World War, some Borneo tribesmen collected Japanese soldiers' heads in order to prove their manhood.

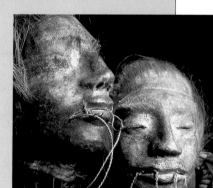

SHRUNKEN TROPHIES Among some South American peoples, heads were carefully shrunken to preserve facial features.

table, as a token of good will. It was a freshly severed human head.

Iselin and his companions leapt to their feet. 'Throw it out!' commanded the colonel. Food was also cleared from the table as none of the officers had any appetite left. It took considerable effort from the interpreters to make the Wa men understand that their present was unwelcome, and even then they failed to grasp the nature of the officers' objection. For when they returned, apologetically, a few minutes later, it was with another gift: a pair of human ears on a bamboo spit.

The head-hunting season

Despite their grisly character, these proffered gifts demonstrated that the Wa were friendly in intention. It turned out that the head-hunters were bitter enemies of the bandits whom Iselin had defeated, and so accepted the explorers as allies. As a result, the colonel and his European companions were privileged to become the first white men to attend a Wa 'Feast of Heads'.

VILLAGE LIFE During the head-hunting season Wa settlements like this would be festooned with macabre trophies.

WA WOMEN Female members of the Wa tribes carry baskets on their backs, in the eastern mountains of Shan State, Burma.

The tribesmen explained that the festivals were held to honour the gods, Ha Mah and Ni Mah, who lived in a sacred mountain lake. According to legend, the supreme god had been pleased when Ha Mah made a plaything of a human head, and so granted him a son. Since then, head-hunting had been a symbol of fertility. Every eleventh day of the third moon, a feast was held at which prayers were said to the heads so that the paddy fields should flourish.

The Wa, in effect, observed a head-hunting season; and because fresh heads were required for the growing crop, strangers entered Wa lands at their peril. As it happened, Iselin's party had arrived when the next festival was just about due. Tribesmen turned up continually with grim trophies, having taken advantage of the bandits' defeat to make surprise attacks on their enemy.

On the feast day, the whole village turned out to admire the fresh skulls, which were displayed in bamboo containers. After a banquet of cooked meats and rice liquors, incantations were made to the heads and the dead were symbolically fed. Then the macabre souvenirs were carried in procession to a sacred alley of skulls in the jungle. The head of a chief was particularly valued and the head of a foreign race prized most highly of all. In the days that followed, as Iselin surveyed the unmapped borderland, there were skirmishes with other, more hostile Wa villages. The colonel realised that the price on his own head must have been enormous – and that he was lucky to keep it on his shoulders long enough to lead his party home.

ASSAULT ON ANNAPURNA

TWO FRENCHMEN CONQUER A HIMALAYAN GIANT – AND PAY A GRUESOME PRICE FOR THEIR VICTORY

The Himalayas – which means 'abode of snows' – are the world's highest mountain range. This gigantic massif boasts 14 peaks higher than 26 246 ft (8000 m) – all of them unscaled during the first half of the 20th century. Sheer cliffs, blizzards and sub-zero temperatures were not the only obstacles to ascent. After the Second World War, roads into the high mountains were barred by political turmoil. Access to Everest lay through Tibet, whose government denied entry to all large expeditions; India and Pakistan were seething with unrest; and Kashmir was also racked by ferment.

For adventurous spirits, a breakthrough came in the autumn of 1949 when Nepal, long hostile to foreign penetration, suddenly relaxed its rules. The maharajah agreed to admit a party of nine French climbers, who arrived aboard a DC-4 in the spring of the following year.

Led by 31-year-old Maurice Herzog, an experienced Alpinist, the French team made their way through the high jungle slopes with 4 tons of supplies and an army of porters and pack animals. Assaults on the world's highest peaks were by now being planned like military operations: climbers would establish a series of camps at intervals up the mountainside, and provision them so that they could rest before the final push on the peak.

The French expedition planned to attempt one of two neighbouring giants: either Dhawalagiri (26 795 ft/8167 m) or the slightly lower Annapurna (26 544 ft/8091 m). But although they could see the mountaintops from a distance, the approach to the lower slopes was problematic. No one, not even the local inhabitants, knew how to reach them through the thickly forested ridges and gorges ahead. By the end of April, Herzog knew that they had to make haste, because climbing was possible only between the spring thaw and the summer monsoon predicted for June.

Having probed for routes and backtracked several times, they decided to concentrate on Annapurna – the Nepalese 'Goddess of Heaven'. The most promising approach was by the north-western glacier, to whose foot they eventually managed to bring supplies and equipment. Next came the gruelling business of setting up a chain of three higher camps. The fifth and last camp was pitched at 24 300 ft (7407 m). By now, the radio in base camp had announced

MAN AND MOUNTAIN French climber Maurice Herzog lost his fingers and toes to frostbite in the conquest of Annapurna.

that the monsoon was on its way – it had already reached Calcutta.

Nonetheless, the day that followed – June 3, 1950 – was sunny, and Herzog, with team member Louis Lachenal, began the final assault, moving up across the blazing white snowfield of the summit dome. They headed for a black patch of rock that guarded the top. Passing through a cleft in the rock's centre, a sudden gust of wind from the other side of the mountain hit them in the face. Dazed though they were, they knew now that they must be close. A few more agonising steps and their goal was attained. They had conquered Annapurna: the first *huit mille* – 'eight-thousander' – ever scaled.

HIMALAYAN HEROES Louis Lachenal (right) recovers in hospital after the 1950 expedition and Maurice Herzog (below, left) during the ascent.

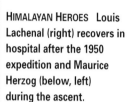

Passing his camera to Lachenal, Herzog took off his gloves and fixed a small French flag to his ice axe. He waved it above his head in a gesture of triumph as Lachenal clicked the shutter. It was then that the true ordeal began. Step by weary step, the two men began to work their way back down across the snowfield. It was a long time before Lachenal noticed something amiss. 'Maurice! Maurice!' he shouted suddenly, and pointed at his companion's hands. Herzog had lost his gloves. The team leader rushed down to Camp 5, his bare hands frighteningly numb. When he reached the tent, two companions were waiting there according to plan. Lachenal, following more slowly, slipped among some ice hummocks and let out a shriek. When they found him, he was bruised and suffering from shock and his feet were badly frozen. That night their companions ministered to the injured men.

The party set out next morning in slightly restored spirits for Camp 4. But the three-hour journey they had anticipated turned into a day-long nightmare as a blizzard erupted and blotted out all landmarks. Groping through the blinding white mist, the mountaineers removed their goggles to try to see better. But to no avail: they completely lost their bearings. At one point, they later discovered, they passed within 300yd (274m) of Camp 4 before wandering off in the wrong direction. When dusk fell, they took refuge in a crevasse where they spent the night tortured by cold, only to wake almost suffocated by a tonnage of snow that had worked loose and slid into their shelter from above.

Amazingly, no lives were lost. One of the men from Camp 4 eventually sighted the four straggling apparitions and helped to guide them to Camp 2. Then, strapped onto makeshift sledges, the two men were taken back to the foot of the mountain they had conquered. It was a famous victory – but the climbers paid a price. Herzog lost all his fingers and toes to frostbite, and Lachenal lost all his toes.

AT THE ROOF OF THE WORLD

ON MAY 29, 1953, HILLARY AND TENZING REACH THE SUMMIT OF THE HIGHEST MOUNTAIN ON EARTH

Chomolungma – 'Goddess Mother of the World' – is the old Tibetan name for the world's highest mountain. The colossus was christened in English after George Everest, a Victorian surveyor-general of India who never attempted to scale the peak that bears his name. In 1921, a British party launched the first assault on the sky-thrust citadel, and many attempts were made in the years that followed. But time after time, the climbers were frustrated by freezing temperatures, avalanches, fierce winds and frostbite. The peak is 29 028 ft (8848 m) above sea level, and the thin air at this dizzying altitude also presents a problem. Oxygen equipment is a vital asset, and only during the Second World War did efficient apparatus become available.

In 1952, a Swiss expedition reached a height of 28 200 ft (8595 m) before ferocious conditions drove them back. But Tenzing Norgay, the leader of the Sherpa porters who carried the Swiss supplies, was to return the following year with a British party headed by the army officer Colonel John Hunt. The 12 climbers who took part in the expedition were organised in pairs, and Tenzing was teamed with Edmund Hillary, a beekeeper from Auckland, New Zealand, who had won his climbing spurs in his country's Southern Alps. Out of this pairing a legendary climbing partnership was formed.

In his early 30s, Edmund Hillary was a climber whose easy-going manner concealed a tough and competitive character. Tenzing Norgay, a seasoned and ambitious mountaineer, had 20 years of climbing experience under his belt. Besides leading the three-dozen Sherpa porters in Hunt's party, Tenzing was a full climbing member of the team.

The gale-torn heights

Hunt was meticulous in his preparations. He minutely studied every previous attempt, made careful observations of the prevailing weather, and had his team spend a month scaling a number of 20 000 ft (6000 m) peaks beforehand, to acclimatise themselves. In addition, Hunt obtained the most up-to-date equipment, including high-altitude nylon weatherproof clothing, and lightweight oxygen appliances for use on the final strike.

For days before the Everest assault, porters and climbers toiled up and down the mountainside, setting up camps and heaving supplies up to them. The expedition launched their attack from the south, and it was Hillary who set up base camp on the mighty Khumbu Glacier, whose course led up amid ice stacks and crevasses to a rising valley called the Western Cwm. Beyond a

MOUNTAIN GROWTH

Mount Everest has grown over 20 in (50 cm) taller since Hillary and Tenzing scaled it in 1953. The Himalayas lie along the edge of two of the Earth's colliding plates, and the pressure is forcing them upwards so that Everest gets higher by about $1/2$ in (13 mm) every year.

gale-torn plateau known as the South Col at 26 200 ft (7986 m) rose the South East Ridge leading up to Everest's South Summit at 28 756 ft (8765 m), an unconquered outcrop below the topmost peak. On May 26, after setting out from Camp 8, team members Charles Evans and Tom Bourdillon became

LONG HAUL Sherpas carrying supplies during acclimatisation exercises in April 1953. Good preparation was the key to the successful conquest of Everest.

FINAL CHECK Hillary and Tenzing examine their equipment before the assault. Oxygen apparatus was thought essential.

the first human beings to attain the South Summit and were sorely tempted to press on to the final goal. But it was getting late in the day and they lacked sufficient oxygen supplies. After a fierce dispute, Evans decided that they must turn back.

Earmarked by Hunt for the final strike, Hillary and Tenzing had watched the two men's progress with mixed feelings, for they were keen to take the laurels themselves. And now that the advance guard had withdrawn, they knew that the prize was in sight.

On May 28, Hillary and Tenzing followed the route Evans and Bourdillon had taken up the South East Ridge, and with their ice axes carved out a small, shelved platform where they pitched their tent. While Tenzing

THE CHOSEN ROUTE Colonel John Hunt's 1953 expedition approached the summit of Mount Everest by way of the South East Ridge.

heated up some soup, Hillary made a tally of their oxygen supplies. Stocks were lower than they had anticipated. They had banked on being able to use 7 pints (4 litres) a minute, but would have to take a chance on 5¼ pints (3 litres) a minute.

That night, Hillary wrote, 'We drank vast quantities of liquid and ate a satisfying meal out of our store of delicacies – sardines on biscuits, tinned apricots, dates, biscuits and jam and honey. Despite our great height our breathing was almost normal until a sudden exertion would cause us to pant a little.' The temperature that night plummeted to –27°C (–16°F) and though the wind dropped, a violent gust shook the tent every 10 minutes or so.

At dawn next morning, the weather was fine. The two men breakfasted on their last tin of sardines and drank copious quantities of lemon juice and sugar to prevent dehydration. Then, having checked their equipment, they hoisted their 30 lb (13.6 kg) of oxygen

gear onto their backs, connected up their masks, and turned on the valves. After a few deep breaths they were ready to go.

It was 6.30 am and they made off, heading ever upwards as the ridge narrowed to a knife edge below their feet. By 9 am they had cramponed onto the South Summit that Bourdillon and Evans had reached. Ahead lay a virgin ridge, frighteningly contorted by twisted fingers of ice and snow that loomed over a 12 000 ft (3658 m) drop. But one white slope offered some promise, and roped together, with Hillary in front, they cut a pathway of steps in the firm, hard snow above the precipice. The weather was still good, though Hillary experienced difficulties when he removed his snow goggles to examine a particularly tricky section: 'I was very soon blinded by fine snow drawn by the cool wind. I hastily replaced my glasses.'

Offerings to the gods

They came next to a 40 ft (12 m) rock wall that appeared at first sight to be impassable. Then Hillary found a crack between the rock and an ice cornice, and he was able to inch his way up it, using crampons, ice axe, knees, shoulders and arms for leverage. At the top he helped pull Tenzing up, and they continued step-cutting laboriously up the ridge, with giant cornices to their right and the ground falling away dangerously to their left.

Suddenly the ordeal was over. Ahead of them the ground started plunging away to

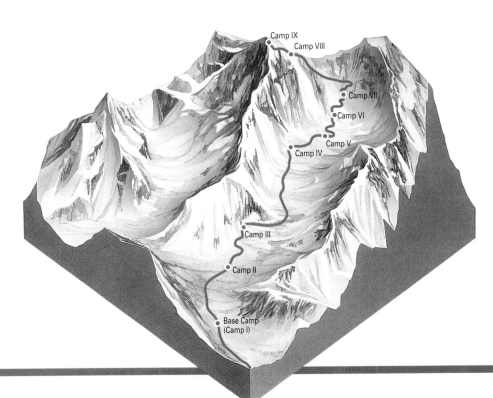

Camp IX
Camp VIII
Camp VII
Camp VI
Camp V
Camp IV
Camp III
Camp II
Base Camp (Camp I)

ATTEMPTS ON EVEREST

THE CONQUEST OF THE WORLD'S HIGHEST MOUNTAIN DID NOT COME EASILY – DISAPPOINTMENT AND DEATH ATTENDED THE EARLY CLIMBS

In tackling Mount Everest in the days of Empire, British climbers had an advantage over rivals from other nations. Because the Himalayan colossus stood within Britain's sphere of influence, it was to Britain that the Dalai Lama gave exclusive rights to the approach via Tibet.

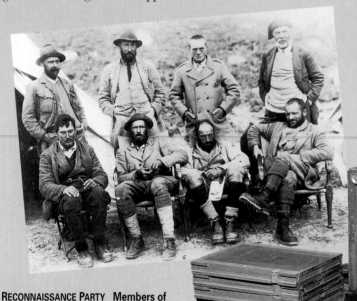

RECONNAISSANCE PARTY Members of the 1921 expedition. The camera belonged to team member Alexander Wollaston (standing, far left).

Mount Everest is roughly the shape of a three-sided pyramid, and it was thought that the northern face presented the only possible route.

The first attempt was made in 1921 by a party known as the Everest Reconnaissance Expedition, under Lieutenant-Colonel C.K. Howard-Bury. The team was eventually forced back by bad weather, but much was learned from this attempt. The climbers established that the proper climbing season should be May or June, before the monsoon. More important, they reckoned that the last push on the summit would not be barred by insurmountable cliffs.

1924 EXPEDITION The ill-fated climbers Irvine and Mallory are standing, first and second from the left.

The conquest was a long time coming, however: a total of seven attempts and three reconnaissance expeditions would be launched before victory was gained. One of the most dramatic assaults was made in 1924 under Brigadier-General C.G. Bruce, a man who had devoted his life to the exploration of the Himalayas. The expedition was plagued at an early stage by violent winds. On June 5, one of the party, E.F. Norton, attained 28 100 ft (8565 m) before he had to be led down, suffering from snow blindness. George Mallory and Andrew Irvine then started for the summit, carrying oxygen equipment. Despite clouds and mist, they were seen by another team member on the ridge leading to the top. The storm was worsening, however, and their colleague lost sight of them. A search the next day revealed nothing. Mallory and Irvine were never seen again. Did they reach the summit before perishing? Speculation was rife after the event, though few authorities have thought it likely.

After the Second World War, political reasons made it impossible to approach Everest through Tibet, but permission was received from Nepal for attempts from the southern side. In 1951, a reconnaissance party marched for the first time up the Khumbu Glacier – the great icefall that would prove the road to success for Hillary and Tenzing two years later.

THE FIRST WOMAN TO CLIMB EVEREST

Declared International Women's Year, 1975 was also the year in which a woman first climbed Everest. Junko Tabei, a 36-year-old Japanese mother, had started climbing as a student and gained early experience among the snowcapped summits of the Japanese Alps. There she learned the cruelties of her vocation, when her experienced female climbing partner, Saso San, was killed trying to save another from a fall. It was not an easy time for Junko whose husband, a climber named Masanobu Tabei, succumbed to frostbite while scaling the north face of the Matterhorn in Switzerland and lost four toes.

In 1970 Junko was one of a women's party that conquered Annapurna III in the Himalayas, and some time afterwards she was invited to join an Everest expedition. She was eager to take part, despite having a 2-year-old daughter, Noriko, by the time the conquest was attempted in May 1975.

Junko headed the all-female climbing team. The expedition followed the same southerly route that Hillary had done. But so buffeted was the team by violent winds and icy snow that on May 3, having struggled up to Camp 4 at the top of the Western Cwm, they were forced to retreat to Camp 2 to recuperate. The next day a thunderous avalanche crashed onto their tent, burying Junko, who lost consciousness, crushed against a partner under the immense snowfall. Junko was badly bruised by the ordeal, and her hip joints were stretched as she was pulled out by her legs.

Press and TV representatives who had gathered at the base of Everest assumed that the attempt would be abandoned. But on May 10, having recovered the strength in her legs, Junko, fellow climber Y. Watanabe and the male Sherpa Ang Tschering returned to the assault. As they struggled back up the icy slopes, they came to doubt whether they had supplies enough for three and, as a result, Watanabe descended, leaving the other two to press on alone. Fighting their way to the South Col, with immense panoramas opening up around them, Junko and Ang Tschering negotiated a knife-edged ridge so sharp that, working along its side and peering over the edge, Junko reflected that her head was in China while her torso was in Nepal.

On May 16, willing herself onwards at every step, Junko at last attained the summit of Everest. The triumph was celebrated all over the world, and especially in her home country where she was fêted with parties, prizes and luncheons. Feminists, meanwhile, proclaimed another victory for Women's Year. But Junko herself was modest about her achievement, seeing Everest only as another stage in her mountaineering career: 'They said it was a fantastic achievement for International Women's Year, but myself, I didn't even know such a thing existed. It wasn't until I got back home and read the newspapers that I realised.'

sweeping vistas of glaciers and slopes below. With a few more blows, Hillary cut steps to the highest place in the world. Tenzing's features, visible behind the goggles and oxygen mask, were contorted with delight. 'We shook hands,' wrote Hillary, 'and then, casting those Anglo-Saxon formalities aside, Tenzing threw his arms around my shoulders and we thumped each other on the back until forced to stop from lack of breath.'

CELEBRATING VICTORY Tenzing (left) plants the flag on the peak. Right: Hillary, Hunt and Tenzing return to Heathrow Airport. Above: The National Geographic Society medal that was presented to the expedition team.

It was 11.30 am, and the two men stayed on the roof of the world for about 15 minutes. Hillary took photographs, including a shot of Tenzing on the summit, raising a string of flags – Nepalese, British, United Nations and Indian – that has become one of the great, heroic images of the 20th century. While Hillary went on to take pictures down the ridges of Everest, Tenzing made a hole in the snow in which he placed candy, a bar of chocolate, and a packet of biscuits as offerings to the gods believed in Buddhist tradition to frequent the peak.

It took them the rest of the day to get back to the advance camp on the South Col, where two companions waited with hot soup and emergency oxygen. News of the triumph was soon radioed to the rest of the world, and the two victors of Everest were rightly acclaimed for their achievement. On June 2, Queen Elizabeth II was crowned in London, and one of her first official acts was to knight Hillary. Tenzing received the George Medal and was fêted throughout India and Nepal. But this was, above all, a team triumph with a long build-up in which scientific preparation had been crucial. It was wholly fitting that Colonel John Hunt was also knighted for his role in the conquest of the world's highest mountain.

THE LOST TRIBE

EDWARD MARRIOTT SEARCHES FOR A STONE-AGE
PEOPLE UNKNOWN TO THE WORLD UNTIL 1993

In October 1993, newspapers announced to an astonished world that a lost tribe of Stone-Age people had been discovered in the dense jungle of Papua New Guinea. The Liawep numbered 79 people who lived in the far north-west of the country, under the shadow of Mount Woraitan (9728 ft/2965 m). The tribe worshipped the mountain as their god, and took cover when planes flew overhead, thinking them to be malevolent sanguma birds; they dressed in leaves and hunted wild pigs with bows and arrows. The people did not appear in the census records.

Of few places on Earth could so bizarre a tale be told in the 1990s. Yet Papua New Guinea shelters some of the last outposts of prehistoric living. Vast tracts of its interior consist of roadless and jungle-choked highland, steaming with mist and mazed with boiling brown rivers. Here, the stilt-rooted pines and strangler figs prevent easy communications, even between neighbouring jungle peoples. Wide marshy lowlands, moreover, prevent easy contact with the coast. In the 1930s, when white explorers began to penetrate the remote valleys of the interior, they found Stone-Age farming communities who had no concept of the sea, let alone of white men.

THE LAST VILLAGE The Liawep villagers, who numbered 79 when they were first visited by Peter Yasaro, had remained unknown to the outside world until the early 1990s.

CULTURE SHOCK In the 1930s, tribesmen living in the remote Mount Hagen region listen to a gramophone brought by explorers. Much of the interior of New Guinea is covered by lush rain forest (right).

The survival of a lost tribe in the 1990s remained a remarkable news item. The story began when a Liawep youth named Kohi, seeking medical help for a dying elder, left his village and made a six-day journey to a government station at Oksapmin. Reportedly, no Liawep had ever walked so far before. The government officer, Peter Yasaro, who found the boy, later mounted a three-week expedition to locate the child's home village – and on his return, proclaimed his discovery of the Liawep in a radio interview. One of the first to follow up the report was a young English writer, Edward Marriott, whose story is told in his book *The Lost Tribe* (1996).

The illegal expedition

Forbidden by the Papuan government from seeing the Liawep, Marriott mounted his own small expedition – a guide and two carriers – and ventured through the jungle illegally. They started out by plane, landing at the airstrip at Wanakipa, a tiny place in the immense rain forest. Then the trek began, along a course roughly parallel to the Lagaip River. 'The jungle was terrifying,' wrote Marriott. 'It was endless and extraordinary, everything outsize. I felt so new, so green, and this place so dark and vast. It was everything I had dreamed and feared, only more grotesque, monstrous: butterflies as fat as soup plates; tree trunks so wide that, up close, they could have been walls.'

For day after day, the party made their way through the murky, creeper-strewn forest, finding sunshine only alongside the river where the jungle canopy and its overlooping vines thinned away, or on ridges where all the vistas were of the same monotonous views of anonymous, treecloaked mountains banked with mist. Once, on a high bank, Marriott missed his footing and plunged 15 ft (4.5 m) head first into a mudswamp, where he had to be rescued by one of the guides, using a walking stick. 'I

would have thanked him, praised him, blessed him,' wrote Marriott, 'had my mouth not been wedged with mud.' On another occasion he slipped on a drowsy gecko and skidded to the bottom of a gully, badly bruising his ribs. Marriott felt himself losing coordination; the jungle was overwhelming him.

At a cluster of straw-roofed huts known to the guide as Kinalipa, the expedition found people who knew of the Liawep. Many a superstitious tale was attached to their lost village, and it was said that their sacred mountain was home to evil beings who feasted on human meat. After four days, Marriott's party caught their first glimpse of it – an enormous upthrust in the jungle, so high that its summit was obscured by cloud. After two more days they reached the lost tribe.

The village stood high on a ridge, almost as if sited for defensive purposes, among groves of banana trees and thickets of tobacco plants. Smoke rose through the roofs of the small wood and straw dwellings. Some of them were mounted on low stilts, with verandahs reached by rickety ladders, and spaces below where pigs were tethered. Inside the dwellings, people lived in a smoky twilight of fug from the fires and tobacco

EXPLORING UNKNOWN NEW GUINEA

STONE-AGE TRIBES IN FEATHERED HEADDRESSES GREETED WHITE ADVENTURERS WITH WONDER AND CURIOSITY – AND WAR-LIKE HOSTILITY

On Easter Monday, 1901, a missionary named Revd James Chalmers was searching the south coast of New Guinea for natives to lead from pagan darkness to the light of Christ. Stepping ashore on Goaribari Island, he was clubbed senseless by local tribesmen, dismembered, cooked and eaten.

New Guinea is a vast Pacific island, divided today between the states of Papua New Guinea to the east and Irian Jaya (part of Indonesia) to the west. The island's spine is a mountain range that lies on a belt of volcanic and earthquake activity. Giant butterflies, flying foxes and birds of paradise haunt the tropical rain forests, which are also frequented by tribes scarcely touched by the 20th century. Stone-Age hunters and farmers still go about clad in traditional garb, with feathered headdresses, penis sheaths and boars' tusks piercing their nostrils. Until quite recently, head-hunting and cannibalism were common.

Captain Cook was among the early European explorers to have a brush with the island's warriors – in 1770 his landing party was repulsed with a hail of arrows. But because New Guinea boasted no apparent riches, its interior was long left unexplored by white men, and only the coming of flight opened some areas of the central highlands to Western eyes. Flying over the unmapped valleys during the 1930s, aviators were astonished to discover a world of Stone-Age farmers whose fields were laid out in squares. When the planes came over, the tribesmen threw themselves to the earth in terror. (They would tell anthropologists that they said among themselves: 'If we look at this thing, we shall surely die.')

Meanwhile, on the ground, adventurers such as the gold prospector Michael J. Leahy and the patrol officer Jack Hides pushed into the remote jungle uplands. They found highlanders who had never seen the coast and thought themselves the only people in existence. The sight of white men astonished them, not least because they believed a person's skin turned white when he passed over to the Beyond. The staple diet of the mountain tribes was sweet potato and, without metal tools, they worked their fields with digging sticks. Pottery was unknown to some – they used lengths of bamboo for cups and cooking pots. But fighting was all too familiar. Tribal warfare was endemic among the people of New Guinea, who wielded spears, bows and arrows, and stone-headed clubs in battle. In many a village stood a sacred 'men's house' adorned with trophies of hunting and war, including crocodile skulls and sometimes a smoked human head. The tribes, then, were war-like. But Hides and Leahy went there gun in hand, and were capable of the most casual murders. In one day alone, the macho Leahy 'bagged' 20 warriors. In 1936, at the League of Nations, his methods of 'pacifying' Papuan tribes were condemned.

Missionaries and anthropologists followed in the footsteps of the explorers, and gradually friendlier relations were established. But to this day, large parts of the highlands can only be reached by aircraft, by boat, or by walking through the jungle. Reports of strange tribes have continued. In 1983, a Baptist missionary saw smoke rising from a valley thought uninhabited, and discovered a previously unknown community of 600 hut-dwelling villagers called the Hagahai. Ten years later came reports of the Liawep – the lost tribe that prompted Edward Marriott's expedition.

GRIM TROPHIES Human skulls were once placed on display in New Guinea villages.

MACHO MAN Prospecting took gold-digger 'Mick' Leahy into highlands where no white man had been before. Too often he let his gun do the talking for him. Above: Tribesmen photographed by Leahy.

VILLAGE LIFE The Liawep women cooked, raised the children and tended gardens in the jungle where the tribe grew food. Right: Liawep villagers pose outside their village church.

smoke from the tapering, fat-ended cigarettes that everyone smoked.

Possessions were kept in string bags hanging from the walls: from treasured hornbill beaks and bunches of emu feathers to staple foods, such as kaukau and taro, which the women would bake at dusk. Life for the women of Liawep was hard. It was they who worked the soil in gardens scattered around the jungle's edge, while the menfolk loitered or hunted in the jungle for black-skinned pigs and other game.

Meeting a cannibal

Marriott was not the first outsider to reach the village after Yasaro's historic patrol. Ahead of him, that same year, had come a Papuan missionary named Herod who had built a small Christian church in the village, made of planks tied by vines, with a bamboo altar. Herod, however, had found the people slow to abandon their pagan ways. They still kept amulets, such as shells and good-luck plants, to ward off evil spirits, and the whole forest around them was charged with religious significance. Moreover, they still worshipped the colossal mountain that loomed

over their village.

Lying in a centre of seismic activity, Mount Woraitan sometimes shook and issued smoke. It also drew storms across the valley and attracted lightning. Marriott found it easy to see how the villagers might believe the mountain to be the centre of the Universe, and confessed that he himself succumbed to an irrational dread of it. 'If I lived

---

MULTILINGUAL ISLAND

About 750 languages have been identified in New Guinea, a consequence of the tribes' isolation from one another. The country's average of one language per 420 sq miles (1090 km^2) would give Britain 211 different native tongues.

---

there I would surely have worshipped it,' he recalled.

He discovered that prayers were offered to Mount Woraitan from a simple clearing in the forest. Tribal lore told how this place was haunted by the spirits of two brothers: one was violent and lived at the top of the mountain, while the other was kindlier and lived

on the lower slopes. In days past, people would come here and speak to the mountain before going out to fight their enemies. The mountain would tell them when to make war, and when to stay at home.

Through an edgy conversation with a group of hunters, Marriott learned that the Liawep were once feared warriors. Their traditional enemies were a tribe from across the Lagaip River, whom they goaded continually with challenges to fight; or they would invite them to a ceremonial feast and ambush them on the way over. That tribe had now vanished – the Liawep had butchered them all. The hunters were not particularly surprised to learn that they had been dubbed a 'lost tribe' because, having killed most of their neighbours, they felt themselves to be alone in the jungle. In recent years no one had dared approach them.

All of the hunters had killed men in their time, a tribesman boasted, though only one of their number was a cannibal. This was Uana, an old man who was painted yellow because he was in mourning for his wife. Asked about the taste of human flesh the cannibal said, 'it's like pork' – an observation which caused his younger companions to rock with laughter, as if speaking the words was an oft-performed party piece. Marriott found the laughter threatening. 'And this was their good side,' he wrote. 'I did not want to encounter them out for blood, worked up into a lather of revenge.'

Lightning strikes

The explorer nevertheless became quite friendly with one of the hunters, named Fioluana. And one day, when the men went off to hunt in the jungle, Fioluana asked Marriott to look after his wife and daughters, who were sick with malaria. The weather was worsening with the onset of the rainy season, and that night a terrifying thunderstorm broke from the clouds weighing low over the village. Lightning flashes built up to one deafening thunderbolt that caused Marriott to spring from his bed and make for the door. Outside, Herod the missionary was shrieking above the storm. It seemed that Fioluana's house had been hit by lightning. The hunter's wife, daughter and three other children were all dead. The scene had the character of a nightmare. With the monsoon rains thrashing down, Marriott rushed across the mud to the house where Herod was now shouting and pointing. Inside, by torchlight, they saw the little bodies and a hole in the roof, singed at the edges. Herod had been praying over the sickly children when the tragedy occurred.

After the shock came feelings

of deep disquiet. Marriott was aware that Fioluana and the other returning hunters would blame him for the calamity. Had he not been charged with taking care of the stricken family? So, with his guides and carriers, he fled before dawn, running in panic back through the jungle, following the now-flooded course of the Lagaip River, with leeches 'hanging like deflating balloons' from his ankles.

At one point on the first day, it seemed that their worst fears had come true. Only 50 yd (50 m) away, through the thick vegetation, they saw Fioluana and the group of hunters – there were 15 to 20 of them and they were closing in. But they turned out to be smiling. The tribesmen were hung with slaughtered game – wild pigs, tree kangaroos and gaudy cockatoos – and on their way back to the village. They had not yet learned of the tragedy.

Marriott and his companions made no mention of it but, after a nervous exchange, moved swiftly on. They knew now that they must continue to keep up their pace, for the hunters moved twice as fast through the jungle and might yet overtake them when they discovered what

DRESS CODE The long, backward-pointing turban worn by this young Liawep tribesman indicates his unmarried status.

FOREST DWELLERS Isolated in their jungle home, the Liawep were suspicious of outsiders. And their reputation for destroying their neighbours had kept people away.

had happened in the village. Fear stopped them from slackening. They sped on for four days, immune to hunger and exhaustion, until they reached Wanakipa with its airstrip and scattering of houses. Even here Marriott did not feel completely safe from the vengeful Liawep, and he had good reason to remain cautious.

Some hours after their arrival, Fioluana and three other tribesmen reached the settlement, full of grief and recrimination. What had Marriott been doing in their village? He had come and five people had died – why? If he had stayed, the tribesmen told him, the villagers would have killed him. But there were only four of the Liawep against Marriott's party and the population of Wanakipa. Eventually, after much argument and patient attempts at reassurance, the quarrel petered out and the outnumbered Liawep shuffled away.

Though relieved, Marriott was left with a sickly sense of guilt. He had hoped to be a dispassionate observer of the Stone-Age tribe, but found himself overwhelmed by ancient superstition and hopelessly entangled in feelings of kinship and responsibility for the people. The jungle stayed with him long after his return to England.

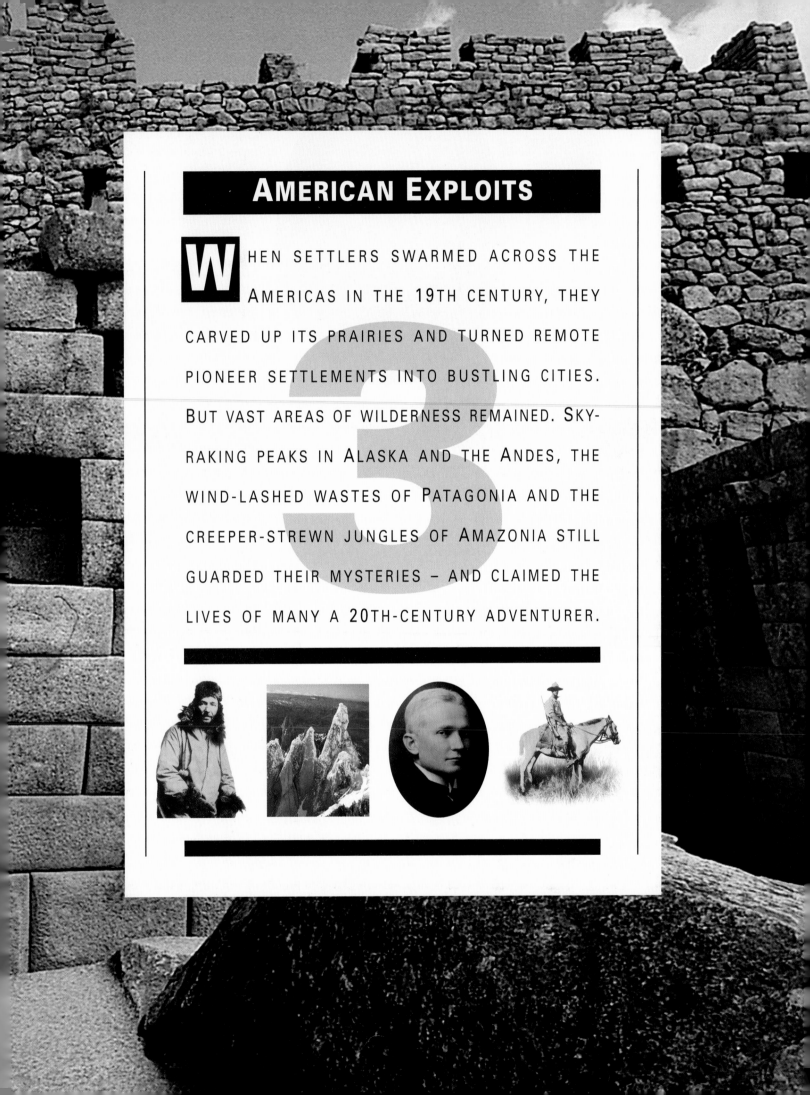

AMERICAN EXPLOITS

WHEN SETTLERS SWARMED ACROSS THE AMERICAS IN THE 19TH CENTURY, THEY CARVED UP ITS PRAIRIES AND TURNED REMOTE PIONEER SETTLEMENTS INTO BUSTLING CITIES. BUT VAST AREAS OF WILDERNESS REMAINED. SKY-RAKING PEAKS IN ALASKA AND THE ANDES, THE WIND-LASHED WASTES OF PATAGONIA AND THE CREEPER-STREWN JUNGLES OF AMAZONIA STILL GUARDED THEIR MYSTERIES – AND CLAIMED THE LIVES OF MANY A 20TH-CENTURY ADVENTURER.

CITY OF THE INCAS

**AMERICAN EXPLORER HIRAM BINGHAM DISCOVERS
A LOST CITADEL HIGH AMONG THE ANDEAN CRAGS**

On a drizzly morning in 1911, a three-man party moving along the forested banks of Peru's Urubamba River emerged from the jungle to vistas of the Andes' spectacular snow peaks. Above them loomed gigantic precipices of many-coloured granite, with glaciers shimmering through clouds that soared high over the river's foaming rapids. The explorers had come in search of a lost city of the Incas – the legendary capital to which the last Inca rulers had fled after they were defeated by the Spanish conquistador Francisco Pizarro.

The party comprised a young American professor named Hiram Bingham, a Peruvian soldier, and a local farmer hired as a guide. Born in Hawaii, Hiram Bingham was the son of retired missionaries and had completed a PhD in Latin American history at Yale University. From 1905 he made several trips to South America. These culminated in his 1911 expedition to seek out the Incas' last

ANDEAN ADVENTURER American Hiram Bingham stumbled on the spectacular ruins of Machu Picchu in 1911.

capital, Vilcabamba, to which the defeated King Manco II is said to have retreated in 1536. Several tales of ruins were current in Bingham's day, but the best guesses located the capital somewhere in the valleys of the Vilcabamba and Urubamba rivers.

The high citadel

Bingham set out from Cuzco with his companion, a sergeant named Carrasco, to explore the Urubamba valley. One night while they were camped near the river, a farmer named Melchor Arteaga came out of his hut to see who the strangers were, and told Bingham of some fine ruins high up in the mountains. Bingham persuaded Arteaga to take him there, and on the morning of July 24 they set out with the sergeant, inching their way across a rickety bridge that spanned the rapids. Rain dripped from tree ferns, and orchids bloomed on soaring trunks, as they clambered up a forest path so steep that Bingham often had to scrabble on all fours. Towards midday it grew exceptionally hot, and they reached a grass hut where some friendly Native Americans gave them gourds full of cool water and a few sweet potatoes. They were above the jungle now, and the views down were magnificent. But what awaited higher up was more remarkable still.

The Native Americans, they discovered, were farming on an ancient terrace that they had cleared of jungle. Struggling up the rest

of the slope, the explorers came upon more terraces and a labyrinth of beautiful stone houses made of white granite blocks fitted together with neat, mortarless joints, perched 4000 ft (1200 m) above the snaking Urubamba. They had stumbled upon an abandoned citadel that was to become the most celebrated ruin in South America.

The lost city stood on a saddle between two colossal peaks: Huayna Picchu to the

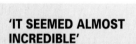

'IT SEEMED ALMOST INCREDIBLE'

Hiram Bingham describes his discovery of Machu Picchu:

'We came to a primitive bridge, made of four logs bound together with vines, and stretching across the stream a few inches above the roaring rapids. On the other side we had a fearfully hard climb for an hour and twenty minutes. A good part of the distance I went on all fours. The path was in many places a primitive stairway, or crude stepladder, at first through a jungle, and later up a very steep, grass-covered slope...We climbed still further up the ridge...and suddenly we found ourselves in the midst of a jungle-covered maze of small and large walls, the ruins of buildings made of blocks of white granite, most carefully cut and beautifully fitted together without cement. Surprise followed surprise until there came the realization that we were in the midst of as wonderful ruins as any ever found in Peru. It seemed almost incredible that this city, only five days' journey from Cuzco, should have remained so long undescribed and comparatively unknown. Yet so far as I have been able to discover, there is no reference in the Spanish chronicles to Machu Picchu. It is possible that not even the conquistadores ever saw this wonderful place.'

north, and the higher Machu Picchu, or 'old peak' to the south. It was from the latter that the ruin took its local name – it had no other title, for none of the old Spanish chroniclers made any mention of the settlement, and it

'THIS WONDERFUL PLACE' Protected by precipices of solid granite, the high Inca citadel was apparently unknown to Peru's Spanish conquerors.

featured on no modern map. Was it, Bingham speculated, the Incas' legendary last refuge? And if not, what was it?

The riddles surrounding this lofty, inaccessible ruin perched among hair-raising precipices caused it to become one of the 20th century's great archaeological mysteries, and the year after his discovery Bingham returned to the site with a larger expedition backed by Yale University and

the National Geographic Society. Members cleared the site of vegetation, and mapped the buildings and the agricultural terraces on which the vanished inhabitants had raised their crops. Most of the farming seems to have been done at the southern end of the settlement, where more than 50 terraces grace the site.

The town itself ran for several hundred yards along the saddle between the two

peaks, and contained a central plaza, royal palace and Temple of the Sun, all built of polygonal dressed stone blocks. Houses on the steeply sloping ground were crowded together around narrow streets, but the multitude of rock-cut flights of stairs made it easy to get about. Machu Picchu boasted over 100 stairways, some with as many as 150 steps.

Why was it abandoned?

Overwhelmed by Machu Picchu's spectacular setting, Hiram Bingham imagined that the entire settlement had been a centre for Sun worship. In expeditions of 1912 and 1915, he found many smaller Inca ruins in the hills nearby, and mapped the Inca roads in the region. The Incas excelled at building highways, and Machu Picchu was reached by a road that had been tunnelled through the cliffs. From his researches, Bingham became more and more convinced that the town was indeed the lost city of Vilcabamba, the Incas' last refuge, and he held to this belief until his death in 1956.

More recent investigation has called this into question. Machu Picchu was not large enough to constitute an Inca capital, and its places of worship were not sufficiently imposing to suggest the ceremonial centre of

SANCTUARY OF THE SUN A stone-built Sun temple was found at Machu Picchu, though the city was not large enough to constitute a religious capital, as Bingham believed.

THE INCAS' LAST CAPITAL

According to Spanish chroniclers, the Incas' last capital, Vilcabamba, was the place to which their ruler, Manco, fled from Cuzco down the valley of the Urubamba River. Christian missionaries railed against it as the Incas' chief town 'and the one in which was the university of idolatry, the professors of witchcraft and teachers of abominations'.

Hiram Bingham wrongly believed that Machu Picchu was Vilcabamba. But he also stumbled on Inca ruins at Espiritu Pampa that were the more likely remnants of the Incas' last capital. In 1964 and 1965 another American, Gene Savoy, returned to the site and discovered that Espiritu Pampa had been a much larger and more imposing city than Bingham had realised. It lay at a lower altitude and had a warmer climate than the mountain outpost of Machu Picchu. Its buildings more closely matched contemporary descriptions of Vilcabamba. And the clinching detail was that the site lay on a river. It is known that Vilcabamba was beside a river for in 1539, according to the Spanish chronicles, Pizarro floated a macabre message downstream to the Inca city: a basket containing the body of Manco's murdered wife, Cura Ocllo.

CAMPING OUT Savoy's expedition at a stopover camp on the journey to Espiritu Pampa, the Incas' last capital.

a religious people. Modern scholars believe that Machu Picchu was a fortress placed high above the Urubamba to control the gateway to the Amazon rain forest from which the Incas obtained a wealth of exotic produce. It also guarded the Inca capital of Cuzco, 70 miles (110 km) upstream, from enemy approaches by river. Quite why the town had been abandoned remains a riddle,

for the inhabitants seem to have deserted the site even before the Spaniards conquered Peru, and there is no evidence of destruction by an aggressor. Did the people succumb to an epidemic, or flee before some Native American enemy? No one can say for sure.

Ironically, Bingham may have discovered Vilcabamba without realising it. In August 1911, only a month after coming upon Machu Picchu, he pressed on into the jungle lowlands and reached a remote sugar plantation whose owner told him of some Inca ruins deep in the forest. After a two-day trip they reached the place, which was called Espiritu Pampa (The Plain of the Spirits), but the guides and porters were impatient to return, and Bingham did not have time to investigate in any detail. Research in the 1960s, however, suggested that the ruins were those of a town much larger than Machu Picchu, and the remnants of the buildings matched contemporary descriptions of the Incas' capital. In all likelihood, Espiritu Pampa was Vilcabamba.

THE CONQUEST OF MOUNT MCKINLEY

FRAUD AND HEROIC FAILURE MARK THE FIRST ASSAULTS ON THE HIGHEST PEAK IN THE USA

concagua (22 831 ft/6959 m), South America's highest mountain, was first scaled in 1897, but it was not until the 20th century that serious attempts were made on Mount McKinley, its North American counterpart. At 20 320 ft (6194 m), the Alaskan giant is lower than Aconcagua, but height alone does not account for the difficulty of a climb. It is possible to reach the summit of Aconcagua without ever touching snow, but Mount McKinley lies within the Arctic Circle, protected by an immense glacier system, in the middle of a then unexplored wasteland of rock and ice. Permanent snowfields cover the whole upper two-thirds of the mountain, so that climbers have to treat an assault on Mount McKinley almost like a polar expedition.

Early expeditions

In the early years of the 20th century, the mountain could only be approached from Glacier City on the remote Alaskan coast to the south. From there, explorers had to undertake a 200 mile (320 km) journey northwards along the turbulent Susitna River to the base of the mountain. A 1903 attempt on the great mountain proved unsuccessful. A 1906 expedition that included Professor Herschel Parker and Belmore Browne fared no better, but in their failure the explorers at least learnt that certain routes were impossible. Having gone upriver with a motor boat and packhorses, the party discovered that the fearsome ridges of the icebound southern face constituted an impassable barrier.

One of the party, a New York physician called Dr Frederick A. Cook, won some brief notoriety by claiming to have made a successful solo conquest after the others returned. His assertion was immediately disputed, however, and when a committee of the Explorers Club investigated the question, Dr Cook refused to give evidence. Later, his photograph of the 'summit' was identified as a small peak at the head of a glacier sited many miles from the main

DOGGED EXPLORERS Herschel Parker (below, left) and Belmore Browne (above and below, right) made two attempts on Mount McKinley, but ran into vicious gales on their way to the summit.

mountain. His case was convincingly disproved – as was his subsequent assertion to have been the first at the North Pole.

In the summer of 1910, another Parker-Browne expedition travelled up the Susitna River in a specially designed boat, heading for the southern face of the mountain. The eight-man team set up a base camp at the foot of the Tokositna tributary, and then approached Mount McKinley by way of a 37 mile (60 km) long glacier, transporting heavy loads of supplies on their backs. Eventually, the glacier led them to a great ice basin that was walled by immense precipices. Through binoculars, they could see a promising north-east ridge, but their way to it was barred by a gigantic ice wall. Storms, icefalls

and avalanches eventually drove them back 'sunken-eyed and lean and hatchet-faced', but still in good enough spirits to launch a third attempt in 1912.

This time the explorers travelled in winter, using Alaskan dog teams to haul their supplies up the broad, level artery of the frozen Susitna. During the early stages, winter travelling proved easier than the summer trek had been and, despite blizzards, they managed to skirt round the north-east side of the mountain and approach the heart via

AVALANCHE IN ALASKA

In 1910, the expedition of Professor Herschel Parker and Belmore Browne was driven back from Mount McKinley by impassable ridges, icefalls and avalanches. Of one incident Browne reported:

'The whole of the great cliffs of the box canyon appeared at first glance to be on fire. Unnumbered thousands of tons of soft snow were avalanching from the southern flanks of Mount McKinley on to the glacier floor 5000 ft [1520 m] below. The snow fell so far that it was broken into heavy clouds that rolled downward like heavy waves. The force of the rolling mass was terrific, and as it struck the blue-green glacier mail [surface] it threw a great snow cloud that raced like a live thing for 500 feet [150 m]; whirling in the wind the avalanche had caused, the white wall swept across the valley, and almost before we were aware of it we were struggling and choking in a blinding and stinging cloud of ice dust.'

the great Muldrow Glacier. On April 24, they established a base camp and began reconnaissance for the assault proper. Day after day, they carried supplies to a series of camps farther up the mountain, which were provisioned with instruments, alcohol lamps, pemmican (a cake made from beef, dried fruit and fat), chocolate, hardtack, sugar and raisins. The glacier rose in steps, like a giant staircase, and by the end of the exercise they had carried many hundreds of pounds' weight of provisions to a height of 15 000 ft (4570 m) in preparation for the final climb.

However, the ordeal had taken its toll on the three-man assault team of Parker, Belmore Browne and Seattle-born Merl La Voy. The climbers were afflicted by snow blindness, and their skin was burnt black by the sun. Their lips, noses and hands were swollen, cracked and bleeding. Unshaven too, their looks were in the words of La Voy 'sufficient to frighten children into the

SNOW GIANT Mount McKinley stands today at the centre of the Denali National Park, so-called after the local Indian name for the mountain, Denali – 'The Great One'.

straight and narrow path'. All suffered violent stomachaches from eating the pemmican and were confined to tea and hardtack. The cold was ferocious; by 10.30 at night, in a tent warmed by the alcohol stove and the warmth of three human bodies, the temperature was –19°C (–2°F). 'Despite elaborate precautions,' reported Belmore Browne, 'I can say in all honesty that I did not have a single night's normal sleep above 15 000 ft [4570 m] on account of the cold.'

By June 29, the trio had attained 18 500 ft (5640 m) and had reached the skyline of the north-east ridge on what seemed a reasonable gradient to the top. Breathing became more difficult at this altitude, and the sky

my body, and I held to my axe with stooped shoulders to stand against the gale; I could not go ahead. . . .'

The climbers were barely 100 ft (30 m) from the top of the highest mountain in North America. And yet they could go no farther in the teeth of that terrible gale. The three carved out a hollow and tried huddling down, but found that they were freezing and were forced to retrace their steps to their upper camp. Their clothes were sodden, rations were running out, and though they made one more attempt on the summit they were again driven off by a storm. Sick at heart, the three men made their way back down the mountain to the foot of the glacier where, after 30 days of lying on snow and ice, they were at last able to lie on bare earth and feel a warm wind fragrant with grass and flowers.

In June the next year, 1913, following the same route up the Muldrow Glacier and central north-east ridge, Dr Hudson Stuck and the Alaskan pioneer Harry Karstens reached the top in clear, bright sunshine. Dr Stuck suggested that the mountain should be known by its traditional North American Indian name of Denali, though this was not taken up. The names of Stuck and Karstens are forever attached to the conquest of Mount McKinley, while the six-year pioneering efforts of the Parker-Browne team – which so nearly took the laurels – do not feature in the record books.

THE CONQUEROR Dr Hudson Stuck, Archdeacon of the Yukon, was the first person to reach the summit of Mount McKinley.

began to darken with threats of bad weather. At 19 000 ft (5790 m), the summit loomed ahead and they hastened onwards through swirling snow to a height of 20 000 ft (6090 m).

'The breath was driven from my body'

And then the nightmare began. As an icy mist descended and the cold began to cut to the bone, they breasted a hummock and met the full fury of a storm wind. Belmore Browne wrote: 'The breath was driven from

THE PRESIDENT'S MEN

FORMER US PRESIDENT THEODORE ROOSEVELT SETS OFF DOWN A TRIBUTARY OF THE AMAZON

In 1901, when US President McKinley was assassinated, he was replaced by the boisterous and controversial vice-president Theodore Roosevelt, at 42 by far the youngest man ever to enter the White House. 'Now look,' fumed Senator Mark Hanna, boss of the Republican Party's national machine, 'that damn cowboy is President of the United States!' One of history's great extroverts, Roosevelt was a robust individualist who had been a cattle rancher in the Badlands of North Dakota and a Rough Rider in the Spanish-American War.

The president's gospel of 'strenuosity', emphasising muscular prowess, can be seen as overcompensation for youthful frailty: Roosevelt had suffered in childhood from asthma and weak eyesight, and

had beefed up his body through incessant physical exercise. But his zest caught the mood of a young nation eager to flex its own muscles. As president, Roosevelt would wholly revitalise the role of Chief Executive and bring a new American assertiveness to world affairs.

Roosevelt served two terms in the White House and was still only 50 on his retirement in 1909. Though he was to lose the Republican nomination for president in 1912, he remained as active as ever – and the next year embarked on what was perhaps his greatest adventure. Roosevelt had planned a speaking trip in South America, which was to be followed by a steamer journey on the Amazon. But the Brazilian government invited him to participate in something

'THAT DAMN COWBOY' US President Theodore Roosevelt jumps hurdles at the Chevy Chase Club, Washington, in 1902. Below: Roosevelt, a keen hunter, bags a jaguar in South America.

much more demanding: the descent of an unknown tributary, dubbed the River of Doubt, in company with Colonel Candido Rondon, a great hero of exploration in the southern Amazon basin.

A military engineer, Rondon had on three occasions penetrated the little-known area called the Mato Grosso, a vast plateau region in the heart of the continent which, at 475 700 sq miles (1 232 000 km²), was as large as France and Spain combined. *Mato grosso* means 'thick scrub', a term descriptive of the forest landscape that contained Native American peoples as hostile as any in South America. Rondon was himself of almost pure Indian blood and extraordinarily enlightened in his attitudes. 'Die if necessary, kill, never', was his motto. It was Rondon who established contact with the warlike Nambikwara tribe, whose practice had previously been to kill all white-skinned people they encountered. It was Rondon, too, who in 1909 discovered and named the River of Doubt, a waterway that had never been heard of by Brazilian geographers.

To the River of Doubt

The Roosevelt-Rondon Scientific Expedition left Tapiripua – the last outpost inhabited by Brazilians – in January 1914, and travelled north-west through dense forests. With horses, pack mules and oxen, the explorers rode

THE HUNTER Roosevelt at Porto Campo on the San Lorenzo River during his Brazilian adventure of 1914. The party caught fish and shot both birds and animals – partly for sport, but also for food.

through torrential rains across 'endless flats of grass and of low, open scrubby forest'. Roosevelt took his son Kermit with him, and they shared a tent into which, early one morning, a pack-ox came and devoured their shirts and underclothes without waking them.

The Roosevelts were keen hunters as well as keen naturalists, and they shot much of the big game that came their way: jaguar, peccary, alligator, tapir and giant anteater. Past huge ant hills and thunderous cataracts, they continued to the Falls of Utiariti – a downpour almost as big as Niagara, where the water plunges 300 ft (90 m) from a mighty shelving rock into the gorge below. And on they pressed through the lands of the Nambikwara until at last they came to the River of Doubt.

Roosevelt wrote: 'On February 27, 1914, shortly after midday, we started down the River of Doubt into the unknown . . . It was interesting work, for no civilized man, no white man, had ever gone down or up this river or seen the country through which we were passing.' The 22 explorers travelled in seven dugout canoes, heavily laden with

food and scientific apparatus. It was the height of the rainy season and the swollen river ran swift and brown, with the forest rising like a green wall on either side, hung with looping, twisted vines, overgrown with plants that grew on the decaying remnants of dead trees. Some, wrote the former president, had huge leaves like elephants' ears.

The Brazilians who paddled the explorers' vessels were, in Roosevelt's words, a strapping set. 'They were expert river-men and

ROOSEVELT ON RONDON

A colonel in the Brazilian army, Candido Rondon was one of the greatest explorers of the 20th century. His expedition partner, Theodore Roosevelt, wrote of him:

'Colonel Rondon is not simply an "officer and a gentleman" in the sense that is honorably true of the best army officers in every good military service. He is also a peculiarly hardy and competent explorer, a good field naturalist and scientific man, a student and a philosopher. With him the conversation ranged from jaguar hunting and the perils of exploration in the "Mato Grosso", the great wilderness, to Indian anthropology, to the dangers of a purely materialistic industrial civilization, and to Positivist morality. The Colonel's Positivism was, in very fact to him, a religion of humanity, a creed which bade him be just and kindly and useful to his fellow men, to live his life bravely and no less bravely to face death, without reference to what he believed, or did not believe, or to what the unknown hereafter might hold for him.'

WILDLIFE OF THE AMAZON

While mapping the River of Doubt, the Roosevelt-Rondon expedition also collected a wealth of information about the flora and fauna of Amazonia. Roosevelt was particularly influential in bringing the piranha to public notice, and a sub-genus, Taddyella, was even named after him. 'The piranha,' he reported, 'is a short, deep-bodied fish with a blunt face and a heavily undershot or projecting jaw which gapes widely. The razor-sharp teeth are wedge-shaped like a shark's, and the jaw muscles possess great power.'

The ex-president was fascinated by the way that the Amazonian snakes had developed their peculiar, venomous specialisation. 'They rely for attack and defense purely on their poison-fangs. All other means and methods for attack and defense have atrophied. They neither crush nor tear with their teeth nor constrict with their bodies.' He also noted another menace: the *Jacaré-uassus*, or black cayman crocodile, which grows to lengths of up to 20 ft (6 m) and might creep up on humans drunk or asleep on the river bank. Numerous in Roosevelt's day, these creatures have been hunted almost to extinction. Roosevelt wrote: 'Caymans were becoming plentiful. The ugly brutes lay on the sand-flats and mud-banks like logs, always with the head raised, sometimes with the jaws open. They are often dangerous to domestic animals, and are always destructive to fish, and it is good to shoot them. I killed half a dozen and missed nearly as many more – a throbbing boat does not improve one's aim.'

GAPING JAWS The red-bellied piranha (*Rooseveltiella nattereri*), one of the species named after the ex-president.

men of the forest, skilled veterans in wilderness work. They were lithe as panthers and brawny as bears. They swam like water-dogs. They were equally at home with pole and paddle, with axe and machete; and one was a good cook and others were good men around camp. They looked like pirates in the pictures of Howard Pyle or Maxfield Parrish; one or two of them were pirates, and one worse than a pirate; but most of them were hard-working, willing, and cheerful.'

The men's cheerful disposition would, however, often be tried, for at the main series of rapids they had to hack their way through the jungle and carry the canoes overland. Sometimes it was possible to avoid a full portage by unloading the canoes so that they rose in the water and could be manhandled through the stream. Often, though, the heavy wooden dugouts had to be taken out of the water and hauled on rollers past the rapids. Where the ground was not flat enough, and the descent long and hilly, they might even abandon their canoes, carry the equipment downstream and build new canoes at the bottom.

Disaster looms

One day, Kermit's canoe overturned in a whirlpool, a porter drowned and he himself barely escaped with his life. Many of the food supplies were lost in this way. The explorers' fears for their safety were aggravated when one of their dogs wandered off and was killed with a poisoned arrow by an unseen American Indian. There was, however, no turning back. Two new dugouts were built and the explorers continued down the river.

A RED LETTER DAY

On April 15, 1913, having endured many ordeals in their expedition, ex-president Roosevelt and his party at last reached an outpost of civilisation.

'We came on a newly built house in a little planted clearing; and we cheered heartily. No one was at home, but the house, of palm thatch, was clean and cool. A couple of dogs were on watch, and the belongings showed that a man, a woman, and a child lived there, and had only just left. Another hour brought us to a similar house where dwelt an old black man who showed the innate courtesy of the Brazilian peasant... We had come over 186 miles (300 km), in 48 days, over absolutely unknown ground; we had seen no human being, although we had twice heard Indians. Six weeks had been spent in steadily slogging our way down through the interminable series of rapids. It was astonishing, when we were on a river of about the size of the upper Rhine or Elbe, to realize that no geographer had any idea of its existence.'

On March 27, while trying to prevent a canoe from capsizing, Roosevelt bruised his leg badly against a boulder and the injury became infected. With dwindling food supplies and half the party now ravaged by dysentery and fever, it looked as if the expedition faced disaster. To cap it all, there was a murder in the party. A European member of the expedition named Julio cracked under the strain and started pilfering rations. After a black American sergeant caught him and knocked him out, Julio ambushed the soldier

AMAZONIAN INHABITANTS An Amazon family photographed by the party – poles and palm fronds provide all the shelter required.

TEAM LEADERS Roosevelt (on the left) with Colonel Rondon, photographed at Navaité on the River of Doubt.

and shot him dead. Then he ran off into the jungle. Three days later, Julio appeared on the river bank shouting that he wanted to surrender. Then he vanished again into the jungle, never to reappear.

Kermit succumbed to a high fever, and his injured father offered to stay behind if it would increase the others' survival chances. Roosevelt wrote: 'No man has any business to go on such a trip as ours unless he will refuse to jeopardize the welfare of his associates by any delay caused by a weakness or ailment of his. It is his duty to go forward, if necessary on all fours, until he drops.'

Fortunately neither he nor his son was put to the test. Travel on the river at last became swifter and easier, and on April 15 they reached a palm-thatched hut – the first house that they had seen in seven weeks.

The explorers had arrived at a little rubber-tapping settlement at the outskirts of civilisation. Its inhabitants at first fled, fearing an Indian raid, for they did not expect anyone to arrive from the unknown regions upstream. But they later returned and offered hospitality and guidance on the course the travellers should take.

By the end of April, Roosevelt's expedition had reached safety at the confluence of the River of Doubt with the Madeira, an immense tributary of the Amazon. In the course of the journey, the explorers had collected 2500 animal and insect specimens and mapped a 948 mile (1525 km) river that had earlier been unknown. It was a formidable achievement, and the River of Doubt was renamed the Rio Roosevelt in honour of the ex-president. Roosevelt himself lived only a few years more. He died in 1919, and it is generally believed that his life was shortened by the sickness he had endured on the river that now bears his name.

ARCHERS OF THE AMAZON A Nambikwara bowman shows off his skill. The expedition passed through the war-like tribe's lands before setting off down the River of Doubt.

THE MYSTERY OF COLONEL FAWCETT

A BRITISH EXPLORER VANISHES WHILE SEARCHING FOR LOST CIVILISATIONS IN THE AMAZON FOREST

Ancient legends of Brazilian lost cities inspired Colonel Percy Fawcett to trek off in search of their alleged splendours. An English explorer who had served 20 years in the British army, Fawcett had surveyed the borders of several South American countries. On a 1908 trip commissioned by the Bolivian government to chart the unknown Verde River, five of his porters died and Fawcett himself almost perished from starvation. But such ordeals sharpened Fawcett's appetite for adventure and, in the course of further work, he came upon rumours of lost cities in the South American interior. One in particular, which he read about in an 18th-century manuscript, boasted columns,

DOOMED EXPLORER Percy Fawcett at camp in the Mato Grosso. The horses were sent back before he set off on his last journey.

statues and 'great arches so high that none could read the inscriptions on them'.

After serving in the First World War, Fawcett got backing from the Brazilian government to search for ruins on the Mato Grosso plateau. Expeditions in 1920 and 1921 ended when his companions could no longer withstand the rigours of the trips. In 1925 Fawcett launched a third expedition, sponsored by the North American Newspaper Alliance, aiming to find a city that he dubbed 'Z'. The party comprised Fawcett, his 21-year-old son Jack, and his son's friend, Raleigh Rimmell. On April 20 they set out from the town of Cuiabá, on the southern edge of the Mato Grosso, on an expedition that Fawcett estimated might last as long as two years.

Dead Horse Camp

Fawcett's party was ravaged by insect bites, to which Rimmell was particularly allergic. The three men are known to have reached a place called Dead Horse Camp, near the headwaters of the Xingu River, for Fawcett

IN THE SADDLE Jack Fawcett accompanied his father into the Xingu jungle and perished there with him.

wrote a letter from there to his wife dated May 30, describing how they had hacked their way through forests of scrub, forded countless streams and climbed forbidding hills. 'We shall not get into interesting country for another two weeks', the colonel wrote.

THE CASE OF RAYMOND MAUFRAIS

Covered with impenetrable equatorial forests, French Guiana contains viciously inhospitable terrain. The notorious former penal colony of Devil's Island lies offshore, while the mountainous interior is the domain of boa constrictors, vampire bats and the predatory piranha fish that frequent its innumerable rivers. Even in the mid 20th century, the jungle was inhabited by Amerindian tribes who had never set eyes on a white man.

French explorer Raymond Maufrais had determined to cross the 2500 ft (760 m) Tumuc-Humac mountains and find a path through uncharted territory to the River Amazon, but in July 1950 his equipment was found abandoned on the banks of the River Tamouri. Of Raymond there was no sign. One man who refused to believe the worst was the explorer's father, Edgar. In 1952 he set out to find his son, starting at the Amazon and working back across the Tumuc-Humacs. That trip ended when his craft was wrecked on river rapids.

In the years that followed, Edgar Maufrais mounted several more expeditions, fuelled by reports of a white man fitting Raymond's description who lived in the forests. And his search was not wholly fruitless; following a trail of clues, he discovered that Raymond had tried to float downstream by raft and that when the raft broke up on the rocks he had tried to continue on foot through the jungle. Not far from Raymond's last known campsite, Edgar came upon a broken screwdriver and a small saucepan that had lost its handle. There, however, the trail petered out, and nothing more was ever heard of the missing explorer.

MISSING MAN Raymond Maufrais disappeared in French Guiana in 1950.

After that, there were no more messages. Fawcett's silence caused no special alarm at first, for he had anticipated a long trip and was entering territory where it would be very hard to send a message. But after three years a search party assembled. Headed by Commander George Dyott, an experienced explorer and pioneer of air routes over the

NOVEL INSPIRATION

The writer Evelyn Waugh was fascinated by the Fawcett case, which helped inspire the ending of his novel, *A Handful of Dust* (1934). The hero, Tony Last, travels up the Amazon, where he falls into the hands of an old, mad recluse called Mr Todd. At the end Last is Todd's prisoner, condemned to read Dickens daily to his captor.

Amazon, the party journeyed beyond Dead Horse Camp and came upon some Anauquas Indians, one of whom wore a brass lapel button belonging to Fawcett as a medallion. The Indians insisted that it had been a gift from the colonel, who had travelled on into the interior where it was likely that he had been killed by hostile Suya tribesmen. During the night, however, the Anauquas chief was over-

heard telling his tribesmen that they should kill this expedition just as they had the last. Dyott's party retreated hastily.

Nothing could be proved against the Anauquas, however – and besides, contradictory reports started to come in, of a demented old white man living among Indian tribes. A Swiss hunter reported in 1932 that Fawcett was being held prisoner in an Indian village in the Mato Grosso near Tapajos; as evidence, the hunter produced a ring identified as one belonging to the colonel. According to a very different report, all three white men were living among the Aruvudu Indians; Jack Fawcett had married a Native American woman who had borne him a white, blue-eyed son. In 1943, an expedition led by journalist Edmar Morel set out on a fruitless quest to locate the child.

In 1950, the riddle seemed solved when a Kalapolo chief confessed on his deathbed to Fawcett's murder. He told the explorer Orlando Villas Boas that the white men had been killed after Fawcett had provoked his tribe by slapping an Indian in the face. Villas Boas dug at the place indicated and recovered human bones, which were returned to England and examined at the Royal Anthropological Institute. Their findings stunned everyone. The bones belonged to a man of about 5 ft 7 in (1.7 m). Fawcett and his son were both over 6 ft 1 in (1.85 m), and Raleigh, too, was much taller than the skeleton. Despite every attempt to solve the riddle, the case remains a mystery.

MACABRE RELIC The supposed skull of Percy Fawcett, unearthed in the jungle in 1951, is shown to Brazilian reporters.

A SCREAM IN STONE

TRIUMPH AND TRAGEDY GREET CLIMBERS TACKLING
THE GALE-TORN SPIRES OF PATAGONIA

SPIDERMAN Italian climber Cesare Maestri
was dubbed the 'Spider of the Dolomites'.

The cold, high deserts of Patagonia cover a vast area of southern Argentina and Chile, and though their mountain peaks are not among the highest in South America, they remained unconquered after the main giants of the Andes had been ascended. One reason for this was the challenging nature of the steep granite spires; the other was the appalling weather. Ferocious winds rushing in from the Antarctic ice cap subject Patagonia's barren heights to incessant storms. Good weather in the area rarely lasts more than three days, and even when conditions are fine at the base they can deteriorate rapidly a mile or so into the mountains.

One of the most dramatic spires is Monte FitzRoy (now known as Cerro Chaltel), which at 10 958 ft (3340 m) dominates the fanged rock peaks all around it. It was attempted many times before the French alpinists Lionel Terray and Guido Magnone finally conquered the summit in 1952. They solved the problems caused by the savage wind by digging ice caves for shelter, but Terray, who had impressive Himalayan conquests under his belt, later confessed that Monte FitzRoy was the climb that pushed him closest to the limits of physical and mental endurance.

Even more dangerous, if possible, is the nearby Cerro Torre, whose nightmarish 10 280 ft (3102 m) spire has been called 'a scream in stone'. Its vertical rock walls plastered with ice soar above a glacier, making it one of the most spectacular peaks in the world. In 1958 two Italian teams tried, and failed, to reach the summit, then a controversial third attempt, via the north-east face, was launched the following year by the Italian Cesare Maestri and Austrian Toni Egger. Six days after setting out on the epic assault, Cesare Maestri was found, dazed and half-buried in the glacier's snow. Egger did not return at all.

According to Maestri they had reached the summit, but during the descent Egger was swept away by an avalanche. Years later, as more climbers were defeated by Cerro Torre's daunting peak, questions were raised as to whether Maestri and Egger could really have got to the top. In 1970, Maestri answered his critics by returning to the spire and bolting his way up the South-east Ridge and East Face with the aid of a compressed-air drill. The ascent, which took many weeks, was an extraordinary test of stamina in atrocious conditions, but the bolt ladder was denounced as unethical by mountaineers all around the world. Moreover, Maestri admitted that he did not surmount an overhanging mushroom of snow at the very top and so was still denied the laurels of the conqueror.

TWIN CHALLENGES The jagged peaks of Cerro Chaltel (left) and Cerro Torre (right) tower over the high Patagonian desert.

20TH-CENTURY TRIUMPHS

1906 Mt Stanley 16 762 ft (5109 m). The highest mountain in the Ruwenzori, Africa's Mountains of the Moon, situated on the Uganda-Zaire border. Its summit (Margherita Peak) was conquered by the Duke of the Abruzzi.

1913 Mount McKinley 20 320 ft (6194 m). North America's highest peak, was ascended by Hudson Stuck and Harry Karstens.

1925 Mount Logan 19 550 ft (5959 m). Canada's highest mountain, in the St Elias range, conquered by Albert MacCarthy and H.F. Lambert.

1928 Lenin Peak 23 405 ft (7134 m). The highest mountain in Russia, in the Pamir Mountains, first climbed by a Soviet-German team led by Rickmers.

1932 Huascarán 22 132 ft (6746 m). Peru's highest mountain, in the Andes, ascended by the German, P. Borchers. (America's Annie Peck had conquered a lesser peak of Huascarán in 1908.)

1933 Communism Peak 24 590 ft (7495 m). The highest mountain in the former Soviet Union, in the Pamirs in Tajikistan. It was ascended by the Russian, Abalakov.

1950 Annapurna 26 544 ft (8091 m). Himalayan peak, in Nepal, the first 26 246 ft (8000 m) mountain to be conquered. It was scaled by Frenchmen Maurice Herzog and Louis Lachenal.

1953 Mount Everest 29 028 ft (8848 m). The highest mountain in the world on the Nepal-Tibet border in the Himalayas. The peak was conquered by Edmund Hillary and Tenzing Norgay.

1954 K2 (or Mount Godwin Austin) 28 251 ft (8611 m). The second-highest mountain in the world, in Northern Pakistan in the Karakorum range. The summit was first ascended by two members of an Italian team, Lino Lacadelli and Achille Compagnoni.

1955 Mount Kangchenjunga 28 208 ft (8598 m). The world's third-highest mountain, in the Himalayas, on the Sikkim-Nepal border. It was ascended by the British duo Joe Brown and George Band, who stopped just short of the true summit out of respect for the religious wishes of the Sikkimese.

During the winter of 1973-4 the summit of Cerro Torre was finally attained beyond doubt by another Italian team, headed by Casimiro Ferrari. Through many searching interviews, however, Maestri has never ceased to defend his own 1959 claim. One find that might have shed light on the mystery proved, in the end, inconclusive. In 1975, Egger's body was discovered 1½ miles (2.4 km) down the glacier. But his camera, which could have held crucial evidence, was never found.

THE ANDES SURVIVORS

AN AIR CRASH LEAVES STRANDED PASSENGERS TO CHOOSE A TERRIBLE ALTERNATIVE TO STARVATION AND PROMPTS A HEROIC TREK THROUGH FROZEN CRAGS TO SEEK RESCUE

On October 13, 1972, a twin-engined Uruguayan Air Force Fairchild F-227 ran into a blizzard high over the Andes mountains. Suddenly hitting an air pocket, the plane went into a dive, plunging some 3000 ft (910 m) in a matter of seconds. When search parties failed to locate the missing aircraft, the 45 Uruguayans on board were presumed dead. Inside the crashed Fairchild, however, a grim ordeal was just beginning.

When the aircraft hit a mountainside its tailplane wrenched off, but snow helped to break the fall of the skidding fuselage. The passengers were mostly young men and members of the Old Christians rugby club, some of whom had brought mothers and sisters with them. The pilot was killed in the crash and 16 others, including most of the women passengers, lay dead or dying around the wreckage. But 28 survived the disaster and, stumbling outside, now felt the impact of sub-zero temperatures. They were stranded amid mountains rising to 21 000 ft (6400 m), in a place of unutterable, icy desolation.

The survivors pinned their hopes on the possibility of rescue by search parties, which they knew from a radio receiver were scouring the mountains for them, and they endured the first days with fortitude. They were healthy, resourceful young sportsmen and they had warm skiing clothes, which they had brought with them for a planned holiday in a Chilean mountain resort. At one end of the wrecked fuselage, the cabin offered some shelter and they blocked up the aperture with an assortment of improvised partitions. The survivors made blankets from seat covers and slept as close as possible to one another to keep warm.

From their few small foraging expeditions they learnt that there was no food to be found – no vegetation, not even lichen, grew at this height, nor did an escape seem remotely possible. All movement was painfully slow in the thin air, and they were not equipped for a long descent. It seemed safest to sit tight, but their meagre food supplies quickly ran out, and on October 21 the survivors heard the news on their radio that they had been dreading. The search parties had been called off. The Chilean Mountain Rescue Service declared that no one could have survived over a week among the frozen crags of the Andes, and that until the spring thaw, no further attempts would be made to locate the wreckage.

As severe hunger pangs set in, the survivors were faced with two alternatives: to die of starvation; or to consume flesh taken from the

WRECKED FUSELAGE A body lies in snow outside the crashed Uruguayan plane that came down in the Andes while flying members of the Old Christians rugby club to Santiago.

NIGHTMARE'S END On December 22, 1972, the Andes survivors wave to greet the rescue helicopter as it arrives to end their ten-week ordeal.

the evening of December 20 when the two ragged figures were seen in the foothills of the Andes by a cattle hand from San Fernando. They were shouting and making gestures of supplication across the River Tinguiririca, but he could not hear what they were saying above the roaring torrent. The following morning he saw them again and this time threw them a piece of paper and a pencil attached to a stone. They threw back a message describing their situation, and ending, 'We have to get out of here quickly because we have nothing to eat. We can walk no more.' Before midnight, patrols had reached the pair and the next day, with helicopter support, most of the survivors were taken off the mountain. Bad weather prevented the last few from being rescued until December 23, but Parrado had kept his promise to get them off by Christmas.

In all, the survivors' ordeal had lasted 70 days, and when all the celebrations were over, a new suffering began – of coming to terms with the memory of what they had done. The Press did not give them an easy time. 'May God Forgive Them,' ran the headline of one Chilean newspaper. But theologians agreed that their actions had been justified under the circumstances, and in a strongly Catholic country believers even found a sacramental element in what had passed. Had not Christ offered his blood and body to the apostles in order that they might find salvation?

AFTERMATH Survivors photographed by a member of the rescue team. It was not yet known that they had resorted to cannibalism.

bodies of their dead companions. It was a hideous decision, but it had to be taken. Strips of frozen flesh cut from the dead were hung to dry until ready for consumption. They were not cooked because, as medical student Roberto Canessa explained, proteins die off at temperatures above 40°C (104°F), and to get the most benefit from meat it must be eaten raw. Rations were presented in small pellets to reduce the ordeal of chewing, but this precaution failed to make the decision acceptable to everyone. Numa Turcatti threw his food away when the others' backs were turned, and allowed himself to die.

Huddled in their shelter, the survivors learnt new terrors. On October 29, nine more died when an avalanche crashed down on the wrecked aircraft and choked the fuselage with an immense tonnage of compacted snow. In the aftermath of this fresh calamity, it was decided that someone must attempt the impossible and try to reach help. The three-man team chosen for this expedition was led by Fernando Parrado, a tall, tough-minded rugby forward who promised his companions that he would have them out by Christmas. Few can have believed him as the trio set out across the snows, wearing improvised mountaineering clothes packed with felt coverings torn from the Fairchild's heating tubes. After three days, one of the trio turned back in order to save rations, but Parrado and his companion, the medical student Canessa, pressed on, scaling ridges never previously attempted even by fully equipped climbers. Canessa later reported: 'We had no idea where we were going, but with the aircraft compass we had to get there. Chile was to the west and we would go there whatever happened.' They accomplished ten days of gruelling travel, enduring intense cold at night and intolerable heat at midday, and they rationed their water and food, telling themselves that if they did not get a certain distance in a certain number of hours they would not eat.

Parrado was the ultimate hero, forever urging his companion on and even carrying Canessa towards the end of their journey. It was

ELUSIVE GIANTS OF THE AMAZON

A YOUNG ENGLISH EXPLORER FALLS VICTIM TO A
STONE-AGE TRIBE HOSTILE TO OUTSIDERS

During the 1950s two Oxford under-graduates, Richard Mason and Robin Hanbury-Tenison, decided to travel by jeep across South America, from Recife on the Atlantic coast to Lima, the Peruvian capital. The journey would take them across the roadless wastes of the Mato Grosso. Jolting and shuddering across the wild scrub, float-ing the jeep on a raft where necessary, they met disaster when the vehicle's chassis broke. Eventually they managed to get it fixed and edged round the piranha-infested swamps of Brazil's Pantanal (an area the size of Britain) before they were hauled by oxen through the Banados del Izozog swamplands in Bolivia to reach their destination on the Pacific.

In 1961, Richard Mason returned to the Mato Grosso to explore the as-yet unmapped headwaters of the Iriri River, which runs through the heart of the wilderness. Two months after setting out from a newly built jungle airstrip at Cachimbo, Mason was found dead, only 30 miles (48 km) from the airstrip. He had been shot with eight Indian arrows, and his skull and left thigh had been broken by clubs.

The tall tribe

Who was responsible? When the arrows were shown to members of the local Txukahamei people, they were identified by their binding and feathering as belonging to a warlike tribe, hitherto unknown to Europeans, called the Kreen-Akrore (which means 'these men whose hair is short'). The Kreen-Akrore were by repute an exception-ally tall people who regularly attacked the Txukahamei villages; investigators believed they were the same people as a club-wield-ing tribe who had been reported clashing with rubber tappers on the River Teles Pires, 100 miles (160 km) to the west.

Gradually, from talk with their neigh-bours, the profile of a Stone-Age tribe emerged. They were, it appeared, hard men and hostile to all outsiders. Among other warring tribes, it was conventional for the victors to carry off the enemies' womenfolk, who would help to breed more children and (incidentally) bring new genes and new ideas to the group. The Txukahamei, for example, learnt how to load and repair captured guns from white women captives. In stark contrast, the prac-tice of the Kreen-Akrore was to massacre enemy women and children.

Investigators learnt that the Kreen-Akrore were one of the peoples who hunted

MURDERED MAN Richard Mason with a member of the Xavantes people. He was killed while leading an expedition sponsored by the Royal Geographical Society. Above: The Paraguay River winds across the Mato Grosso plateau.

in the deep forest, travelling on foot. Unlike those who lived on the rivers, they had no canoes and could not even swim. 'In water,' said one of their neigh-bours, 'Kreen-Akrore sink.' Their houses were small and shabby, with sloping roofs and no walls. But the tribe laid out planta-tions of banana, potato, maize and manioca in geometric patterns of circles and crosses, which astonished the first aerial reconnais-sance party to locate a Kreen-Akrore village.

In 1968, an expedition was sent out to locate the Stone-Age tribe. It was headed by the brothers Claudio and Orlando Villas

as we walked; angry spider monkeys rained dead wood on our heads. Oblivious of our existence all the game of the forest seemed to parade to and fro across our trail.'

'They just vanished into the jungle'

The Kreen-Akrore proved extraordinarily elusive. When, eventually, their villages were located, the inhabitants abandoned them and melted into the jungle as the expedition approached. The explorers left gifts: mirrors, beads, knives, pans, even toy aeroplanes, symbolic of the craft that the tribes must sometimes have seen flying over their land. Sometimes the gifts were taken away at night by unseen warriors, who left war clubs in return. But by day the tribesmen themselves kept away.

One time, three Kreen-Akrore

Boas, recognised as Brazil's greatest living explorers, who had spent many years working with the jungle tribes, championing their cause and shielding them from the first shock of civilisation. The quest for the Kreen-Akrore is described in *The Tribe that Hides from Man*, by Adrian Cowell, a member of the party, and it proved a fascinating, frustrating journey. They entered what the Indians called black jungle. Cowell wrote: 'This is the name given by the Txukahamei to forest which is so high that humans seem to live in an underworld of semi-darkness; we were not to see the sun for months, and our skin was to become so pale that it was almost green. In this world every sound we made produced an echo, every movement disturbed a life. Jaguars stalked through our camps; coati scampered beside us

HELPING HAND Claudio Villas Boas giving medicine to a Txukahamei villager. He wanted to accustom the tribes to medical treatment before settlers brought disease.

walked calmly out of the jungle and stood on a sandbank 600 yd (550 m) away. 'It was an unexpected, and therefore frightening, confrontation . . . the three black figures stood like a line of Toltec statues. They did not call. They made no gesture. And after a few minutes of tension, they just turned and vanished into the jungle.'

By January 1969, when the Kreen-Akrore had rejected all approaches, a decision was taken to suspend activities for the time being. But in 1972 the Villas Boas led another expedition, and in February the following year contact was made with the elusive tribe. After an episode when Claudio was met with a volley of arrows, 25 Kreen-Akrore warriors entered his camp on the Braco Norte River. 'GIANT INDIANS DEMAND TRINKETS', reported *The Times*, noting how the tribesmen were on average a foot taller than their neighbours, and how there were fears that if denied more trinkets they might turn nasty. 'The giant Indians are feared by other tribesmen, who also say that the Kreen-Akrore women are just as tall and

CITY BOUND Orlando Villas Boas on a flight to a Brazilian city with an Indian child. The brothers educated youngsters to lead the tribal relations with the outside world. Below: An abandoned Kreen-Akrore village.

THE FATE OF THE TRIBE

In 1967, before the first expedition went out to find the Kreen-Akrore, their nine jungle villages contained an estimated 600 people. In January 1975, when the survivors were transferred by aircraft to the Xingu National Park, there were only 79. Epidemics of white men's diseases – especially influenza – account very largely for the death toll. In a 1994 interview, an elder named Tesseya described how, after the first contact with the Villas Boas party, he and his family returned by night to one of the villages. 'When we arrived, my grandfather, Sewakri, died. He was the first one to die. We had just arrived, and we still had the fear of the white people on us, and my mother died. Everyone came to that village and got sick. People were too weak to get up, and the others scattered in all directions in the forest. First one died, then another, and another. Everyone was sick. "What is happening to us?" the people said, "It must be because of the white people." Everyone died there.'

Survivors were too sick and debilitated to bury the dead and when mothers died, nursing infants perished with them for lack of milk. Corpses were eaten by vultures and turtles. Matters were worsened by the traditional belief that such visitations resulted from sorcery – and many tribespeople were executed as witches. Evacuated to Xingu, however, the hungry, anaemic population riddled with malaria gradually recovered. In 1994 the Kreen-Akrore (or Parana, as they were now known) were granted an area of more than 1.2 million acres – more than 488 000 hectares – of their traditional land, in Mato Grosso and Para states.

powerful as their menfolk. One woman is reported to have battered to death four enemy tribesmen with a war club 4 ft 6 in (1.4 m) in length before 15 members of the opposing army put her out of action.' Nevertheless, *The Times* reported, they let Villas Boas embrace them and hand them gifts in exchange for bows and arrows during a 20 minute encounter.

Who were these tall people? And why had they been so hostile to contact, not only with white men, but with other Indian tribes? The Kreen-Akrores' name for themselves was Parana. Their own oral history told how, in the distant past, they had moved westwards, away from a savannah homeland overrun by white men with guns, to settle in the forest. Studies of their language confirmed the tribal narrative. It appeared that the Parana were the last survivors of a once-widespread people known to Brazilian historians as the Southern Cayapo. They had fought fiercely with the gold-hungry Portuguese in the 18th century. Fleeing westwards into the remote forests of the Mato Grosso, the people had retained a strong sense of their otherness from the local tribes, and a particular hostility to white men. When Richard Mason succumbed to their clubs and arrows in 1961, he fell victim to a 200-year-old group memory of Portuguese slaving raids and massacres, which had caused all white men to be thought of as savage and dangerous enemies.

THE FROZEN LANDS

RELENTLESS FREEZING WINDS CRACKED THE FACES OF THE 20TH-CENTURY EXPLORERS WHO VENTURED TO THE EARTH'S NORTHERN AND SOUTHERN EXTREMITIES. IN THESE UNMAPPED WHITE WASTES, FROSTBITE, SNOWBLINDNESS AND SCURVY WERE RECURRENT HAZARDS. FOR ANTARCTIC EXPLORERS, THE SHEER SIZE OF THE CONTINENT WAS DAUNTING, WHILE ARCTIC ADVENTURERS HAD OTHER PERILS TO CONTEND WITH, FROM SWIRLING ICE FLOES TO MARAUDING POLAR BEARS.

THE FIRST TO THE POLE?

IS IT REALLY TRUE THAT ROBERT E. PEARY WAS THE FIRST PERSON TO REACH FARTHEST NORTH?

In 1887, Robert E. Peary wrote: 'I must have fame, and cannot reconcile myself to years of commonplace drudgery and a name late in life when I see an opportunity to gain it now and sip the delicious draughts while yet I have youth and strength . . . I want my fame now.'

Venerated by Americans as the first man to reach the Earth's northernmost extremity, Peary is also revered as a patriot who nailed the Stars and Stripes to the North Pole for the glory of his country. There is nothing unusual in an explorer possessing the sort of personal ambition to which Peary confessed. The myth of Robert Peary, however, has been scrutinised on other grounds. Serious doubts have been expressed as to whether he reached the North Pole at all.

Born in western Pennsylvania in 1856, Peary joined the US navy and after doing survey work for a canal through Nicaragua, turned his thoughts towards exploration in the frozen north. In 1891, accompanied by his valet, a young black American named Matthew A. Henson, Peary led an expedition to Greenland, where he studied the survival techniques of the Inuit people. On this trip, too, went a man who was to play a notorious role in the North

MEN OF DESTINY Robert E. Peary, photographed with sledge dogs below, won fame as the first conqueror of the North Pole. Right: Matthew A. Henson accompanied Peary on his 1909 journey to the Pole.

CIGARETTE CARD The *Theodore Roosevelt*, specially designed to withstand being crushed by polar ice, carried Peary's expedition to the edge of the Arctic ice cap.

Pole saga – a Brooklyn doctor named Frederick Albert Cook.

During later voyages, the conquest of the North Pole became Peary's obsession, and on a northward push in 1899 he experienced the true savagery of the Arctic cold. When Peary's feet began to bother him, Henson removed his master's boots to find both legs a bloodless white up to the knee. Then Peary's rabbitskin undershoes were removed – and several toes snapped off with them. Frostbite had taken its toll. 'My God, Lieutenant! Why didn't you tell me your feet were

COOK'S CLAIM

Frederick Cook was astonishingly successful in his fraudulent claim to have reached the North Pole. He was fêted by crowds of thousands wherever he went; tall, brown 'Dr Cook' fur hats were all the rage in women's fashion in London and New York, while miniature fur-clad 'Dr Cook' figures on sledges were bestsellers in the toy shops. In September 1909, when Peary challenged Cook's claim to have reached the Pole, most Americans were inclined to believe Cook.

frozen?' Henson asked. Peary's reply was terse: 'There's no time to pamper sick men on the trail. Besides, a few toes aren't much to give to achieve the Pole.' After that trip all but two of Peary's toes had to be amputated, and it was hobbling on maimed feet that he made his later Arctic expeditions.

Following a failed attempt on the Pole in 1902, Peary became discouraged, feeling that he was getting too old for the quest and writing that 'The game is off'. But he bristled when he discovered that an Italian party headed by the Duke of the Abruzzi had surpassed the existing farthest-north record. Spurred on by the competition, he was soon back in harness. Peary built lighter, broader sledges to improve performance over rough ice fields. He also worked on what was to be called 'The Peary System', which involved sending advance parties to break the trail and build igloos as depots; support groups to shuttle supplies forwards; and a main assault team which, with its energies conserved, would make the final dash to the Pole.

Peary's detractors have claimed that there was nothing new about the system – much had been standard among 19th-century Arctic explorers, as had his practice of wearing Inuit clothing and using Inuit survival techniques. Nevertheless, Peary's were state-of-the art preparations for polar exploration, and they were enhanced when he ordered the building of a specially designed schooner to carry the expedition to the very edge of the frozen Arctic Ocean. The double-framed hull of the *Theodore Roosevelt*, as the vessel was christened, was designed to withstand the worst polar winter.

On a 1905-6 expedition, Peary claimed to attain latitude 87°6', beating the Italian record by 36 miles (58 km). However, his records on this trip were so vague that his claims have always been controversial. Though he was well enough received on his return to the United States, a book he wrote about the expedition sold poorly and funds for another attempt dried up. It was the competitive spirit, again, which caused him to renew his efforts. Peary learned that his former companion, Frederick Cook, was now planning an attempt on the Pole, and with rekindled enthusiasm he scrounged around to find financial backing for what was now his sixth Arctic expedition.

Amazing news

On July 6, 1908, the *Roosevelt* set sail from New York harbour, skippered by Newfoundland-born Bob Bartlett, who would also be a key member of the polar assault

THE DEBONAIR DOCTOR Frederick Cook claimed to have reached the North Pole with two Inuit companions on April 21, 1908.

team. The ship stopped at Etah, Greenland, to take on huskies to haul supplies and Inuit to construct the igloos. While they were there, Peary learnt that Cook had set off for the Pole in March. 'Dr Cook's action in going north,' Peary told *The New York Times*, 'for the admitted purpose of forestalling me is one of which no man possessing a sense of honour would be guilty.' But such fulminations had no effect. On September 2, the world's press splashed out the amazing news that after braving all the perils of travel across the Arctic ice, Cook had reached the North Pole.

The story received sensational coverage, with many papers celebrating the triumph in banner headlines, double-page features and editorials. But from the outset, one or two journals remained sceptical, and while Cook's bandwagon rolled on, following a triumphant press conference in Copenhagen, a handful of writers and scientists began to ask for evidence. Cook promised that he would

THE RIVALS A French magazine cover of 1909 shows Cook and Peary fighting for the glory of conquering the North Pole.

generally acknowledged to be a fraud, and in the meantime Peary had everything to prove.

Peary himself was out of contact with civilisation when Cook's story hit the headlines. His 24-man party, with 19 sledges and 133 dogs, had set up base at Cape Columbia on Ellesmere Island, and the advance parties were hindered early on by the opening of wide 'leads' or channels in the ice. These are the bane of all explorers on the Arctic's polar ice cap, which is supported by no solid rock but floats over the sea, cracking at times to leave waterways between the expanses of frozen crust. Sometimes, Peary's men were able to get across by moving from one floating ice floe to the next; on other occasions, they were halted by leads as much as 1/4 mile (400 m) across, and were forced to wait until they closed up.

By March 31, 1909, Peary, Henson and Bartlett, with a handful of Inuit, had reached the last advance base, 133 miles (214 km) from the Pole, and were ready for the final push. It was then that Peary made a highly controversial decision: he told Bartlett to go back. Bartlett himself was angry about the order, believing that he was entitled to complete the conquest, and indeed it is hard to justify Peary's decision. Peary's story was that Henson was the better dog team driver. But was that the real reason? Critics have speculated that Peary did not want to share the credit with another white man – or that he did not want Bartlett to be around to verify the positions he was noting down.

Whatever the truth, Bartlett turned back. And on April 2, Peary pushed farther north with Henson and four of the Inuit: Egingwah, Seeglo, Ootah and Ooqueah. With five sledges and 40 dogs, they made a last dash during which, if Peary's figures are to be believed, they averaged 29 miles (47 km) a day. This was an extraordinary rate considering that they had earlier struggled to maintain a daily average of 10 miles (16 km).

FROZEN WILDERNESS Peary's expedition trudges north. He believed in using the best resources available: the Inuit and their dogs, the best-quality sledges and skin clothing, and concentrated rations.

supply proofs in due course, but was never, in fact, able to produce even a diary he had promised – or any other satisfactory records for inspection. In reality, he was almost certainly lying (as it was later learned that he was lying about his conquest of Mount McKinley, the highest peak in the United States). But it was years before Cook was

Peary was to explain later that the polar ice now became unusually smooth and easy for the sledges (though this has not been confirmed by later explorers).

The conquest

'The bitter wind burned our faces so that they cracked,' Peary wrote, 'and long after we got into camp each day they pained us so that we could hardly go to sleep. The Eskimos complained much, and at every camp fixed their fur clothing about their faces, waists, knees and wrists. They also complained of their noses, which I had never known them to do before. The air was as bitter as frozen steel.'

At last, on April 6, 1909, Peary told his companions that they had reached the North Pole, and he marked the achievement with a famous diary entry that ran: 'The Pole at last! The prize of three centuries. My dream and ambition for twenty years.' The team stayed at the place they had reached for 30 hours, and Peary took a photo of Henson and the Inuit, posed before a large ice hummock surmounted by the Stars and Stripes.

Then they returned to the last advance camp – at a pace even speedier than the

HOW COULD THEY KNOW?

How did Peary or Cook decide they had reached their goal? Geographically, the North Pole is the northern extremity of the Earth's axis of rotation. A compass is of only limited value in trying to find it, because a compass needle points to the magnetic pole – a point that does not coincide with the North Pole and which, moreover, shifts its position from time to time. To locate the North Pole proper, Arctic explorers have to take regular sightings of the sun to determine latitude and longitude. The Pole is at latitude 90°N.

Cook was discredited after he failed to produce his logbooks for verification (he claimed to have left them behind in the Arctic). But Peary's own logbook was not much more rewarding. When it was examined in 1985 by British explorer Wally Herbert, he found that there were nine blank pages for the time spent in the vicinity of the Pole, and that the entry recording Peary's triumph was a loose-leaf one that could have been a later insertion.

Peary had taken only three sightings for latitude on the way to the Pole, and none for longitude. His basic method was to take a compass reading, and then to strike out in a straight line towards the Pole until he had marched the required distance. This rough-and-ready approach did not take into account the fact that the ice covering the Pole is drifting. Herbert concluded that Peary may well have gone the right distance but in the wrong direction, and ended up at best 50 miles (80 km) to the west of the Pole.

When Peary did take his sun sightings, he would have discovered that he had not yet reached latitude 90°N. Herbert speculates that Peary could not bring himself to tell his exhausted companions the truth – and faked his log to substantiate his claim.

PLANTING THE FLAG In a contemporary German illustration, Peary erects the American flag at the North Pole, watched by Matthew Henson.

PLACE NAMES

Peary's credibility as a polar explorer was damaged by the fact that he invented some fictional places. On a trip across Greenland in 1892 he claimed to have seen a channel, which he named Peary Channel, separating the mainland from another island. Later explorers discovered that no such channel exists. On his 1906 expedition, he named an island Crocker Land, after George Crocker, one of his financial backers. Again, it was discovered that no such land exists.

outward journey, taking only three days. Peary then hastened back to his main base at Cape Columbia. The *Theodore Roosevelt's* return to civilisation was long delayed by ice, but on September 6, 1909, from a telegraph station on the coast of Labrador, Peary announced to the world that he had reached the North Pole.

There followed a furious controversy. When Peary learned of Cook's claims, he made savage attempts to discredit them. Cook himself was initially anxious to avoid a quarrel, writing that 'there is glory enough for us all', but Peary was brutal in his attacks,

and the ferocity of the dispute was heightened by the fact that two great newspapers lined up behind the rivals, the *New York Herald* having exclusive rights to Cook's story and *The New York Times* backing Peary. 'Do not trouble about Cook's story,' Peary wrote in the *Times*, 'or attempt to explain any discrepancies in his statements. The affair will settle itself. He has not been at the Pole on April 21st, 1908, or at any other time. He has simply handed the public a gold brick.'

In the end, Cook's claims were totally undermined by the growing doubts about his conquest of Mount McKinley. And when he supplied his

EAGLE'S PERCH *'Peary or Cook? Either way it's America's Pole!'* proclaims a *Punch* cartoon of 1909. Below: Captain Bartlett and his party photographed by Peary, who sent them back before the final assault on the Pole.

own much-vaunted 'proofs' of his polar feat to a commission of enquiry at the University of Copenhagen, the authority's findings were damning: 'The data in the documents submitted to us are of such an unsatisfactory character that it is not possible to declare

AN UNDISPUTED CLAIM.
AMERICAN EAGLE "MY POLE, ANYWAY!"

'THE POLE AT LAST!'

In a passage from his book, *The North Pole*, published in 1910, Robert E. Peary purports to describe his conquest. But the book was ghost-written – and its version of events has since been called into question:

'The last march northward ended at ten o'clock of the forenoon of April 6. I had now made the five marches planned from the point at which Bartlett turned back, and my reckoning showed that we were in the immediate neighbourhood of the goal of all our striving. After the usual arrangements for going into camp, at approximate local noon, on the Columbia meridian, I made the first observation at our polar camp. It indicated our position as 89 degrees 57'.

'We were now at the end of the last long march of the upward journey. Yet with the Pole actually in sight I was too weary to take the last few steps. The accumulated weariness of all those days and nights of forced marches and insufficient sleep, constant peril and anxiety, seemed to roll across me all at once. I was actually too exhausted to realize at the moment that my life's purpose had been achieved. As soon as our igloos had been completed, and we had eaten our dinner and double-rationed the dogs, I turned in for a few hours of absolutely necessary sleep, Henson and the Eskimos having unloaded the sledges and got them in readiness for such repairs as were necessary. But, weary though I was, I could not sleep long. It was, therefore, only a few hours when I woke. The first thing I did after awaking was to write these words in my diary: "The Pole at last. The prize of three centuries. My dream and goal for twenty years. Mine at last! I cannot bring myself to realize it. It seems all so simple and commonplace."'

with certainty that the astronomical observations referred to were actually made; there is likewise lacking details in practical matters – such as sledge journeys – which could furnish some control. The Commission is therefore of the opinion that the material transmitted for examination contains no proof whatsoever that Dr. Cook reached the North Pole.'

In contrast, Peary's claim was accepted in America by the National Geographic Society and in England by the Royal Geographical Society, so that his became the name that entered the textbooks as conqueror of the North Pole.

Continuing doubts

Disputes, however, never fully died out. Peary's critics have noted that several members of the National Geographic Society were friends and admirers, and that they gave his evidence only the most cursory examination. 'We simply sat down with him

PEARY'S JOURNEYS Reaching the North Pole became an obsession for Robert Peary. After several failed attempts he finally achieved his ambition in 1909.

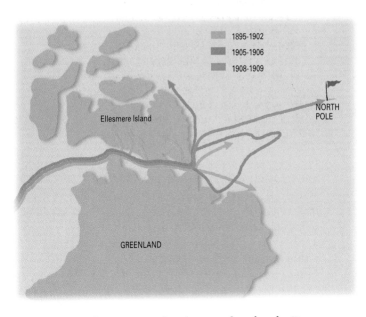

and read his journal from his original records,' one later reported. When Peary's submission was later inspected by the Royal Geographical Society, only 17 of the 35 appointed committee members were present, and their approval was hardly wholehearted. Eight voted for Peary, seven voted against, and two abstained. Peary never allowed the University of Copenhagen to examine his proofs as they had done Cook's. Indeed, he would not even release his observations to the US navy – a body which, after all, paid his salary.

Peary campaigned so hard for recognition – and a state pension – that he provoked a backlash even in his own day. As early as 1916, Henry Helgeson, a US Representative from North Dakota, brought a bill before Congress to the effect that Peary 'never reached, discovered, nor was approximately near to' the North Pole. Peary's alleged speeds in the final days nearing the Pole were queried around the same time.

In 1985, British Arctic traveller Wally Herbert concluded that the explorer was miles off target; permitted to study all of Peary's remaining personal papers, diaries and observations, Herbert reckoned that Peary probably failed to get closer than 50 miles (80 km) to the North Pole.

However, a reappraisal in 1989 of Peary's notes, made by the Navigation Foundation (which is sponsored by the National Geographic Society), decided that his final position was in reality only 5 miles (8 km) from the exact geographical location of the North Pole – giving a moral victory to Peary, even if he lacked the instruments to take absolute readings of

SOUND OF SUCCESS A music publisher cashes in on Peary's newsworthy achievement.

his position. The photographs taken by Peary were scrutinised with favourable results. In addition, his measurements of the Arctic Ocean depths near his estimation of the position of the Pole compare well with modern findings.

Still, Peary's status as the first conqueror of the North Pole is today best described as questionable. We will probably never know the truth for sure, for his notes on the journey were incomplete, and, more importantly, there was no one to crosscheck his readings of his final position – which was, after all, no more than an invisible point on a constantly moving ice pack, adrift on the Arctic Sea.

THE FORERUNNER

ERNEST SHACKLETON DISPLAYS COURAGE AND
RESILIENCE IN AN ATTEMPT ON THE SOUTH POLE

Bleak, deserted and cruelly inhospitable, Antarctica has witnessed some of the most dramatic events in the history of world exploration. Ernest Shackleton, a British sailor, made four voyages to the ice-bound continent and exhibited heroism as great as any known in the polar regions.

Born in Ireland in 1874, Shackleton left school at 16 and joined the merchant marine. As third lieutenant on Captain Scott's scientific expedition of 1901-4, he was one of a three-man team that sledged across the Ross Ice Shelf to reach 82°17'S – the farthest point south yet attained. On the way back, Shackleton succumbed to scurvy and had to be sent home. Undaunted, he determined to return and continue with the Antarctic quest.

In 1907, he declared his intention of mounting a privately financed expedition that was to assault both the South Pole and the South Magnetic Pole. His plan was to use Captain Scott's base at Hut Point, but when Scott learnt of this he informed Shackleton that he, too, was planning another expedition and asked Shackleton to leave the base free. Disappointed, Shackleton agreed. However, when his expedition reached Antarctica in January 1908, his proposed landing place was still frozen, and he had to land near Hut Point after all.

From Cape Royds, one of Shackleton's teams climbed 12 450 ft (3795 m) Mount Erebus, an active volcano on Ross Island,

ANTARCTIC HERO Ernest Shackleton
pioneered the route that Scott would later
use to reach the South Pole.

and went on to map a large amount of new territory before reaching the South Magnetic Pole on January 16, 1909. The supreme challenge, though, was the South Pole itself. Shackleton himself led this attempt, and began by setting up supply depots. On October 29, 1908, with three companions and four sledges drawn by Manchurian ponies, he set out on what he calculated should be a 1600 mile (2575 km) journey to the Pole and back. The team took provisions

for 99 days, hoping to maintain an average of 20 miles (32 km) a day. The going proved hard on the ponies, the first of which had to be shot after five weeks, with two more following suit soon after. Nonetheless, on November 26 Shackleton passed Scott's farthest point south.

The great Ross Ice Shelf had provided them with a fairly smooth highway during the long approach. But in December they reached the beginning of the continental landmass and came upon a huge glacier grinding its way down from the inland ranges to meet the Ross Ice Shelf. Shackleton named it the Beardmore Glacier after the industrialist William Beardmore, his main financial backer. The glacier would provide access to the 10 000 ft (3050 m) high Antarctic plateau, but the ascent was painfully slow. Progress slowed to 5 miles (8 km) a day and the last pony fell into a crevasse. They reached the plateau on Christmas Day, but rations were very short and they all began to suffer from gruelling headaches. On January 4, 1909, as a searing wind drove temperatures down to −26°C (−14°F), Shackleton wrote: 'The end is in sight. We can only go for three

more days at most, for we are weakening rapidly.' On January 9, 1910 he ordered his men to turn round and head back. They had got to within 97 miles (156 km) of the South Pole.

The return nearly ended in catastrophe. The expedition ship *Nimrod*, which had orders to leave Antarctica by March 1 at the latest to avoid getting iced in, had already dropped back when Shackleton reached Hut Point on February 28. On seeing no ship along the coast, Shackleton and one of his

THE VOYAGE TO SOUTH GEORGIA

After Amundsen and Scott had conquered the South Pole, Shackleton, ever eager for glory, planned something even more ambitious. In an expedition of 1914-16 he proposed a coast-to-coast crossing of Antarctica, from the Weddell Sea to the Ross Sea. However, his ship, the *Endurance*, became trapped in the Antarctic ice and began to buckle and leak under pressure. After 281 days, he and his men were forced to lower boats and evacuate the ship, which eventually sank leaving them marooned on a large ice floe.

There followed one of the greatest of all polar adventures. Shackleton decided that they should make their way over the ice to Paulet Island, 350 miles (560 km) away. They set out on December 20, 1915, hauling their boats with them, but found the ice so soft that they could barely manage a mile a day. Their dog teams were shot for food, and they were reduced to eating what seal meat they could hunt. On April 9, the ice pack began to break up and they took to their boats, which they threaded among the icebergs by day,

hauling them out by night to rest on the unstable floes. One night a floe split in half, and Shackleton had to drag a man out of the water by clutching at his sleeping bag.

Eventually the party reached bleak, ice-bound Elephant Island. With five others, Shackleton then took to a boat and journeyed some 700 miles (1100 km) to get help. Braving blizzards, storm waves and tormenting thirst, Shackleton at last reached South Georgia Island and walked across it – a 24-hour journey that had never been accomplished before – to find help at the small whaling station of Grytviken.

Shackleton faced appalling difficulties in trying to get a ship to relieve the remainder of his expedition on Elephant Island, but on August 20 a Chilean steamer at last picked up the stranded men. Incredibly, they were all still alive.

GLACIAL CREVASSE Two members of Shackleton's 1914-17 expedition negotiating an Antarctic glacier.

companions lit fires and hoisted flags to signal their return. It worked: the next morning the *Nimrod* came back to pick them up and all four exhausted explorers were carried safely back to England.

CRUSHING POWER The *Endurance* trapped in the Antarctic ice, 1915. Above: The Royal Geographical Society medal awarded to Shackleton for his 1908-9 expedition.

Knighted for his feat, Shackleton was also granted £20 000 by the British government to help pay off his expedition debts. He made two further trips to Antarctica, attempting coast-to-coast crossings of the continent. The first came to grief when his ship *Endurance* was crushed by ice, and resulted in an epic open-boat odyssey to South Georgia. In 1922, during the second attempt, Shackleton died of a heart attack.

THE RACE FOR THE POLE

TRIUMPH AND TRAGEDY AS AMUNDSEN AND SCOTT COMPETE FOR ANTARCTICA'S ULTIMATE PRIZE

It was one of the greatest dramas of the 20th century. In the winter of 1911-12, two rival expeditions reached the South Pole within 34 days of one another: the first a Norwegian team led by Roald Amundsen; the second a British party headed by Captain Robert Falcon Scott. And although the Norwegian won, the heroic manner in which Scott's expedition faced defeat and death won them so great a reputation that it constituted a victory in itself – a victory for the human spirit. Shortly before his death, Scott scribbled a message to the public that read, 'For my own sake I do not regret this journey, which has shewn that Englishmen can endure hardships, help one another, and meet death with as great a fortitude as ever in the past. We took risks, we knew we took them; things have come out against us, and therefore we have no cause for complaint, but bow to the will of Providence, determined still to do our best to the last.'

The rivals

Some years before his fateful last expedition, Scott had become known to the British public through his bestselling book *The Voyage of the Discovery*. This described a National Antarctic Expedition of 1901-4, in which he had been commander of a ship specially designed for polar seas. Sponsored by the Royal Geographical Society, Scott's party (which included Ernest Shackleton) built a winter base at a place called Hut Point on Ross Island, carried out scientific investigations, and sledged across the Ross Ice Shelf to reach the farthest point south yet attained. Scott also went up in a balloon tied to the *Discovery* to make the first aerial ascent in Antarctica.

Welcomed on his return as a popular hero, Scott was promoted to full captain. In April 1907, he learnt about Shackleton's plans to reach the South Pole, and he declared his own intention of trying for the same goal. When Shackleton came back without having reached the Pole, Scott knew the way was clear for his own attempt and on June 1, 1910, with a naval crew and a party of scientists, he set out for the Antarctic in the steam whaler *Terra Nova*.

In October, when Scott reached Melbourne, Australia, he received a cable from Madeira that read: 'Beg leave to inform you proceeding Antarctica. Amundsen.' The news came as a bolt from the blue. Norwegian explorer Roald Amundsen was a veteran of Arctic, rather than Antarctic, exploration and was renowned as the first man to sail the Northwest Passage. He had then borrowed the *Fram*, the vessel belonging to the Arctic explorer Fridtjof Nansen, with the intention of trying to drift across the North Pole. When he heard of Peary's conquest of the Pole, he had immediately turned and headed south. It was not until he reached Madeira that he announced his intention of trying for the South Pole.

A race was now on to see who could get there first. After provisioning in New Zealand, Scott's vessel reached Cape Evans on Ross Island 14 miles (23 km) north of Hut Point on January 4, 1911, and the party began to bring materials ashore to establish a winter station. Only seven days later, Amundsen reached the Bay of Whales 500 miles (800 km) to the east, on the other side of the Ross Ice Shelf.

During the autumn and winter, Scott's party set up a chain of supply depots across the ice shelf. Food and fuel for their primus stoves were the main materials deposited. Though tents, sleeping bags, cameras and theodolites accounted for some of the weight, food took up three-quarters of the payload on a sledge among polar explorers of the pioneer age. The staple was a pounded dried meat known as pemmican. Otherwise, supplies included onion powder to flavour

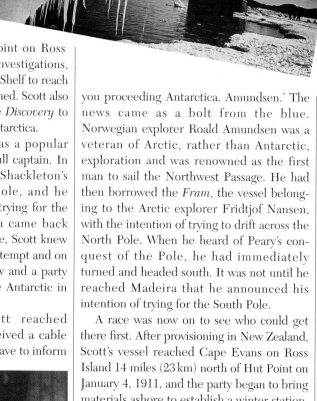

COLD HARBOUR The *Terra Nova* anchored near an iceberg off Cape Evans, Antarctica, during Captain Scott's last expedition.

CARVE UP Members of Scott's 1910-12 team cutting up pemmican in preparation for the polar assault. Left to right: Lieutenant Bowers, Dr Atkinson and Dr Cherry-Garrard.

stews, biscuits, oatmeal, pea flour, cheese, chocolate, cocoa and tea.

On November 1, Scott's expedition set off for the Pole in three teams of four men each. Siberian ponies drew most of the sledges, but the expedition also had two dogsleds and two motor vehicles on tracks. The motor sledges gave out within a couple of days and so – more calamitously – did the ponies. As a result, the party ended up man-hauling their sledges over vast distances, using up precious reserves of physical energy.

WINTER STATION Scott's den at the Cape Evans base on Ross Island, where the party spent the autumn and winter of 1911 establishing a string of supply depots stretching across the Ross Ice Shelf.

Scott had studied Shackleton's reports and followed much the same route, hoping to achieve the same speeds as his predecessor. But he drove his men very hard trying to match the schedule, and the strain began to tell as they struggled through blizzard snows up the Beardmore Glacier. By the evening of December 14 they had reached only 2000 ft (610 m) – and what they did not know was that on that day Roald Amundsen's men were already raising the Norwegian flag over the South Pole.

On skis to the Pole

From the outset, Amundsen was a shrewd and determined rival. His base at the Bay of Whales was 60 miles (97 km) closer to the

THE NORTHWEST PASSAGE

From the earliest days of New World exploration, navigators had looked for a sea route along the north coast of America that would connect the Atlantic Ocean with the Pacific. It was while searching for a Northwest Passage, as it was called, that John Cabot in 1497 became the first European since the Vikings to visit Newfoundland. But it was only in the 20th century that a route was found.

Norway's Roald Amundsen, the future conqueror of the South Pole, was the man who opened the way. In June 1903, he set out from Oslo in the single-masted *Gjøa* with a 13 horsepower engine and a crew of six. Having passed through Baffin Bay, they entered the passage at the Lancaster Sound and on September 12, facing the onset of the first winter storms, they dropped anchor off King William Island in a small harbour that Amundsen named Gjøa Haven. King William Island was a name with its own dark resonance in the history of exploration. Here, in 1859, was found the body of Sir John Franklin, who had tried to navigate the passage with two vessels and 137 crew members. From the frozen skeletons and the records found on the island, it became clear that the expedition had become icebound and that its members had died either of scurvy or starvation. The Norwegians spent two years on King William Island, making scientific studies and getting to know the Inuit, from whom they learnt many techniques for survival in the frozen lands.

On August 12, 1905, the *Gjøa* left its haven and sailed westwards through Simpson Strait into an unknown waterway, which Amundsen named Queen Maud Gulf after the Queen of Norway. This was the mystery stretch of the passage, and it was a good thing that Amundsen had only been able to afford a small vessel – for he had to thread his way through very narrow, shallow waters where concealed rocks threatened to rip the hull apart. But on August 26 the *Gjøa* rounded Banks Island and entered an area of open water later named Amundsen Gulf. There he met an American trading vessel whose captain knew about the expedition and greeted him with the words: 'I am exceedingly pleased to be the first one to welcome you on getting through the Northwest Passage.' Later, the ship got trapped in ice, and it was not until September 1906 that Amundsen struggled through the Bering Strait to reach Nome, Alaska. The whole town turned out to welcome the explorers, and as the Norwegian national anthem was played the hard-bitten Amundsen burst into tears.

ARCTIC CRAFT Amundsen's vessel the *Gjøa*, in which the Norwegian explorer opened up the Northwest Passage.

NORWEGIAN CONTENDER Born in the town of Borge, near Oslo, Roald Amundsen was a shipbuilder's son who had dreamed of polar exploits from the age of 15.

The dog teams had particular difficulties here, but by the time they reached the top many of the dogs were no longer needed, and 40 were shot and fed either to the other dogs or to the men. They called the camp The Butcher's Shop; Amundsen remained in his tent while the killing was done.

The Norwegians were now 10 000 ft (3050 m) above sea level, advancing into the teeth of a south-east blizzard, and facing

Pole than Scott's station, and like Peary he employed dog teams to draw his sledges, sacrificing them en route for food. The Norwegians cheerfully ate dogs' flesh themselves. Amundsen wrote: 'If we ourselves wanted a piece of fresh meat we could cut off a delicate little fillet; it tasted to us as good as the best beef.' Amundsen also used Inuit clothing, which was warm, loose-fitting and lightweight. Each suit weighed about 10 lb (4.5 kg) – half that worn by Scott and his men, who were dressed in heavy woollens with thin overclothes of proofed gaberdine, which got wet and froze solid. Additionally, Amundsen's party had set out earlier than their British counterparts. After making an over-eager false start when the first thaws began at the end of August, they launched their definitive attempt on October 20, 1911.

The Norwegian party consisted of five men: Amundsen, Olav Bjaaland, Helmer Hanssen, Sverre Hassel and Oscar Wisting. Their four sledges, each drawn by 13 dogs, made very good time over the snows of the Ross Ice Shelf, which were so smooth in places that they were able to travel on skis, pulled along behind the dogsleds. 'And there I stood,' wrote Amundsen, 'until we reached 85 degrees 05'S – 34 miles (55 km). Yes, that was a pleasant surprise. We had never dreamed of driving on skis to the Pole.'

The going got tougher on November 17, when they left the ice shelf and broached the steep Axel Heiberg Glacier (which Amundsen named after one of his backers).

'ONE BLOW ON THE SKULL'

Amundsen's success was due in part to his matter-of-fact approach to the employment of sledge dogs as food once they had outlived their usefulness hauling supplies. A sacrifice was made immediately after planting the Norwegian flag on the South Pole:

'Everyday life began again at once. When we had got the tent up, Hanssen set about slaughtering Helge, and it was hard for him to have to part from his best friend. Helge had been an uncommonly useful and good-natured dog; without making any fuss he had pulled from morning to night, and had been a shining example to the team. But during the last week he had quite fallen away, and on our arrival at the Pole there was only a shadow of the old Helge left. He was only a drag on the others, and did absolutely no work. One blow on the skull, and Helge had ceased to live. "What is death to one is food to another" is a saying that can scarcely find a better application than these dog meals. Helge was portioned out on the spot, and within a couple of hours there was nothing left of him but his teeth and the tuft at the end of his tail.'

new hazards in the form of big, hard snow waves known as *sastrugi*, aligned like desert dunes by the prevailing wind. Because they were blinded by thick, whirling snow, the explorers continually walked into them unawares, getting bowled over; three or four paces was often the most they could manage before falling down. 'The *sastrugi* were very high,' wrote Amundsen, 'and often abrupt; if one came on them unexpectedly, one required to be more than an acrobat to keep one's feet.'

The high altitude made each fall worse, for the explorers had to stand and gasp every time they fell. Hanssen, the Norwegians' dog-team driver, led the way through this white hell, and Amundsen afterwards wrote that he deserved special praise for his perseverance in the appalling conditions. 'One would not think it possible to keep an approximately right course when the uneven ground gives such violent shocks that the needle flies several times round the compass, and is no sooner still again than it recommences the same dance; but when at last we got an observation, it turned out that Hanssen had steered to a hair, for the observations and dead reckoning agreed to a mile.'

PROOF POSITIVE Amundsen's team using a sextant and artificial horizon to confirm that they have reached the South Pole; the Norwegian flag was raised over the spot.

Gradually the *sastrugi* levelled out and they made good progress over the smoother ground. On December 7, they passed the farthest point attained by Ernest Shackleton, and Amundsen fixed a Norwegian flag to the leading dogsled. They were farther south than any other human had been, and, watching the rustling silk shake itself out, flapping in the pure, clear air, Amundsen found himself more moved than at any other point in the whole expedition. To enhance their delight, the weather kept improving all the time; it was calm and radiant now – almost summerlike. Amundsen wrote that inside the tent it felt quite sultry.

Five weatherbeaten fists

But the struggle was by no means over yet. The dogs were getting ravenous and would swiftly devour any loose objects left lying about: ski bindings, whips, boots – even the ebonite points of their ski sticks. Serious worries arose when the dogs started to gnaw at the sledge

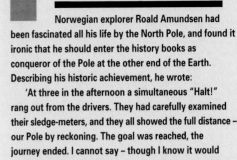

lashings, and every evening, on halting, the explorers buried the sledges in the snow for safety. Curiously, the dogs never tried to dig at the snow to get at them; and more curiously still, they never made any attempt to break into the provision cases despite the sight and scent of the pemmican.

Amundsen and his men were now suffering badly from frost sores, which seemed to have been brought to a head by the relative warmth of the weather. 'These sores were a great trouble to us during the latter part of the journey. The slightest gust of wind produced a sensation as if one's face were being cut backward and forward with a blunt

knife.' The explorers nonetheless knew that the prize was now within their reach, and on December 13 they camped at latitude 89°45' S. They knew that the next day should bring them victory, and Amundsen wrote that as he went to sleep that evening he experienced the same intense excitement that he could remember as a little boy on the night before Christmas Eve.

The next day, at three o'clock in the afternoon, their sledge-meters told them they had reached the Pole and together they raised the Norwegian flag. 'Five weather-beaten, frostbitten fists they were that grasped the pole, raised the waving flag in the air, and planted it', wrote Amundsen. 'Of course, there was festivity in the tent that evening – not that champagne corks were popping and wine flowing – no, we contented ourselves with a little piece of seal meat each, and it tasted well and did us good. There was no other sign of festival indoors. Outside we heard the flag flapping in the breeze. Conversation in the tent was lively that evening, and we talked of many things. Perhaps, too, our thoughts sent messages home of what we had done.'

The Norwegians knew that without time and very sophisticated instruments, it would be impossible to gauge the precise location of the geographical Pole, so to place the issue beyond any doubt, they made a circle round the place of 12½ miles (20 km) radius. Amundsen's party were

ENGLAND'S PRIDE Robert Falcon Scott, photographed on skis, has been immortalised as the very model of the English gentleman explorer.

at the Pole for three days and left a tent there, containing a record of their presence and a letter from Amundsen to his rival, Scott. Then they headed back, driving into their old tracks and following them. The return was uneventful and after detouring much of the Axel Heiberg Glacier, the Norwegians got back safely to the Bay of Whales, reaching the station with two sledges and 11 dogs at 4 am on January 25, 1912.

'An awful place'

Scott and his men, meanwhile, were tested to the limits of endurance – and beyond. By New Year's Day they had at last surmounted the Beardmore Glacier and caught up with Shackleton's schedule. But the last support team was almost exhausted, and on January 4 it turned back to base, leaving a five-man party

HISTORIC IMAGES Scott's photographer, Ponting, produced many fine images of the last expedition, including the view (right) from a grotto in an iceberg. Far right: Petty Officer Edgar Evans, the first of Scott's party to perish on the return journey.

to make the final assault. They were 178 miles (286 km) from the Pole. With Scott went his team members Dr Edward Wilson, Captain Lawrence 'Titus' Oates and Petty Officer Edgar Evans; and they also took a marine called Lieutenant Bowers, one of the support team members who was noted for his strength. This was unwise as the extra man was a drain on rations and caused congestion in their only tent.

On January 7 they reached 10 560 ft (3219 m), their highest point, and began the descent to the Pole. Despite blizzards and everything else that they had endured, their spirits were sustained by the increasing belief that they would reach their goal, a belief that was only shadowed by what Scott called the 'appalling possibility' – the sight of the Norwegian flag forestalling their own. On Tuesday, January 16, that possibility turned

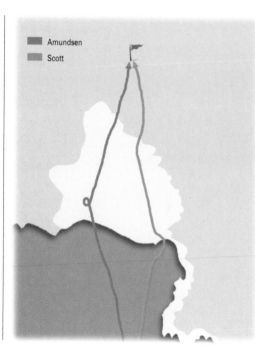

Amundsen
Scott

TWO ROUTES Both expeditions set out from the edge of the Ross Ice Shelf, but Amundsen's base at the Bay of Whales was 60 miles (100 km) closer to the Pole than Scott's starting point.

into a reality. Bowers' sharp eyes picked out a black speck ahead, and as they marched on, they discovered that it was one of Amundsen's markers, a black flag tied to a sledge bearer near the remains of a camp. They saw ski and sledge tracks, and the footprints left by many dogs. It was, in Scott's words, a terrible disappointment.

Next day, the British party followed the Norwegian sledge tracks towards the Pole, discovering two small cairns besides. The explorers stood at the heart of a white nothingness, facing a savage wind and temperatures of –30°C (–22°F). 'Great God! This is an awful place,' Scott wrote in his diary.

The photographs they took at the Pole betray both their weariness and their anxiety. Though they tried to celebrate that night, an overwhelming apprehension is evident in Scott's diary entry: 'We have had a fat Polar hoosh [a thick soup made from pemmican and broken biscuits] in spite of our chagrin, and feel comfortable inside – added a small stick of chocolate and the queer taste of a cigarette brought by Wilson. Now for the run home and a desperate struggle. I wonder if we can do it.'

Next day, they came upon Amundsen's little gaberdine tent, with the Norwegian flag and a pennant with *Fram* painted on it, and Amundsen's letter to Scott inside. They turned and headed back for their base some 800 miles (1300 km) away, all suffering from frostbite and scurvy. Petty Officer Edgar

THE DEATH OF CAPTAIN OATES

In 1912, during the Scott expedition's harrowing march back from the South Pole, Captain Oates became badly stricken by frostbite. Scott's diaries record:

'*Friday 16 March or Saturday 17*. Lost track of dates, but think the last correct. Tragedy all along the line. At lunch, the day before yesterday, poor Titus Oates said he couldn't go on; he proposed we should leave him in his sleeping-bag. That we could not do, and induced him to come on the afternoon march. In spite of its awful nature for him, he struggled on and we made a few miles. At night he was worse and we knew the end had come.

'Should this be found I want these facts recorded. Oates' last thoughts were of his mother, but immediately before he took pride in thinking that his regiment would be pleased with the bold way in which he met his death. We can testify to his bravery. He had borne intense suffering for weeks without complaint, and to the very last was able and willing to discuss outside subjects. He did not – would not – give up hope to the very end. He was a brave soul. This was the end. He slept through the night before last, hoping not to wake; but he woke in the morning – yesterday. It was blowing a blizzard. He said, "I am just going outside and may be some time." He went out into the blizzard and we have not seen him since.'

Evans was the first to succumb; weakened by hunger and exhaustion, he died at the Beardmore Glacier on February 17. His companions stayed with the body for two hours after the death, then shuffled onwards on frozen feet towards the base they now feared they would never reach. A month later, severely frostbitten, Captain Oates told his companions that he could not go on, and asked to be abandoned. They induced him to press on for a few more miles, but in the tent that night he parted from them and walked out into the blizzard, never to return.

The three remaining explorers were in terrible shape, too. Towards the end, Scott himself knew that

PICTURE OF DEJECTION Four of Scott's party pose by Amundsen's tent at the South Pole. From left to right: Scott, Oates, Wilson and Evans. Lieutenant Bowers – the fifth man – took the photograph.

both his feet were so afflicted by frostbite that even if he pulled through they would require amputation, and that the trouble might well be spreading farther. His party set up their last camp on March 21, just 11 miles (18 km) from One Ton Depot, where they knew there were plenty of supplies. However, an unrelenting gale prevented them from going any farther.

On March 29, Scott made his last diary entry: 'Every day now we have been ready to start for our depot 11 miles away, but outside the door of the tent it remains a scene of whirling drift. I do not think we can hope for any better things now. We shall stick it out to the end, but we are getting weaker, of course, and the end cannot be far. It seems a pity, but I do not think I can write more.' Then, after signing his name, Scott added a postscript: 'For God's sake look after our people.'

The three men were eventually found dead in their sleeping bags by a search party on November 12.

FLIGHT OVER THE POLES

**AMERICAN NAVAL PILOT RICHARD EVELYN BYRD
BECOMES THE FIRST MAN TO FLY OVER BOTH POLES**

Born into a prominent family in Winchester, Virginia, in 1888, Richard E. Byrd wrote in his diary at the age of 15 that he intended to be the first man to reach the North Pole. Robert Peary's conquest put paid to that dream; but later, as a naval pilot, Byrd's ambition took new shape as he became determined to be the first to travel over the Pole by aircraft.

He was not alone in dreaming of such a flight. In 1925, the ever-competitive Norwegian Roald Amundsen teamed up with the American millionaire Lincoln Ellsworth to attempt a flying expedition to the North Pole. Using two Dornier-Wal flying boats with twin Rolls-Royce engines of 360 horsepower each, Amundsen and Ellsworth set out from the island of Spitsbergen on May 21. However, one of their planes developed engine trouble, and with fuel running low they were forced to land in a 'lead', or stretch of open sea between the floes. Then the water iced up and crushed one of the aircraft. The two men only just managed to take off in the other plane and head back to Spitsbergen.

Undeterred by the setback, Amundsen planned a second attempt the following year, this time in a dirigible, and a new race for the Pole was on as Richard E. Byrd launched his own assault. Backed by John D. Rockefeller and Edsel Ford (son of motor magnate Henry Ford), Byrd set off from King's Bay, Spitsbergen, with Warrant Officer Floyd Bennett as co-pilot. Their aircraft, the *Josephine Ford*, was a Fokker monoplane with three 200 horsepower engines and, after a difficult takeoff, they found themselves speeding over vast

HIGH FLIERS Roald Amundsen (above, on the left), with his pilot Omdahl, made a failed attempt to fly to the North Pole in 1925. Below: Richard E. Byrd in Arctic kit, with sundial compass, in 1926 – the year he flew his Fokker monoplane *Josephine Ford* over the North Pole.

expanses of sea, snow and ice. Byrd wrote: 'To the right, somewhere, the rays of the midnight sun shone down on scenes of Nansen's heroic struggles to reach the goal that we were approaching at the rate of almost 100 miles (160 km) per hour. To our left lay Peary's trail.'

About an hour from the Pole, Byrd noticed through the cabin window a leak in

DEATH OF THE EAGLE

Aerial exploration of the Arctic began with a hot-air balloon flight by Swedish aeronaut Solomon Andrée, who set out from Spitsbergen in 1897 – and vanished over the frozen Arctic. In 1930, the remains of Andrée and his two companions were found by Norwegian sailors on White Island, not far from their departure point. Their diaries told how their balloon, *The Eagle*, had come down on an iceberg farther to the north-west, and the men had sledged as far as the island, where they died.

the oil tank of the starboard motor. Bennett suggested that they try to land to fix it, but Byrd decided that they should press ahead – on the grounds that they would be in no worse difficulties should they come down near the Pole than they would be if they had a forced landing where they were. All the same, he kept an eye on the leak and the oil-pressure indicator throughout the rest of the flight, feeling sure that at some stage they would have to make an emergency landing.

They reached the North Pole at 9.02 am on May 9, 1926, and circled it several times, taking both still and moving pictures as they went. Byrd later wrote that thus 'we made a

THE CRASHED DIRIGIBLE

On May 11, 1926, two days after Richard E. Byrd had made the historic first flight to the North Pole, Roald Amundsen reached it in a dirigible named *Norge*. Powered by two 250 horsepower engines, the airship had been designed by the Italian engineer Umberto Nobile, who was also pilot of the craft.

On the 71 hour flight, ice formed on the propellors and was constantly being flung loose to bombard the airship, cutting a hole in the hull. Fog seriously reduced visibility, and the radio stopped working when the aerial frosted up. Nonetheless, Nobile managed to steer them to safety at Point Barrow, Alaska. Altogether they had flown 3180 miles (5118 km), crossing much previously unknown territory. The *Norge* was so badly damaged that it had to be scrapped, but the flight made Amundsen the first man to reach both of the Poles, an achievement for which he received great acclaim.

Nobile, who had hardly slept on the entire journey, felt that his own contribution had not been fully recognised. Back in Rome he won support from Mussolini's new Fascist government to carry out an entirely Italian flight to the Pole where, this time, he intended to land. His new airship the *Italia* set out on May 23, 1928, and did reach the North Pole; a Fascist flag and papal cross were thrown out and a gramophone played the Italian national anthem. However, the airship was unable to land because of bad weather. On the way back, amid worsening storms, the *Italia* was forced to crash-land on the polar ice north-west of Spitsbergen. On impact, the gondola holding Nobile and nine companions broke away and skidded to a halt. Much lighter now, the *Italia* rose into the air with the remainder of the crew on board – they were never seen again.

The marooned survivors, the injured Nobile among them, set up camp with a red tent they hoped would be conspicuous from the air and tried to send out radio messages. No acknowledgment was received; and when they tuned in to broadcasts, it became clear that the search was going on in the wrong area.

Some time later, in Oslo, Amundsen was attending a banquet when he was handed a telegram announcing that the *Italia* had

DOOMED ATTEMPT Nobile's airship *Italia* flies poleward over Spitzbergen in 1928.

been officially declared lost. 'I am ready to go at once', the 56-year-old explorer announced. He then flew from Bergen to Spitsbergen to join the search, in which 16 ships and 21 aircraft were taking part. One of the aircraft, a Swedish seaplane, spotted the crashed *Italia*'s red tent and was able to rescue Nobile. Amundsen's own aircraft, however, went down over the sea, and the great explorer perished in the wreck.

nonstop flight around the world in a very few minutes. In doing that we lost a whole day in time; and, of course, when we completed the circle, we gained that day back again.' Then they flew back to base, without mishap from the oil leak. On their return they were met by Roald Amundsen, who was just about to take off for the Pole in his airship, and the Norwegian asked Byrd what his next target was. 'The South Pole', Byrd replied.

Fêted as a hero back in the United States, Byrd set sail for Antarctica in August 1928, and in December set up his base camp at a

TICKERTAPE WELCOME Byrd and his pilot, Floyd Bennett, march in triumphant procession up Broadway on July 2, 1926, after returning from the North Pole.

THE SACRIFICE

During Byrd's flight to the South Pole in 1929, the crew had to ditch all their emergency food supplies in order to gain the height needed to clear a glacier:

'McKinley shoved a second bag through the trapdoor, and this time we saw it hit the glacier, and scatter in a soundless explosion. Two hundred and fifty pounds [114 kg] of food – enough to feed four men for a month – lay strewn on the barren ice. The sacrifice swung the scales. The plane literally rose with a jump; the engines dug in, and we soon showed a gain in altitude from 300 to 400 ft [90-120 m]. It was what we wanted. We should clear the pass with about 500 ft [150 m] to spare. Balchen gave a shout of joy. It was just as well. We could dump no more food. There was nothing left to dump except McKinley's camera. I am sure that, had he been asked to put it overboard, he would have done so instantly; and I am equally sure he would have followed the precious instrument with his own body…'

POLAR SQUAD Richard Byrd (second left) with his South Pole team. On the left is Bernt Balchen, the pilot of the plane.

place on the Ross Ice Shelf, which he named Little America. One of the two aircraft he brought with him was wrecked in a storm and the other, a Ford tri-motor, suffered engine damage during an early attempt to attain the required altitude. Nonetheless, Byrd persevered with the plane, which was named *Floyd Bennett* after his former co-pilot, who had died in a crash earlier that year. At 3.29 pm on November 28, 1929, accompanied by a crew of three, Byrd took off.

Approaching the pass at Liv's Glacier they met a crisis. The plane would not rise high enough to clear it, and Byrd knew that they must shed some weight swiftly, ditching either fuel or food bags. If they dropped fuel, he knew, they might as well turn back now, for they would never reach the Pole. If they dropped food, their lives would be jeopardised in the event of a forced landing. 'It really took only a moment to reach the decision,' Byrd wrote. 'The Pole, after all, was our objective. I knew the character of the three men. McKinley, in fact, had already hauled one of the food bags to the trapdoor. It weighed 125 pounds [57 kg]. The brown bag was pushed out and fell, spinning, to the glacier. The improvement in the flying qualities of the plane was noticeable. It took another breath and resumed the climb.'

The explorers had to shed still more weight before safety was guaranteed, but after that the flying was smooth and they reached the South Pole at 1.14 am on November 29, 1929. Byrd opened the trapdoor and dropped a small flag weighted with a stone from Bennett's grave. There was no remnant now of Amundsen's tent in which Scott had read the note the Norwegian had left for him. The Pole lay in the centre of a limitless plain, its white desolation and solitude were disturbed only by the sound of their engines. 'And that, in brief, is all there is to tell about the South Pole,' Byrd wrote. 'One gets there, and that is about all there is for the telling. It is the effort to get there that counts. We put the Pole behind us and raced for home.'

MOVING TRIBUTE In November 1929, Byrd dropped a Stars and Stripes over the South Pole. The flag was weighted with a stone from his former partner's grave.

ACE AGAINST TIME

**LLY HERBERT MAKES THE FIRST SURFACE
OSSING OF THE ARCTIC OCEAN**

On February 21, 1968, Wally Herbert, an English explorer, set out on what travel writer Eric Newby has called the Arctic's 'last great heroic journey'. The aim of his British Trans-Arctic Expedition was to cross the frozen Arctic Ocean on dog sledges, by way of the North Pole. It had never been attempted before, and the members of the expedition knew that if Robert Peary had been wrong in his calculations and had failed to reach the Pole, they would be the first to get there across the ice.

Herbert with three companions and four teams of dogs, set out from Point Barrow, Alaska, and travelled 1200 route miles (1930 km) before setting up their summer camp on an ice floe on July 4th. As the floe drifted north, they made scientific studies of sea, weather and geophysical conditions, and when the sea iced up again in the autumn they continued their journey. At latitude 85 degrees they set up their winter camp, and with an airdrop of six months' supplies, they drifted on an ice floe that was constantly fracturing throughout the long polar night.

On February 24 they set out for the North Pole and reached it on April 6, 1969, after a journey of 408 days – and considerable difficulties in trying to locate their goal. The ice was drifting all the time so that they would awake to discover that their camp was in a different position from the night before. Also, if a calculation of longitude was slightly out, it could set them off in the wrong direction, increasing their error the farther they went. Once, they travelled for what they estimated was 7 miles (11 km) and stopped. They set up a theodolite, did a rough calculation, and found they were still 7 miles from the Pole, because they had spiralled in an almost complete circle.

To add to their disorientation, the dateline runs through the Pole so they could find themselves walking from Sunday into Saturday and back again. After they finally reached their goal, exhausted, with temperatures at –37°C (–35°F), Herbert wrote: 'Trying to set foot on it had been like trying to set foot on the shadow of a bird circling overhead. The surface across which we were

BRITISH TEAM Wally Herbert (right) and other members of his Trans-Arctic Expedition discussing plans before leaving Point Barrow, Alaska, on their 3500 mile (5600 km) hike to Spitsbergen.

moving was itself a moving surface on a planet that was spinning about an axis. We were standing approximately on that axis, asleep on our feet, dog-tired and hungry. Too tired to celebrate our arrival on the summit of this supermountain around which the sun circles almost as if stuck in a groove.'

Knowing that they were behind schedule, they prepared for the journey south to Spitsbergen. The last part of the trip

SLEDGE RUN The Trans-Arctic Expedition crossing the frozen Arctic Ocean. Herbert and his three companions were supported by airdrops.

ICE STATIONS

The Arctic ice pack is a key element in the world's great weather machine. Though the cold air mass above is fairly stable, it is influenced by upflows of air from the relatively warm ocean currents flowing below. The margins of the ice pack are, moreover, in constant flux, with floes freezing and melting, grinding together and splitting apart. Investigation of these phenomena helps to predict future weather, and when Wally Herbert and his team set up their drifting ice station in 1968, they made vital studies of marine and air temperatures, wind circulation, atmospheric pressure and so on.

Theirs was not the first such outpost. In 1937, a team of Soviet scientists had set up an ice station named 'North Pole 1' on a drifting floe that moved steadily towards the Greenland Sea, where they were picked up by an icebreaker.

Fixed stations have played their part, too. In Antarctica, polar flyer Richard Byrd came close to death while making studies at the Bolling Advanced Weather Station. A tiny prefabricated hut buried in the snow of the Ross Ice Shelf, it was the explorer's home for seven months in 1933-4 and he lived there entirely alone. It could only be entered by a hatch, which was faulty, and Byrd once found himself stranded outside in the full fury of an Antarctic blizzard. 'It is more than just wind,' he wrote, 'it is a solid wall of snow moving at gale force, pounding like surf . . . you can't see, you can't hear, you can hardly move.' Somehow, though, he managed to find a shovel, dig his way to the hatch and get it open – he survived.

ROTHERA BASE An ice station set up on Adelaide Island to make scientific studies in Antarctica.

involved a series of forced marches as the onset of summer sunshine caused the Arctic sea ice to disintegrate all around them. Cracks appeared, calling for long detours; then closed up again, forming pressure ridges that posed serious obstacles – colliding floes in the Arctic can create upthrust ridges as high as four-storey houses.

Adrift on the floes, the explorers were prey to every caprice of the elements. 'The whole vast area,' wrote Herbert, 'was a confusion of currents, counter-currents and winds which moved the sea ice like brittle scum.' In the end, with the ice melting all around them, the explorers had to be rescued by helicopter just a few miles short of Spitsbergen. Herbert had planned for a trip lasting 130 days; in fact, it had taken 476 days. And, with detours, they had travelled more than 3500 miles (5600 km) – nearly twice the distance from Point Barrow to Spitsbergen as the crow flies.

ARCTIC HERO Wally Herbert with one of the huskies that took him and his team across the treacherous ice landscape of the Arctic.

OF SEA AND SKY

SHIFTING WINDS AND ROLLING SEAS ARE NOT AS EASILY MAPPED AS THE PLANET'S FIXED CONTINENTS. YET THE CONQUEST OF THE AIR AND EXPLORATION OF THE OCEANS WAS JUST AS MUCH AN ACHIEVEMENT AS THE PENETRATION OF ITS JUNGLES, DESERTS AND ICE CAPS. THE NAMES OF SUCH PIONEERS AS CHARLES LINDBERGH, AMELIA EARHART, WILLIAM BEEBE AND JACQUES COUSTEAU BELONG IN THE SAME PANTHEON AS THOSE OF EDMUND HILLARY AND CAPTAIN SCOTT.

THE CHANNEL ADVENTURE

FRENCHMAN LOUIS BLÉRIOT BECAME A HERO WHEN HE CROSSED THE CHANNEL IN A MONOPLANE

In 1909 the English newspaper the *Daily Mail* offered a £1000 prize to the first person to fly across the English Channel. By midsummer, two of Europe's top aviators were leading the challenge: Hubert Latham and Louis Blériot. Both were French (though the former was of English descent), and both had had recent mishaps. Latham had ditched into the sea when his 50 hp engine failed during an attempted Channel flight; Blériot had been badly burned by an engine fire, and was on crutches at the time of the challenge.

The rivals were both ready on July 24 but they were kept on the ground by high winds that looked set to continue the next day. However, one of Blériot's business associates, Alfred Le Blanc, had a sleepless night in their Calais hotel and got up in the small hours of Sunday the 25th. As the gales had died down he woke Blériot, and while Latham and his companions were still wrapped in slumber, the two men left for the garage at Les Baraques where the monoplane, *Blériot XI*, was kept. On arrival, Blériot discarded his crutches proclaiming,

as he was helped to his aircraft: 'I won't want them again until I come back from England.' He could not take off immediately; the *Daily Mail* had insisted that the flying must be done between sunrise and sunset. But at 4.35 am, with the dawn light breaking all around, Blériot took flight.

Driven by a three-cylinder, 25 hp engine, the monoplane was the eleventh aircraft that

LICENCE TO FLY   Louis Blériot's aviation document, issued by the Aero-Club of France. In 1909 Blériot was already known as one of Europe's leading flyers.

Blériot had constructed. All widely differing from one another, the models included several prototypes that had never got off the ground. But *Blériot XI* rose steady and sure above telegraph wires at the cliff edge and headed out over the sea. Below him, the aviator could make out the destroyer *Escopette* which had been laid on by the French gov-

READY TO GO   The French airman in his three-cylinder monoplane, *Blériot XI*, at Calais. His flight across the Channel took little more than 36 minutes – yet it changed aviation history.

ernment to assist in the event of an accident. Spotting the monoplane, the ship made full speed ahead, but was soon overtaken by Blériot who was travelling at a height of 260 ft (79 m) and a speed of 26 mph (42 km/h).

Suddenly, the plane entered a cloud and Blériot lost all bearings. He later told the *Daily Mail*: 'I am amazed. There is nothing to be seen, neither the torpedo-destroyer, nor France, nor England. I am alone. I can see nothing at all – *rien du tout!* For ten minutes I am lost. It is a strange position, to be alone, unguided, without compass, in the air over the middle of the Channel. I touch nothing. My hands and feet

AN HISTORIC LANDING

Early in the morning of July 25, 1909, French aviator Louis Blériot approached the gusty cliffs at Dover and prepared to land, at the end of the first aircraft flight across the English Channel.

'Once more I turn my aeroplane, and, describing a half-circle, I enter the opening and find myself again over dry land. Avoiding the red buildings on my right, I attempt a landing; but the wind catches me and whirls me round two or three times.

'At once I stop my motor, and instantly my machine falls straight upon the land from a height of 20 metres [65 ft]. In two or three seconds I am safe.

'Soldiers in khaki run up, and a policeman. Two of my compatriots are on the spot. They kiss my cheeks. The conclusion of my flight overwhelms me. I have nothing to say, but accept the congratulations of the representatives of the *Daily Mail* and accompany them to the Lord Warden Hotel.

'Thus ended my flight across the Channel. The flight could be easily done again. Shall I do it? I think not. I have promised my wife that after a race for which I have entered I will fly no more.'

rest lightly on the levers. I let the airplane take its own course. I care not whither it goes.'

At last the plane emerged from the disquieting mist and Blériot sighted white cliffs ahead. There lay Dover with its castle and, to the west, the spot where he hoped to land. It was clear that the wind had taken him off course, and he veered sharply left as he came in towards the chalk cliffs. On approaching them, he noticed his speed dropping, for the wind resistance was much stronger here and he briefly considered a return to Calais. But he could not miss this chance. Fiercely buffeted by the wind, with red buildings looming to the right, Blériot

switched off his motor and crash-landed with a jolt on the turf. As he emerged in his wool-lined khaki jacket, a crowd quickly assembled to cheer the hero, and cameras clicked, immortalising the beaming, moustached aviator in his moment of triumph.

Back in France, Hubert Latham was shattered by the news. He had woken up to discover his rival already en route for glory, and when he tried to take flight himself, found that the wind had got up again, preventing takeoff.

The Calais correspondent of the *Daily Mail* wrote that Latham looked on the verge of a breakdown: 'His back was curved almost to a hump. There were deep lines around his mouth. His eyes were narrowed to a slit. More than once he brushed away a tear.'

HERO'S WELCOME Blériot's monoplane photographed on its historic flight. Below: After the crossing, the Frenchman waves to crowds at Victoria Station, London, seated beside Lord Northcliffe, the *Daily Mail* publisher, who organised the Channel Challenge.

THE SPIRIT OF ST LOUIS

**IN 1927 CHARLES LINDBERGH OPENED THE
SKIES TO AN AGE OF INTERNATIONAL TRAVEL**

A quiet midwesterner, raised in Minnesota, Charles A. Lindbergh made an unlikely world hero. Yet in 1927, the 25-year-old pilot achieved a feat that caused one of the greatest traffic jams in French history. Hundreds of thousands of Parisians turned out to greet him as the first man to fly solo across the Atlantic Ocean – and his life would never be the same again.

Trained at a flying school in Lincoln, Nebraska, Lindbergh first took to the air in 1922, and four years later was making regular air mail service flights between Chicago and St Louis. It was on one of these trips that he decided to try for the $25 000 prize offered by a rich New York financier, Raymond Orteig, for the first person to fly nonstop from New York to Paris. Lindbergh found backing for the venture from a group of St Louis businessmen who were eager to promote their city as an aviation centre, and in tribute to them he named his specially constructed Ryan monoplane *Spirit of St Louis*.

'He has tried too much'

The Atlantic had been crossed in a nonstop flight once before – in 1919 when Britain's John Alcock and Arthur Brown flew from Newfoundland to Ireland. The New York-Paris run was much more ambitious, and the solo nature of the flight made it a feat of heroic individualism. In preparation for the epic, Lindbergh gave himself training in sleep deprivation, staying awake for stretches of up to 40 hours at a time.

Lindbergh's aircraft was constructed in San Diego, California, and when it was ready he flew it via St Louis to New York. After some days of rest and preparation, he took off from Roosevelt Field, Long Island, at 7.52 am on May 20, 1927. Lindbergh had been so nervous on the night before takeoff that he barely slept a wink – a fact that was to make staying awake at the controls all the more difficult. The plane was unwieldy too; overloaded with fuel at takeoff, it barely cleared the trees at the end of the runway. According to a British newspaper report, the crowds who gathered along the American coast to watch Lindbergh's departure were pessimistic about his chances: 'That's the last of him. He has tried too much.'

Lindbergh's route took him over Newfoundland; by the time he reached Alcock and Brown's starting point, he had already been flying for ten hours. Then, leaving behind a black silhouette of mountains and a scattering of lights, he was over the vast Atlantic, and flying by dead reckoning for Europe. He ate homemade sandwiches and steeled himself for the ordeal.

By the 13th hour, with fog and darkness shutting off even the view of his own wingtips, Lindbergh was already experiencing the strain of flying with his eyes always on the instrument board, 'with nothing more to stimulate my mind than the leaning of a needle'. The monotony eased as daylight dawned and strange cloudscapes emerged, spread out below in grotesque canyons and crevasses. But now he found himself wondering whether he was a living, breathing person or perhaps a spirit in a spirit world. There was no radio aboard the plane. No one on either side of the ocean knew if he was alive or not.

As the hours passed, the desire to sleep became overwhelming. In attempted remedies, Lindbergh slapped himself fiercely on the cheek; or cupped his hand into the slipstream diverting an air current into his face.

MAN AND MACHINE Charles Lindbergh (right) and the *Spirit of St Louis* in flight in 1927. After his solo transatlantic flight, Lindbergh made a series of goodwill flights in Europe and America.

Occasionally he let his eyelids fall shut for five seconds before raising them against what seemed like tons of weight. To no avail; Lindbergh dozed off several times and once awoke to find himself skimming the Atlantic waves. By the 26th hour, he had raided his medicine box and was crushing capsules of smelling salts under his nose; but he found that his senses were so deadened by now that he could smell nothing.

'Which way is Ireland?'

In the 27th hour, as he flew almost in a dream, a black speck on the water caught his eye; he blinked his tired eyelids and looked again. It was a boat – in fact, several small boats scattered over the surface of the ocean. Seconds passed before he took in their full importance; then, banking his plane towards them, he nosed down and saw

that they were fishing boats – the coast of Europe could not be far away!

Lindbergh circled over the boats and at one point glided down within 50 ft (15 m) of a cabin, closed the throttle and shouted as loudly as he could 'WHICH WAY IS IRELAND?' But he could not raise the crew and so straightened out the *Spirit of St Louis* and flew on eastwards.

During his 28th hour in the air, Lindbergh struck a foam-edged coast that he knew must be that of Ireland. All wish to sleep left him now, as he sped over hilltop farms and sheep-nibbled pastures. There would be more sea to cross before he

reached his goal, but the end was now approaching. Lindbergh reached the Normandy coast towards nightfall, and found his way to Paris by following the course of the River Seine. Although he was not aware of it, his plane's arrival had been spotted from the ground, and news of his approach raced ahead of him to the French capital via radio and telephone. Parisians teemed out of the city and made their way to his scheduled landing place, Le Bourget Airdrome, choking the roads all around. As Lindbergh brought his aircraft down he was

SAFELY DOWN Lindbergh's arrival at Le Bourget, on May 21, 1927. His approach had been widely reported, and crowds of Parisians around the airfield caused the biggest traffic jam in French history.

baffled by the immensity of the crowds and thought something must be amiss – he could not believe that they had come for him. When he got out of the tiny cockpit, the mob surged forwards, sweeping aside two compa-nies of French troops, but he was so cold and numb that he could not speak to them.

The historic flight had covered 3610 miles (5085 km) and taken 33 hours, 29 minutes and 30 seconds. And it caught the imagina-tion of a generation worldwide. A few days later, Lindbergh flew to Croydon in England where wildly cheering crowds burst through the fences as his plane landed, so that the aviator had to wait for ten minutes in the cockpit while police cleared a way through the tumultuous mob. 'Heaven help my machine', was his first remark. He was received by royalty and heads of state throughout Europe, and received numerous

awards. Back in the United States, Lindbergh had the biggest reception of all. Brought home in a warship, he stayed at the White House with President Coolidge then went to New York where nearly 2 million people gathered along the 3 mile (4.8 km) route to and from City Hall, showering bliz-zards of tickertape on their hero.

An intensely private person, Lindbergh found all the attention hard to cope with. He later married and settled down as a technical adviser for commercial airline companies, but his tranquillity was destroyed in 1932 when his one-year-old son was kidnapped and killed in a case that made national head-lines. During the late 1930s, he travelled in Europe and caused great controversy by commenting favourably on the German Luftwaffe and advocating US neutrality in the Second World War. However, he later contributed to the Allied cause, so recover-ing his popularity with the American public.

'HEAVEN HELP MY MACHINE' When Lindbergh flew to Croydon in England, shortly after crossing the Atlantic, the crowds were so vast that he had serious concerns for his aircraft.

LANDFALL

After 28 hours of flying, fighting desperate sleepiness over the desolate Atlantic Ocean, Lindbergh at last reached a coastline. But which?

'A fjorded coast stands out as I approach. Barren islands guard it. Inland, green fields slope up the sides of warted mountains. This must be Ireland. It can be no other place than Ireland. The fields are too green for Scotland; the mountains too high for Brittany or Cornwall.

'Now I'm flying above a foam-lined coast, searching for prominent features to fit the chart on my knees. I've climbed to two thousand feet [610 m] so I can see the contours of the country better. The mountains are old and rounded; the farms small and stony. Rain-glistened dirt roads wind narrowly through hills and fields. Below me lies a great, tapering bay; a long, bouldered island; a village. Yes, there's a place on the chart where it all fits – line of ink on line of shore – Valentia and Dingle Bay, on the south-western coast of Ireland!

'I can hardly believe it's true. I'm almost exactly on my route, closer than I had hoped to come in my wildest dreams back in San Diego . . . I spiral lower, looking down on the little village. There are boats in the harbour, wagons on the stone-fenced roads. People are running out into the streets, looking up and waving. This is the earth again, the earth where I've lived and now will live once more. Here are human beings. Here's a human welcome. Not a single detail is wrong. I've never seen such beauty before – fields so green, people so human, a village so attractive, mountains and rocks so mountainous and rocklike.'

WOMAN FLYER

HOW AMELIA EARHART VANISHED DURING AN ATTEMPT TO FLY AROUND THE WORLD

On June 1, 1937, a Lockheed Electra plane set out from Miami, Florida, to make a round-the-world flight from west to east. At the controls were Amelia Earhart and co-pilot Fred Noonan. South America, Africa, India, New Guinea – all were reached before the aircraft began the last lap, heading for Howland Island, a tiny air-base in the middle of the Pacific Ocean. Earhart and Noonan never reached the island, however – and to this day no one can say with certainty what happened to them.

Born in 1898 at Atchison, Kansas, Amelia Earhart first considered learning to fly during the First World War, while on a tour of duty as a military nurse in Canada. A $10 joyride at an airshow convinced her. She took flying lessons, bought a small plane with a loan from her mother, and in 1922 made her first solo flight. Not long afterwards, in her own aircraft, she set a new altitude record of 14 000 ft (4267 m). In 1928 Earhart was chosen by the publicist George Palmer Putnam to be the first woman passenger on a flight across the Atlantic. Flown by a male pilot and navigator, she nonetheless received much press coverage for enduring the trip. 'I would sooner fly the Atlantic ten times than face all this publicity and fuss again', she told reporters. But fame was to be her lot for the rest of her life. With Putnam as her manager, she began to make a name for herself as the voice of female aviation in America. Solid achievements backed up the ballyhoo: before the year was out, she had flown from New York to Los Angeles and back again, becoming the first woman to fly solo both ways across the United States.

Earhart and Putnam married in February 1931, and through a multitude of stunts and record-breaking feats he made her one of America's best-known celebrities. In 1932 Amelia attempted a solo flight across the Atlantic. She took off on the evening of May 20, from Harbor Grace, Newfoundland, on what proved to be a more hazardous trip than Lindbergh's. Following an electrical storm and altimeter failure, ice on the wings sent her into a 3000 ft (914 m) tailspin. After the exhaust manifold also caught fire, it became clear that she

must shelve her original plan of flying to Paris, and she brought her plane down in Ireland, landing in a field after 14 hours and 56 minutes in the air. Although the trip was curtailed, it brought her world renown as the first woman to fly solo across the Atlantic.

Into oblivion

In January 1935 Earhart flew solo from Hawaii to California. Inspired by the experience, Earhart was determined to attempt a round-the-world flight. On June 1, 1937, she set off from Miami, Florida, with an experienced airman, Lieutenant Commander Fred Noonan, as her navigator. But after negotiating more than two-thirds of the distance, she disappeared somewhere in the vicinity of Howland Island in the Pacific Ocean.

AT THE CONTROLS Amelia Earhart in 1937, the year she mysteriously disappeared on a flight over the Pacific Ocean.

This stretch of the ocean had never before been flown, and Earhart had taken off from Lae, New Guinea, into bad weather. Ships in the vicinity of Howland Island picked up staccato messages from her plane, indicating that their position was uncertain and fuel was running low. Then all contact was lost – the couple vanished into oblivion.

ENGLAND'S QUEEN OF THE AIR

Britain's equivalent to Amelia Earhart was the English flyer Amy Johnson. A fish merchant's daughter from Hull, she took up flying at the age of 25 and only two years later, in May 1930, put the cover on her typewriter in a London solicitor's office and set off from Croydon Aerodrome to become the first woman to fly solo to Australia. Her plane was a secondhand Gipsy Moth named *Jason* which she had painted bottle green. Amy had prepared herself well, having studied map-reading, meteorology and even jujitsu in case she was forced to come down, as one writer put it, 'in some place where men were swine'. Nonetheless, her lack of flying experience alarmed her fellow aviators. At that time she had had only 75 hours in the air – and she had never before flown over water.

From England Johnson flew via Vienna for Istanbul, consuming a packet of sandwiches and a Thermos of tea on the way. Something about the ordinariness of the Yorkshire tomboy caught the public imagination, and by the time she reached Karachi – the halfway mark on her journey – she was already an international heroine. The Press at that time was turning once-shy aviators into celebrities comparable with Hollywood film stars, and huge ads now appeared in the *Daily Mail* paying tribute to her chief sponsor Lord Wakefield, an oil magnate: 'Am delighted with the Wakefield Organisation and Castrol XXL Motor Oil gave magnificent and faultless lubrication – Amy Johnson.'

On she flew, through monsoon storms en route for Rangoon, and over Java where bamboo stakes raked her wings, making holes that had to be patched up with sticking plaster. Once, in Timor, she missed the airfield and landed in a field of ant mounds. On May 24, however, she touched down at last in the northern Australian town of Darwin, to be greeted by a vast, cheering crowd. At the Town Hall, she delighted everyone by declaring 'Don't call me Miss Johnson, just plain Johnnie will do, that's what my English friends call me.' A song called 'Johnnie's in Town' was immediately composed, while back in England Tin Pan Alley offered 'Queen of the Air', 'Aeroplane Girl' and 'Amy, Wonderful Amy'.

Congratulated by her king, queen and prime minister, Amy Johnson enraptured the British public on her return home. She was to marry aviator Jim Mollison, and the pair became known as the Flying Sweethearts to the Press. During the Second World War she worked for the RAF as part of the Air Transport Auxiliary. Amy Johnson died in January 1941 when a plane she was delivering from Scotland crashed into the estuary of the River Thames.

'AEROPLANE GIRL' England's Amy Johnson, with the secondhand Gipsy Moth she flew to Australia in 1930.

WORLD FIRST

The first person to fly solo around the world was American Wiley Post. He took off from New York in the aircraft *Winnie Mae* at 5.10 am on July 15, 1933, and accomplished the feat in 7 days 18 hours and 49 minutes. During an earlier round-the-world flight with navigator Harold Gatty, he had been forced to come down in a field in England's West Country. 'I don't think we can honestly say we were lost,' he said later, 'we just didn't know where we were.'

According to one theory which became widespread during the Second World War, Earhart had been on a surveillance mission for the US government, with orders to spy on the Japanese-mandated Pacific islands. It was also rumoured that the woman aviator had been brought down and held captive by the Japanese.

Speculation about Earhart's fate has been rife, but the official verdict remains the likeliest; that she and Noonan simply ran out of fuel and drowned at sea.

HALF A MILE DOWN

IN AUGUST 1934 AMERICAN WILLIAM BEEBE MADE THE DEEPEST OCEAN DESCENT YET ACHIEVED

Though explorers had circumnavigated the surface of the globe in sailing ships hundreds of years before the dawn of the 20th century, the vast undersea world remained mysterious. The submersibles of Victorian times could go down only a few yards below the surface, and science knew little of the teeming life of the deep ocean, apart from stray specimens brought up from time to time in fishing nets.

The man who opened the fathomless depths to exploration was American naturalist William Beebe. Associated for many years with the New York Zoological Society, he was primarily interested in undersea fauna and flora. In 1930 he tried out a diving bell he had invented with engineer Otis Barton for the purpose of studying deepwater life. His large, strong submersible sphere had a steel shell 1½ in (38 mm) thick. Portholes were made of molten quartz to withstand the phenomenal pressures experienced in the abyssal zone, the regions of eternal darkness which lie so deep that the sun's rays never penetrate them. The craft, named a bathysphere, was suspended by a cable which ran down from a surface vessel; the two vessels were also connected to each other by telephone.

Underwater fireworks

By 1934 Beebe and Barton were making impressive descents in the sea off the coast of Bermuda. On the morning of August 11, with the sun blazing over the ocean, they plunged into the green underworld that deepened to turquoise as they went down. Swarms of small crustaceans known as copepods could be seen through the portholes, and other creatures too were readily identified by the naturalist. 'At 320 feet (98 m) a lovely colony of siphonophores drifted past.

RARE SPECIMEN Underwater explorer William Beebe with a sand shark, photographed during a six-month Zoological Society cruise of the Atlantic and Pacific oceans, in 1925.

PERILOUS DESCENT An Italian magazine of 1932 shows Professor Beebe descending below the surface of the Atlantic in his strong, steel-clad bathysphere.

At this level they appeared like spun glass', Beebe wrote. Lower still a pilot fish looked in on the explorers who were already learning much about the vertical distribution of fish in the sea. 'My next visitors were good-sized yellow-tails and two blue-banded jacks which examined me closely at 400 and 490 feet (122 and 149 m) respectively. Here were so-called surface fish happy at 80 fathoms. Several silvery squid balanced for a moment, then shot past, and at 500 feet (152 m) a pair of lanternfish with no lights showing looked at the bathysphere unafraid.'

Lower down the sea became a dark, luminous blue – a strange colour which appeared bright to the eye, but so lacked power that it was useless for reading and writing. At 1000 ft (305 m), the naturalist noticed that the steel shell of the bathysphere was becoming very cold to the touch. Through the porthole the blue was now fading through grey to black. When they switched off their lights, they saw swarms of marine creatures glowing phosphorescent in the twilight zone. These were species that had evolved their own luminosity to cope with the abyssal dark. One such is the bizarre anglerfish which

A NEW FISH

During his record-breaking descents of 1934, William Beebe observed several new species of fish through the porthole of his bathysphere. On August 11, for example, he reported:

'Suddenly I leaned forward, banging my head against the steel but not losing a second of observation. A small school of luminous fish had just passed when, fortunately at a moment of suspension, came a new and gorgeous creature . . . a fish almost round, with long, moderately high, continuous, vertical fins; a big eye, medium mouth, and small pectoral fins. The skin was decidedly brownish. We swung around a few degrees to port, bringing the fish into the dark blue penumbra of the beam, and then I saw its real beauty. Along the sides of the body were five unbelievably beautiful lines of light, one equatorial, with two curved ones above and two below. Each line was composed of a series of large, pale yellow lights, and every one of these was surrounded by a semicircle of very small, but intensely purple photophores.

'The fish turned slowly and, head on, showed a narow profile . . . My name for it is *Bathysidus pentagrammus*, the Five-lined Constellationfish. In my memory it will live throughout the rest of my life as one of the loveliest things I have ever seen.'

appears to have a fishing line suspended from its head, dangling a luminous 'bait' to tempt prey into its wide mouth. Other species which Beebe saw were previously

unknown to science. On their three-hour dive that day, the explorers attained a depth of 2510 ft (765 m) – just 130 ft (40 m) short of the half mile mark on which Beebe had set his heart. But that depth was achieved only four days later, on August 15. Diving in more or less the same spot as before, Beebe got a clear view of an extraordinary phenomenon. At 1680 ft (512 m) he saw a creature several inches long dart towards the porthole, turn sideways – and explode. The flash was so strong that it lit up the inner sill of the window. Similar small explosions against the glass had baffled the scientists before, but this time Beebe was able to identify the cause. It was a great red shrimp – one of several deep-sea shrimps that have evolved the ability to vent a glowing flame as a defence mechanism. Sometimes the flash diffused in a glowing mist; on other occasions it went off like a Roman candle.

Just after 11 am that morning, with the cable on its winch almost run out, Beebe and

his companion touched down on the ocean floor at 3028 ft (923 m). They had reached a zone of unutterable darkness – it was jet black outside. Afterwards, wrote Beebe, 'I could never again use the word BLACK with any conviction.' At this depth the water was exerting a monstrous pressure of 19 tons on each porthole. Beebe's fingers were numb from the cold steel of the windowsill, and the metal floor was like a cake of ice. From the surface ship, by telephone, the crew asked if they

PLUMBING THE DEPTHS

On January 23, 1960, Swiss scientist Jacques Piccard and American Don Walsh plunged into the Pacific's Marianas Trench, the deepest place in the world. Descending in a bathyscaph, the two men touched bottom at 35 813 ft (10 916 m). At the bottom the water was exerting a pressure of 7.55 tons per sq in (1.17 tonnes per sq cm). Nonetheless, their searchlights picked out the bulging eyes of a flatfish which had learned to survive in the abyssal deep.

wanted to come up. Yes, Beebe replied. They were ready to be pulled up at once!

During the return to the surface, the explorers heard something snap suddenly; up on deck there were real fears that the cable had given way with consequences of unimaginable horror for the bathysphere's occupants. But it turned out to be only one of the guy ropes used in spooling the cable onto its drum, and not the all-important cable itself. Beebe and his partner returned to the surface safely and blinked into the Bermuda sunshine after returning from the ocean floor half a mile down.

LIGHT IN THE DARKNESS The deep sea anglerfish *Linophryne polpogon*, with its luminous 'bait' for smaller fish.

N THE SILENT WORLD

**ACQUES COUSTEAU OPENED THE EYES OF THE
WORLD TO THE MARVELS OF MARINE LIFE**

Jacques Cousteau once said: 'We did not dive to make films. We made films to record dives.' Nonetheless, his screen evocations of the underwater world introduced global audiences to marine scenes of exquisite beauty – and thrilling danger, too. Cousteau's team of 'menfish' swam unprotected among sharks, giant whales, manta rays and moray eels, braving also the menace of fire coral and sea poison ivy which can inflict burns that may last for days. Audiences learnt of other dangers too; like the 'rapture of the depths', in which a diver equipped with breathing apparatus may become so intoxicated by nitrogen that he offers his mouthpiece to a passing fish. Cousteau's film *The Silent World* won the Grand Prix at Cannes and an Oscar, and he also hosted the most popular documentary series in TV history. Through his questing spirit, his bravery and his sheer, instinctive showmanship, he became the most famous underwater adventurer in the world.

Flying in the ocean

Marine exploration was severely limited in the 19th century. Victorian treasure hunters investigating sunken ships had to wear bulky diving suits with a rigid spherical helmet, into which air was pumped from the surface through a tube. It was all very cumber-

some, and divers were not truly liberated until effective transportable breathing equipment was devised. The big breakthrough came during the Second World War when Jacques-Yves Cousteau, then a French naval captain, invented the aqualung, or scuba (self-contained underwater breathing apparatus). In 1942-3, Cousteau was in

DEEP-SEA HAZARDS

Decompression sickness is a serious hazard for deep-sea divers. It is caused by too quick a return to normal atmospheric pressure after a stint in deep water. The high pressure at depth causes large quantities of gases to accumulate in the blood. If a diver ascends too rapidly, nitrogen bubbles up in the blood, interrupting supply to the tissues and producing the joint pains known as the 'bends', as well as breathing difficulties known as the 'chokes'.

Toulon where the French navy was interned, and he teamed up with a control-valve engineer, Emile Gagnan, to solve a problem that had bedevilled earlier designs. Their patent aqualung comprised a canister of compressed air, a mouthpiece and a demand regulator that could supply a constant flow of oxygen at the same pressure as the water around the

diver. This was a vital element in the design, for a person's lungs are not powerful enough to expand against the pressure of the sea at depth. To breathe, a diver must receive air at the same pressure as the surrounding water – or risk lung collapse.

Freed from constraining cables, divers could now 'fly' in the ocean and perform a wealth of tasks that had earlier been problematic. During tests in June 1943, Cousteau wrote, 'I experimented with all possible manoeuvres of the aqualung – loops, somersaults and barrel rolls. I stood upside down on one finger and burst out laughing, a shrill distorted laugh. Nothing I did altered the automatic rhythm of the air. Delivered from gravity and buoyancy I flew around in space.'

How far could divers descend with the device? By October, a colleague named Frédéric Dumas had gone down to 210 ft (64 m) in a carefully planned experiment. But his dive revealed the undersea danger of nitrogen narcosis. About half way down, Dumas began to notice a strange, blissful sensation. He felt drunk and carefree; a buzzing filled his ears and his mouth tasted bitter. This dizzy elation continued as he descended farther, but vanished when he dropped his weights and soared to the surface. Cousteau, too, came to know the peril,

THE SUBMARINER Jacques Cousteau enters a bathyscaph, in 1959. From the research vessel *Calypso*, he and his team explored coral reefs and ancient shipwrecks, bringing back much dramatic film footage.

which has no relation to the bends but results from the effects of nitrogen saturation on the central nervous system. 'I like it and fear it like doom,' he admitted. 'It destroys the instinct of life.'

Deep dives held other dangers. Cousteau's worst experience did not occur in the ocean but in the inland water cave of Fontaine-de-Vaucluse, not far from Avignon. An underground spring erupted here every year for about five weeks towards the end of winter, for reasons no scientist could determine. Cousteau believed that there must be a huge inner reservoir, and with several companions descended into its dark, cold waters in the summer of 1946. In the course of their exploration, all succumbed to an enigmatic stupor that nearly killed them. It transpired that their cylinders contained a small excess of carbon monoxide which became lethal at a depth of 160 ft (49 m) – where the effect of carbon monoxide is magnified sixfold.

Shark attack

Despite all the dangers, the aqualung provided a key to a hidden world of wonders: with one small piece of 20th-century technology Cousteau and Gagnan had opened up a vast portion of the globe to human exploration.

OCTOPUS CITY

In his book *The Silent World* Jacques Cousteau describes many undersea creatures in their own living environments, including a whole metropolis of octopuses:

'On the flat shallow floor northeast of Porquerolles we came upon an octopus city. We could hardly believe our eyes. Scientific credence, confirmed by our own experiences, holds that the octopus lives in crannies of rock and reef. Yet here were strange villas, indisputably erected by the octopuses themselves. A typical home was one roofed with a flat stone two feet [0.6 m] long and weighing perhaps twenty pounds [9 kg]. One side of the stone had been raised eight inches [20 cm] and propped by two lintels, a stone and a red building brick. The mud floor inside had been excavated five inches [13 cm]. In front of the lean-to was a wall of accumulated debris: crab and oyster shells, stones, shards of man-made pottery, sea anemones, and urchins. A tentacle extended from the dwelling and curled around the rubble, and the owl-like eyes of the octopus peered at me over the wall. When I went closer, the tentacle contracted, sweeping the debris up against the door, concealing the inhabitant. We made colour photographs of an octopus house.'

Jacques Cousteau continued with test dives to improve his equipment, and developed an underwater camera that could go down as far as 1970 ft (600 m) to yield fascinating images of flora and fauna.

The shark, above all, symbolised the heightened contrasts of undersea life. On the one hand Cousteau spoke of the sleek, streamlined fish as ranking among the most perfect and most beautiful creatures developed in nature. Yet he could also describe a pack of sharks in a feeding frenzy as 'demons incarnate'. Once, off the west coast of Africa, he had an almost fatal encounter. As Cousteau and Dumas were filming an 8 ft (2.4 m) grey shark, two more sharks – 15 ft (4.6 m) blues – loomed from the darkness.

The three great fish slowly closed a circle around the divers. Cousteau tried shark repellant (cupric acetate tablets which copper-stain the water around) but the sharks swam on through the clouded sea. Cousteau then tried flailing his arms and releasing a stream of bubbles, but the monsters came closer still. In the end, the grey shark broke loose and sped towards Cousteau who beat him off with his camera – while still filming the oncoming beast. He felt the smashing impact of its snout, and for what seemed like

CLOSE ENCOUNTER The great white shark *Carcharodon carcharias* proved in one early encounter to be more alarmed by Cousteau than the marine explorer was by the shark.

an eternity the two divers continued to repel the trio of sharks. They were nearing exhaustion, with diminishing air supplies, when at last the shadow of their launch fell over them. The crew had seen the bubbles and recognised their distress; the sharks grew agitated and fled the scene.

Often sharks proved surprisingly shy. On an early encounter with the feared *Carcharodon carcharias* – the man-eating great white shark – Cousteau and Dumas were totally unprepared for the monster's response. When it spotted the divers, the great white stopped in its tracks, released a cloud of excrement, and sped away. The two men burst into nervous laughter. Cousteau said that the shark was no more a 'killer' in the criminal sense than the housewife who served bacon at the family breakfast. Nonetheless, the powerful, unpredictable carnivores remained a disquieting presence in the undersea habitat. 'The better acquainted we become with sharks,' he said, 'the less we know them, and one can never tell what a shark is going to do.'

In 1951, while still serving in the French navy, Cousteau commissioned a research vessel to be converted from a wartime minesweeper. Stripped and totally refurbished with improved navigational aids, enlarged crew quarters and a crane on the port afterquarters, she was christened *Calypso*, after the beautiful sea maiden of Homer's *Odyssey*. Her supreme attribute was an underwater observation chamber at the front of the ship and below the waterline,

CLASSIC FOOTAGE A scene from the TV series *The Underwater World of Jacques Cousteau*, which brought his aquatic adventures to millions.

with the steel chamber and entry tube outside the hull so as not to weaken the bow structure. Inside the 'false nose', two members of the crew were able to observe and film underwater life through five circular windows.

In this vessel, painted a sparkling white instead of battle grey, Cousteau began systematically to explore the world's oceans, starting with the coral reefs of the Farasan Bank off the Saudi Arabian coast in the Red Sea. Using soundings, scientists aboard the *Calypso* were able to demonstrate that the Red Sea floor contained volcanic basins, while divers took thousands of underwater photographs and identified previously unknown species of marine life.

Soon afterwards Cousteau turned to underwater archaeology and his *Calypso* team explored the wreck of a large Roman ship which had sunk in the Mediterranean off the rocky island of Grande Conglué 12 miles (19 km) from Marseilles. Working in 140 ft (43 m) of water, his divers began by

THE CONSERVATIONIST In his later years, Cousteau became concerned about environmental issues and campaigned to protect Antarctica from ecological dangers.

raising thousands of ceramic pots and dishes in baskets. Later they used an underwater vacuum cleaner, operated by a colossal pump onshore, that hoovered sand, fish, shells and ancient relics to the surface where they could be sifted at leisure. So powerful was the pipe that if its mouth had been accidentally grabbed by a diver, it would have sucked the blood from his body.

In 1957 Cousteau was made director of the Oceanographic Museum of Monaco in which capacity he launched several new scientific projects. The most innovative involved seeking ways for humans to live for weeks at a time beneath the sea. Developed

during the 1960s, Cousteau's Conshelf stations were the first underwater living environments, and inspired the US navy to develop similar experimental stations called Sealab. In the same period, Cousteau campaigned against the French government's decision to dump nuclear waste in the Mediterranean and became a spokesman for a variety of environmental causes.

Cousteau the campaigner

During the 1980s, Cousteau developed a windship called *Alcyone* whose turbosails lowered fuel costs by up to 40 per cent. He completed a two-and-a-half year voyage in the wind-powered vessel to support fuel economies and protest against nuclear weapons. He also took the *Calypso* up the Amazon River which, sustaining the world's largest forest, represented for Cousteau the world's supreme ecological wonder. One of the animals he filmed in the Amazon was the mysterious pink dolphin, a graceful mammal whose unusually flexible body is adapted to manoeuvre like a gymnast around the river's flooded vines and branches.

Tireless even as he approached the age of 80, Cousteau led a campaign in 1989 to protect the continent of Antarctica from commercial exploitation. He died in Paris in the early morning of June 25, 1997, and was accorded a memorial mass at the Cathedral of Notre Dame, an honour usually reserved for heads of state.

UNDERSEA HABITATS

After the Second World War, scientists' impulse to explore outer space was matched by a desire to colonise the underwater world. Fantastic ideas were proposed to answer possible overpopulation, by farming underwater crops and even milking whales in underwater dairies. But how would men adapt to the rigours of life in seafloor habitats? Jacques Cousteau was among the first to investigate the possibilities. In 1962, two members of his team, Albert Falco and Claude Wesly, stayed for a week in a small

CONSHELF 3 Lowering the underwater station into the Mediterranean at Nice, 1965.

chamber sunk 33 ft (10 m) into the Mediterranean Sea. Dubbed Conshelf 1 (Continental Shelf Station Number One), the cylindrical dwelling was only 17 ft (5.2 m) long and 8 ft (2.4 m) high. Though the pair ate gourmet meals sent down in pressure cookers and enjoyed hot freshwater showers piped from the surface ship, they sometimes fell prey to irritability and claustrophobia.

Underwater experiments with later Conshelf stations were more elaborate: in Conshelf 2, situated in the Red Sea, five men lived in a complex equipped with full living and working facilities, as well as luxuries which included hi-fi music. In 1965 in Conshelf 3 six oceanauts worked for three weeks in chilling darkness 325 ft (99 m) below the surface of the Mediterranean. Because the nitrogen in air is lethal at this depth, they breathed a mixture of 98 per cent helium and only 2 per cent oxygen. This heliox, as it was called, made their vocal cords vibrate rapidly, so that their voices sounded like Donald Duck when they talked. It also had the strange effect of dulling their senses so that they could not taste foods or smell odours. 'On air,' said one of them, 'we find everything so beautiful, but with heliox, the reality is there, grey and sad.'

Despite the problems, however, Cousteau and his team had proved that semi-permanent undersea habitats, similar to space stations, were feasible. And his achievements inspired many other submerged habitats in the waters of Japan, Great Britain, Italy, the United States, the Soviet Union, West Germany, Canada, the Bahamas, the Netherlands and Cuba.

SINGLE-HANDED SAILOR

AT 65, FRANCIS CHICHESTER WON INTERNATIONAL RENOWN FOR SAILING SOLO AROUND THE WORLD

Within 24 hours of leaving Sydney in his yacht *Gipsy Moth IV*, round-the-world sailor Francis Chichester hit one of the gales known to mariners as a Tasman terror. In the storm, he wrote, 'the white breakers showed in the blackness like monstrous beasts charging down on the yacht'. When the craft ran into an exceptionally large wave, she rolled over onto her side; crockery smashed and cutlery rattled as water poured in through the forehatch. Though the yacht righted herself again, Chichester contacted Sydney on the radio distress frequency. All the next day the storm howled on. 'Let's face it,' wrote Chichester, 'I was frightened.'

Francis Chichester was not a seaman of long experience. Born in 1901, he had first made his name as a pioneer of long-distance aviation in his tiny plane, *Gipsy Moth*. He gave up flying after a crash in Japan in 1931, and had already reached his fifties before his thoughts turned to yachting. *Gipsy Moth II*, an 8 ton cutter, was the first of his boats and in 1960, in *Gipsy Moth III*, he won the first solo Transatlantic Race. But he had long been nursing a more ambitious project which he disclosed to his wife Sheila: 'I want to try a very fast sail round the world alone.'

'A sort of pilgrimage'

For this adventure Chichester had a new boat designed, one with an unusual hull constructed from six thin skins of laminated plywood, only 7/8 in (22 mm) thick but immensely strong. He also wanted a watertight bulkhead forward, which would offer some hope of survival even if she crashed into an iceberg. Long and sleek, she was clearly going to be a very fast boat; but no one quite knew how the single-handed sailor would be able to manage her in the Antarctic seas.

Building work began on *Gipsy Moth IV* in December 1964 and was completed 15 months later. At 11 am on August 27, 1966, a gunshot echoed at the Royal Western Yachting Club's race-starting line in Plymouth, and Chichester set out to take on 28 500 miles (45 865 km) of ocean. In the lee

LONE YACHTSMAN Chichester with *Gipsy Moth IV*, heading towards Cape Liptrap, Australia, three months into the first leg of his round-the-world voyage.

of Madeira, he met his first squalls and learned how alarming it could be when his long, speedy, lightweight vessel met rough weather. But she bore up well, and Chichester himself felt braced by the challenge of the seas. He had embarked on what his wife called 'a great spiritual adventure, a sort of pilgrimage'.

On September 17, as the bucketing boat sped south at 7 knots (13 km/h) Chichester celebrated his 65th birthday. That evening in the cockpit, he donned a famous green velvet smoking jacket which he had already carried six times across the Atlantic, and opened a bottle of champagne. 'This must be one of the greatest nights of my life,' he wrote. 'I don't think I can escape ageing, but why beef

ROUND THE WORLD RECORDS

Francis Chichester was not the first man to sail solo around the world. That title belongs to America's Captain Joshua Slocum in his oyster boat, *Spray*. Slocum took more than three years, returning to Fairhaven, Massachusetts on July 3, 1898. Chichester took nine months and made only one stop – at Sydney, Australia. The first solo circumnavigation without stopping was in 1969 by Britain's Robin Knox-Johnston in his 32 ft (10 m) ketch *Suhaili*.

about it? Our only purpose in life, if we are able to say such a thing, is to put up the best performance we can – in anything – and only in doing so lies the satisfaction of living.'

Gipsy Moth IV had set sail without proper trials, and though many of her design features proved successful, the vessel behaved like a thoroughbred racehorse: she was as temperamental as she was fast, and prone to heel over in the slightest breeze. She also had a tendency to whip around and lie broadside to the waves. Coursing down through the South Atlantic, Chichester found himself tiring because of the number of sail changes needed to cope with winds that grew suddenly stronger or lighter. By October 11, he was over half way to Sydney and being rushed along in the great westerlies known as the Roaring Forties. But the going was rough, and he succumbed to a curious sensation of solitude which he had never known in the North Atlantic. 'This Southern Ocean was totally different; the seas were fierce, vicious and frightening . . . The incessant squalls had one unexpected quality – often the sun would continue to shine brightly while the wind whipped the sea to fury.'

Chichester's aim was to reach Sydney in the same time as the great clipper ships of the past. They averaged 100 days, but when

raging seas cracked the steel frame of his self-steering gear he lost some time improvising workable repairs, and it was not until early December that he reached the shipping lanes of South Australia. Days before he expected them, boatloads of journalists and cameramen drew near. One motor launch came so close that it bumped *Gipsy Moth*'s stern, causing Chichester to hurt his elbow and issue his first direct words to a fellow human after three months alone at sea: 'go away' (a more emphatic two-word expression according to his biographer). To make matters worse, the winds dropped just before his landfall and *Gipsy Moth* lay becalmed for a time before Chichester at last entered Sydney Harbour on December 12.

The voyage had taken 105 days 20 hours, and though he had lost his wager with the

ARRIVAL AT SYDNEY *Gipsy Moth IV* entered Sydney Harbour on December 12, 1966, having negotiated an armada of vessels loaded with journalists and cameramen.

clipper ships, he had gone much longer distances at much higher average speeds than any other single-handed sailor. Press barrages and TV conferences ensued. Journalists suggested that the exhausted yachtsman should conclude his voyage in Australia and not tempt fate by attempting a return around the Horn, but Chichester was determined to press on. On January 27, 1967, while still in Australia, Chichester learnt that he had been awarded a knighthood. Then a couple of days later he was off again.

After being capsized by the Tasman terror, which he ran into almost immediately,

CHICHESTER ROUNDS THE HORN

Flown through storm winds aboard a tiny Piper Apache aircraft, *Sunday Times* journalist Murray Sayle obtained exclusive pictures of Chichester's *Gipsy Moth IV* rounding Cape Horn:

'As I flew by Cape Horn, its grey pyramid could be seen lashed by heavy seas . . . South of the Horn the waves were driving eastward in long ridges of white and grey-green. Overhead were black driving clouds driven by the gale and a mile or two ahead the clouds were joined to the sea by rain in a black, impenetrable barrier towards the south and the pole . . . Then I picked out the salt-grimed hull of *Gipsy Moth* lurching forward as the seas passed under her . . . It was a flight I am not anxious to repeat, but the sight of *Gipsy Moth* ploughing bravely through this wilderness of rain and sea was well worth it.'

so particularly fascinating was its slight, bespectacled 65-year-old hero. By the time Francis Chichester entered Plymouth harbour on May 28, he had been making headlines for weeks. Half a million people had crowded into the city to witness his homecoming after the 119 day nonstop voyage from Sydney. Admirers waved from hundreds of boats in the harbour and a special reception was held for him by the Lord Mayor of Plymouth. There were messages from the Queen and Prince Philip, and a telegram of congratulations from Prime Minister Harold Wilson.

In July, in a formal ceremony of knighthood, a red carpet was laid over a pontoon by the *Gipsy Moth* at Greenwich. Chichester was knighted by the Queen with a sword which Elizabeth I had used to knight Francis Drake after his circumnavigation in the *Golden Hind*.

Chichester removed cutlery from his sodden bunk and managed some sleep before sailing on through further gales. They blew so strong that he found himself rushed 1115 miles (1794 km) in seven days towards the voyage's ultimate peril. Cape Horn, the most southerly point of mainland America, is a notorious graveyard of mariners. Here the Atlantic and Pacific Oceans meet in a wild embrace, and as Chichester approached, the icy winds rose to 40 knots (74 km/h) amid huge breaking seas. Suddenly, Chichester wrote, 'there was the Horn, quite plain to see. It stood up out of the sea like a black ice-cream cone.' A tiny yellow aeroplane, carrying two terrified BBC men and a *Sunday Times* journalist, braved the storm to obtain a scoop sighting of *Gipsy Moth IV* as she threaded her lurching path through the immense, battering waves. Chichester survived the mountainous seas and headed for warmer waters. On April 24 he crossed the Equator and began what turned out to be a fast run home. The whole adventure had now fired the imagination of a worldwide public and as *Gipsy Moth IV* sped northwards, the excitement grew. What made the epic

ROYAL ACCOLADE Using a sword that belonged to Sir Francis Drake, Elizabeth II knights Francis Chichester at Greenwich.

OPERATION TITANIC

THE WRECK OF THE LUXURY LINER IS DISCOVERED DEEP BELOW THE SURFACE OF THE ATLANTIC OCEAN

It was the ultimate feat of underwater exploration. At 1.05 am on September 1, 1985, far out in the Atlantic, crewmen in the control room of the research vessel *Knorr* gasped in amazement. From the ocean floor deep below them, the robot submarine *Argo* was transmitting images of giant rivets from what looked like a boiler. Someone punched a button and telescopic views flashed up on the screen of strewn wreckage …bedsprings, chamberpots, bottles of ale … then empty lifeboat davits. The unthinkable had occurred, and the news was quickly picked up by communications satellites and the radio traffic of merchant ships in the area. In no time at all the whole world knew that a French-American team had found the wreck of the *Titanic* – an incredible 2¹/₂ miles (4 km) below the surface of the Atlantic.

It is hard, today, to recapture the impact of the reports. When the great luxury liner sank in 1912 with the loss of 1513 lives, it seemed that she had plunged into a fathom-

ROBOT CAMERA In 1986 Ballard returned to the *Titanic* in the submarine *Alvin*, from which he could remote control Jason Jr, a robot with cameras that could explore the wreck.

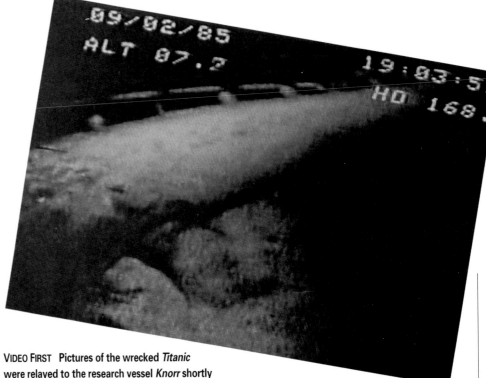

VIDEO FIRST Pictures of the wrecked *Titanic* were relayed to the research vessel *Knorr* shortly after midnight on September 1, 1985.

less realm never to be seen again. Now that realm was accessible; once as remote as the moon it had, like the moon, succumbed to hi-tech equipment. 'If they can find the Titanic, they can find anything', was the verdict of many.

'I was in tears'

The *Titanic* disaster had been one of the great, tragic news stories of the 20th century. Pride of the White Star fleet, the ship had been the largest and most luxurious ever built. Because of her special design, with a steel hull divided into 16 watertight compartments, she had been proclaimed 'unsinkable' and carried enough lifeboats for only half of the passengers. As a result, when she hit an iceberg off Newfoundland and went down on her maiden voyage, it was a scandal as well as a

RECORD WRECK

In June 1989, Robert Ballard caused another sensation by locating the wreck of Hitler's flagship, the *Bismarck*. Sunk during the Second World War, the battleship went down 600 miles (960 km) west of the French port, Brest, with the loss of more than 2000 German seamen. Filmed by the submersible *Argo*, she lay on the ocean floor half a mile (1 km) deeper than the *Titanic*. An incredible 3 miles (4.8 km) down, this was the deepest shipwreck ever found.

---

catastrophe. Afterwards, new safety regulations for ships at sea were drawn up by an international convention, and an international ice patrol established. Precisely how the iceberg had managed to sink the great liner remained, however, an unanswered question; and without access to the wreck, it seemed destined to remain an enigma forever.

The man determined to locate the *Titanic* was Robert Ballard of the Woods Hole Oceanographic Institute in the United States. He had been working since 1967 on deep-sea diving submersibles, and especially on the refinement of a three-man submarine named *Alvin*, which had been used in

THE MASSIVENESS OF IT

John Salzig, who went down to explore the *Titanic* in the submarine *Alvin*, compared the experience with earlier investigations of underwater volcanoes:

'For me, as a very new pilot, it was a challenge because on earlier dives I had climbed around on things that were pretty much rock piles – scarps and lava pillows and the calderas of dead volcanoes. This was different. There's manmade objects down there. And this hull! Going to the stern section in the debris field – this hull that extended as far as I could see in any direction. And that's what gave me the sense of awe: the massiveness of it. I never got that feeling on top of a volcano. You expect volcanoes to be big. You're used to gliding along the bottom and seeing piles of rocks stretching on for miles and miles. You don't expect to go down there and find the whole world filled with manmade objects. It never really happens. A volcano is a thousand times bigger than the Titanic; but it was the Titanic that made me feel insignificant.'

Project FAMOUS to help to explore the Mid-Atlantic Rift Valley. The *Titanic* adventure involved years of preparation for his Deep Submergence team, and a long search after the expedition put to sea. It focused on the Grand Banks region of the Atlantic.

From June 1985 a French research vessel *Le Suroit* crisscrossed the area using deep-sea sonar equipment and had scoured more than 80 per cent of the target area before August 9, when Ballard's *Knorr* arrived. After ten days of fruitless search on the bottom with his robot submarine *Argo*, the American began to suspect that they might be looking in the wrong area. Now and again hopes rose as search equipment registered abnormal magnetic readings, only to be dashed as they turned out to have been prompted by deep-sea sand dunes or rock formations. Morale was low by the start of September, when the *Argo* suddenly started transmitting images of the *Titanic's* boiler.

Within a few days of the discovery, helicopters bearing camera crews were flying out across the sea to get pictures of the *Knorr*, while the ship's radio was jammed with calls from pressmen. Bombarded with questions, Ballard was overwhelmed, not only by fatigue but by a sense of the tragedy he was exploring. He and other scientists examining *Argo's* first pictures of the wreck burst into tears, and some suffered what they later called minor nervous breakdowns. 'Finding the ship, I did not expect it to hit me in such a tragic sense,' Ballard later said. 'I did not expect to feel the disaster to the

level I felt it. I was in tears. I must have looked like a real crybaby. I just – I was really depressed . . . I wanted to run away from the *Titanic*. I wanted it out of my life.'

The roving eyeball

In July 1986, Ballard returned to the scene and, with two companions, explored the wreck of the *Titanic* at close quarters, in the tiny submarine *Alvin*. The craft was a titanium bubble just 7 ft (2 m) across, equipped with a mechanical arm. The pilot sat in the middle of the cramped sphere, with his two passengers crouching at the port and starboard view ports, surrounded by TV monitors and video cassette recorders.

On the day of the first descent, the *Alvin* sank by gravity for two hours through the abyssal darkness. When at last they approached the bottom, they switched on the floodlamps and saw some nameless creature skitter away from the craft; the deep

SEABED WRECKS

In the quest for sunken ships, with their promise of sunken treasure, 20th-century searchers have a range of hi-tech devices. Sonar apparatus uses sound waves to locate objects on the ocean bed (the name comes from Sound Navigation and Ranging). Sub-bottom Profiling Sonar, a specialised type of sonar, can detect the remains of shipwrecks buried as much as 98 ft (30 m) deep in the mud of a harbour or estuary. Another aid is the proton magnetometer, which detects ferrous metal, and can locate a large steel ship up to a quarter of a mile (400 m)

SHIP'S TOUR The Mary Rose is the only 16th-century warship on display in the world – in Dry Dock No. 3 at Portsmouth.

away or, at closer range, identify a cannon or anchor. If a shipwreck site is covered with a large quantity of sediment, it can be removed with the aid of a prop-wash. This is a giant piece of apparatus that is attached to the salvage vessel's propellor and blows mud and sand away from the wreck.

Besides the *Titanic*, HMS *Bounty* (1957), the Tudor galleon *Mary Rose* (1971) and Hitler's *Bismarck* (1989) are just three of the historic vessels which have been located by modern searchers. In 1971, Florida treasure-seeker Mel Fisher located a shipwrecked Spanish galleon, the *Atocha*. The wreck was first detected by magnetometer, and when divers saw nothing on the bottom they used a prop-wash to uncover the site. Don Kincaid, the first diver to go down into the hole, saw a large iron anchor. Fanning sand from the area around, he then spotted a shining chain.

'In the green light it looked like brass at first, then suddenly I knew it was gold and I fought against the falling sand and dug frantically with my hands and ended up with an eight-foot [2.4 m] gold chain, the first of tons of treasure to be eventually discovered on the fabled *Atocha*.' Tragedy marked the discovery; three

members of the salvage team drowned when their boat capsized, and it took 14 years of further search before the galleon's mother lode was located. But the reward, then, was astonishing. Fisher's divers brought to the surface a haul of silver coins, gold bars, emeralds and other artefacts, valued at around $25 million.

BURIED BATTLESHIP The *Bismarck* was found off the French coast in 1989.

ocean mud was etched with the trails of crabs and worms.

The *Titanic* appeared to them as a huge mound of grey, rusted steel. The ship's hull had broken in two during the disaster, and the two halves lay at some distance from one another in a half-mile-wide debris field strewn with wine and champagne bottles, gleaming cutlery, copper buckets – even carpetbags and leather suitcases. Despite the passage of 75 years, many perishable items had been preserved by the near-freezing waters. Ballard's team saw beautiful silverware but had made a promise to themselves not to take anything, and left them where they lay.

'The stern is hardly recognisable,' Ballard later told reporters. 'It is just a tremendous pile of twisted wreckage that is very difficult to manoeuvre in because it is so irregular and overhanging. Still, we inspected a large part of it, almost the size of a city block, it seems, and radiating out around it is a tremendous series of artefacts. It is actually like going to a museum, there are just thousands and thousands of items that were laid all over the bottom.'

When the submarine touched down on the forecastle roof of the *Titanic*, the crew felt like Armstrong and Aldrin making the first landing on the Moon. Later the craft glided up the vestige of the promenade deck and parked on the bridge, where the bronze post of the ship's wheel loomed outside the forward view port. Jason Jr, a robot camera,

PROJECT FAMOUS

Before locating the *Titanic*, Robert Ballard had been closely involved in organising deep-sea dives to explore the Mid-Atlantic Ridge. Called Project FAMOUS (French-American Mid-Ocean Study), the operation was mounted in 1972-5 to investigate the huge fracture that runs the length of the ocean, from Iceland to the Antarctic. Through it, volcanic lava oozes continually onto the ocean floor, along the dividing line between two of the Earth's plates. The lava, quickly cooling and solidifying on contact with the cold water, has created a submerged mountain range – the Mid-Atlantic Ridge – whose central crest is divided by a wide rift valley.

The manned, deep-sea submarine *Alvin* was used to explore areas of volcanic activity where the crew found glassy lava lakes, with hydrothermal vents and fantastic towers. The towers rise from the ocean floor as water, heated in the fissures along the plate boundary, deposits these 'mineral chimneys'. Bacteria flourish near the hot springs of sulphide-laden water, providing food for worms, giant species of shrimp, blind crabs and other marine creatures.

Project FAMOUS yielded vital information about the mechanism of the Earth's plates, but synchronising the actions of the various submersibles and support vessels proved something of a nightmare. 'It was exhausting,' wrote Ballard, 'sort of like being a symphony conductor orchestrating ships, French and American submarines, scores of people. All the machines and all the people were tuned to do something. There was the brass section, the woodwinds – they all had to do it right. And we had to make them do it.'

explored the Grand Staircase and the staterooms. This 'roving eyeball', attached to *Alvin* by a cord, consisted of a propellor-driven video camera that was guided like a remote control toy. Everywhere,

stalactites dripped from the rusted hull contributing to the ghostliness of the scene.

The photos from the ocean bed amazed the world, and one thing became clear as a result of the investigation. Historians had believed that when the iceberg hit the *Titanic*, it had cut a long gash in the hull, as if with a mighty sword. Illustrations of the gashed side appeared in school textbooks and even graced the logo of Woods Hole's Operation Titanic logo.

But the wreck's explorers could see no evidence of any such wound. Instead, the ship seemed to have buckled so that steel plates had sprung, rivets popped, seams split. Individually, the cracks had been no more than a few inches wide – yet they had been enough to pierce the giant's armour, allowing 24 000 cu ft (680 m³) of water to enter the *Titanic* during the first hour of her sinking. Tilting then began, and as the anchor holes slipped beneath the surface, more sea rushed in through the apertures. Flooding at the prow caused the stern to be lifted out of the water – and under strain, the great ship had snapped in two.

TREASURE TROVE Delicate porcelain plates (above) rest undamaged in the silt on the seabed. Rust hangs from a pair of bitts on the forward deck of the *Titanic*.

UNUSUAL ADVENTURES

CROSSING THE OCEANS OF THE WORLD BY BALLOON OR BY BALSA-WOOD RAFT, OR DESCENDING INTO THE FIERY MOUTHS OF VOLCANOES OR INTO THE BLACK DEPTHS OF ABYSSAL CAVE SYSTEMS . . . 20TH-CENTURY ADVENTURERS HAVE NOT LACKED FOR WAYS OF TESTING THEIR METTLE. IN AN AGE WHICH HAS SEEN THE EARTH'S LAST WILDERNESS EXPLORED AND MAPPED WITH PINPOINT ACCURACY, BOLD SPIRITS HAVE SOUGHT OUT NEW CHALLENGES.

BALLOONACY

DAREDEVIL BRAZILIAN ALBERTO SANTOS-DUMONT PIONEERED AIR TRAVEL BY BALLOON

One of the world's first wristwatches for men was created for Alberto Santos-Dumont. The Brazilian aeronaut discovered that he could not check his pocket watch because he was using both hands to steer a balloon, and in 1901 his friend, the jeweller Louis Cartier, came up with a novel solution. Originally intended as a one-of-a-kind creation, it was square-faced – unlike all previous watches which had been round – with Roman numerals and a simple, sturdy leather strap. Dubbed the Santos, the wristwatch remained a curiosity available only for private customers until commercial production began during the First World War.

The youngest son of a Brazilian millionaire, Santos-Dumont was the very archetype of the wealthy eccentric. Fired as a child by the science fiction novels of Jules Verne, he was a resident of Paris from the age of 18 and there determined to realise his own dreams of flying. At the beginning of the 20th century, the French capital was a centre for experiment and innovation. The Eiffel Tower had recently punctured the

DEBONAIR ADVENTURER Alberto Santos-Dumont, Brazilian-born pioneer of aviation, with one of his balloons (above). Note the aeronaut's high, white 'Santos-Dumont collar' which was emulated by fashionable Parisians.

skyline, the first automobiles were rumbling along the boulevards, daring cancan dancers appeared at the Folies Bergère, while a young painter named Pablo Picasso painted his first acrobats and harlequins. Meanwhile, the dapper young Brazilian aeronaut became a familiar sight over the Parisian chimney-pots. His first balloon, which he called the *Brazil*, was a tiny affair of Japanese silk and bamboo, weighing only 44 lbs (20 kg) and so compact that he could carry it around in a valise. Many devices followed, sustained by hydrogen gas and powered by petrol engine – a potentially catastrophic combination, as concerned friends pointed out. He was

LES BALLONS DIRIGEABLES
Les Expériences de M. Santos-Dumont

one point he climbed out of the gondola and clambered across the Tower's girders to attend to a misfiring engine. Crowds of Parisians 1000 ft (304 m) below gasped – then cheered – as the flight continued. 'Have I won? Have I won?' Santos-Dumont asked the throng as he brought the balloon down – for he had no free hand to check his pocket watch. The crowd answered by carrying him shoulder-high to the waiting judges – and the age of flight dawned.

TOWERING ACHIEVEMENT In 1901 Santos-Dumont (below) made a balloon flight around the Eiffel Tower. Onlookers held their breath as the daredevil left the craft and climbed onto the tower to make a repair.

LUNCHING ABOVE THE CLOUDS

Wealthy balloonist Alberto Santos-Dumont enjoyed lavish champagne lunches while making his pioneer flights in France:

'A joyous peal of bells mounted up to us. It was the noonday Angelus, ringing from some village belfry. I had brought up with us a substantial lunch of hard-boiled eggs, cold roast beef and chicken, cheese, ice cream, fruits and cakes. Champagne, coffee and Chartreuse. Nothing is more delicious than lunching like this above the clouds in a spherical balloon. No dining room can be so marvellous in its decoration. The sun sets the clouds in ebullition, making them throw up rainbow jets of frozen vapour like great sheaves of fireworks all around the table. Lovely white spangles of the most delicate ice formation scatter here and there by magic, while flakes of snow form by moment out of nothingness, beneath our very eyes, and in our drinking glasses!'

certainly courageous.
'One only had to see him in a little wicker basket next to a motor going full out and vomiting flames beneath a balloon full of hydrogen gas to be convinced of that', declared his contemporary, Louis Blériot.

Crashes were frequent. Once he hit the roof of the Trocadero Hotel and he had to be got down by firemen. Smartly moustached, with neat, centre-parted hair, the young Brazilian remained indifferent to danger, setting standards in fashion as well as ballooning.

On October 19, 1901, Santos-Dumont achieved his supreme triumph, winning a 100 000 franc prize offered by the Paris Aero-Club for the first man to make a half-hour controlled flight around the Eiffel Tower in a powered balloon. Several others had been killed in attempts, and the Brazilian's own flight was a heartstopping achievement. At

HIGH FLYER

Santos-Dumont experimented with winged aircraft as well as balloons. On November 12, 1906, watched by the Aero-Club of France, he flew 722 ft (220 m) in 21 seconds in a heavier-than-air craft. He was celebrated at the time for establishing the world's first aviation record. It was only later that the public learnt of the Wright brothers' historic *Kitty Hawk* flights of 1903, which had gone largely unreported at the time. The Brazilian accepted the Wrights' claim with admirable good grace.

UP, UP AND AWAY

FROM PIONEER FLIGHTS IN BASKETWORK GONDOLAS TO MODERN HOT-AIR ODYSSEYS, BALLOONS HAVE MADE A FASCINATING CONTRIBUTION TO THE CONQUEST OF THE AIR

In 1901, the year of Santos-Dumont's prize-winning feat, two German scientists named A. Berson and R. Suring ascended in a balloon to a height of 34 550 ft (10 530 m) above Berlin; they may even have risen 1000 ft (305 m) higher but could not take readings for, despite having oxygen equipment, they were unconscious during the highest part of their climb.

Manned balloons have been floating through the skies since the Montgolfiers' ascent in 1783, and it is easy to forget that during the first decades of the 20th century they seemed to represent the best hopes for the conquest of the air. The big 'dirigibles' – balloons capable of being guided – were a streamlined cigar shape, driven by propellers and steered by a rudder. They were quieter and more spacious than the first winged aircraft, could carry heavier loads, and did not have to stop so often to refuel. It was in a dirigible that, in 1926, Roald Amundsen and Umberto Nobile made their flight over the North Pole. Extraordinary feats of altitude were registered, too. In 1927 a balloon manned by US army captain Hawthorne C. Gray reached 42 470 ft (12 945 m). Tragically, he was found dead on the floor of his gondola when the balloon came down – the record height was registered on his barograph.

The luxurious airships of the 1920s and 30s were sustained by inflammable hydrogen gas, and their era ended with a series of spectacular crashes that included the disaster of the *Hindenburg* in 1937. Ballooning has continued to play a part in aerial exploration, but in general, hot-air balloons have superseded the gas types. In 1987 the young British tycoon Richard Branson with his pilot Per Lindstrand became the first to cross the Atlantic in a hot-air balloon

ZEPPELIN POSTER Giant airships seemed to offer the best hopes for luxury air travel until a series of disastrous crashes brought their heyday to an end.

and, in 1991, two hot-air balloons flew over Mount Everest for the first time. The ultimate achievement came in 1999, when Bertrand Piccard and Brian Jones completed the first non-stop round-the-world flight.

The hot air principle may have been observed by early man watching dry leaves, or straw, rising above the heat of their camp fires. Did our ancestors also experiment with smoke-filled bags – even learn to fly themselves, 2000 years ago? The Nazca Plains in Peru contain mysterious designs of birds and other creatures forming patterns which can only be seen from the air. Some people believe that the Nazca people of the area may have made and flown hot-air balloons from which they were able to plan their pictures. In 1975, using materials which would have been available to the Nazca people, a balloon called *Condor 1* was built. The basic design followed a pattern seen on a piece of Nazca pottery and represents a very simple way of folding an uncut piece of material. Balloonist Julian Nott and co-pilot Jim Woodman climbed astride the reed gondola and rose gently into the sky. They attained a height of about 300 ft (91 m) before the cooling air caused a descent. After touch-down, the two aeronauts got off the gondola and let the balloon fly off of its own accord. *Condor 1* soared to about 1700 ft (518 m) before landing undamaged 20 minutes later. Evidently, balloons could have been made and flown above the plain in ancient times.

BALLOON TRAVELLERS Richard Branson (left) and his Swedish pilot, Per Lindstrand, crossed the Atlantic in a hot-air balloon, the *Virgin Atlantic Flyer*, in 1987.

THE *KON-TIKI* EXPEDITION

THOR HEYERDAHL TRAVELLED TWICE THE DISTANCE COLUMBUS DID ON A BALSA-WOOD RAFT

One morning in 1947, far out on the vast Pacific, explorer Thor Heyerdahl wrote in a dew-damp logbook: '17th May. Norwegian Independence Day. Heavy sea. Fair wind. I am cook today and found 7 flying fish on deck, one squid on the cabin roof, and one unknown fish in Tortsein's sleeping bag . . .' Heyerdahl sat bobbing on a balsawood raft, 850 sea miles (1573 km) from the coast of Peru, with five companions and a green parrot. And just for a moment he found himself asking what in the world he was doing there.

He was attempting to solve one of the great riddles of Pacific settlement. The Polynesian islands towards which he was sailing are situated in the middle of the immense ocean, isolated from each other by vast tracts of featureless sea. Yet the islands are fully inhabited, some containing ancient temples, pyramids and paved roads. Easter Island is the most puzzling of all; a mere pinprick on the map of the Pacific, far to the east of the main group, it boasts hundreds of giant heads, cut from single blocks of dark volcanic rock. Who erected them? And why?

Orthodox history taught then, as it does today, that Polynesia was settled in prehistory by people from Indonesia. The settlement of the Pacific islands was a long process; the great adventure began about 3500 years ago, and it was not until AD 500 that the voyagers reached Easter Island. Norwegian Thor Heyerdahl took a different view. He saw striking similarities between the stone figures of the Pacific and the monoliths which survive from the lost civilisations of South America. Pre-Inca Peruvians, he believed, could have settled the islands from the east.

Certain Polynesian legends speak of a sun-god, Tiki, who brought skills from the islanders' old home beyond the sea. Curiously, there are legends of a god called Kon-Tiki, in South America. He was reportedly driven out of Peru and sailed off with his followers to vanish beyond the western horizon. Heyerdahl believed that the two gods must be one and the same. And he was determined to prove that the long voyage from Peru to Polynesia could be accomplished using the technology known to the ancient South Americans.

Encounter with a whale shark

The natives of Peru had only clumsy balsa rafts for coastal navigation. Assembling his five-man team, Heyerdahl set to work building a 45 ft (14 m) raft modelled on those of ancient times, using balsa logs lashed together with hemp rope. The two masts were cut from mangrove wood and a hut was erected towards the stern, made of split bamboo with banana leaves for roofing. The raft was named *Kon-Tiki* and its big square sail bore the image of the Peruvian god's face.

On April 28, 1947, the raft was towed by tugboat out of the port of Callao in Peru and set adrift in the hope that the wind and currents would carry it out into the open ocean. Sceptics claimed that they would be picked up off the coast in a few days – or would never be seen again.

LIVING HISTORY   *Kon-Tiki* photographed off Callao in Peru, prior to its epic journey. The raft was made using materials and methods known to ancient peoples of South America.

The explorers, however, had no difficulty travelling westwards, for a strong east wind and the powerful Humboldt Current made it hard to steer in any other direction. The distance to be travelled, though, was a daunting 4000 miles (6500 km). The entire vessel was held together without nails or wire, and Heyerdahl worried that the hemp ropes, squeaking incessantly in the tossing sea, might perish. Then again, the porous balsa might become waterlogged and sink beneath the explorers' feet.

But they found that the balsa remained buoyant, and that the wood was too soft to chafe the ropes as Heyerdahl feared. After

FULL SAIL Decked with modern flags, its square sail adorned by the ancient Peruvian sun-god's face, Thor Heyerdahl's balsa raft *Kon-Tiki* breasts the Pacific waves.

the first weeks, the explorers reached calm seas with long swells on the ocean. The cold Humboldt Current gave way to the blue and increasingly warm South Equatorial Current where they found themselves travelling as far as 72 miles (116 km) a day.

Their first real drama came when they found themselves chased by a whale shark, a giant among fish that 'bumped into the steering oar and placed its huge, froglike head, with tiny eyes and a five-foot (1.5 m) mouth, right up against the raft'. The huge creature kept them company for several hours, while the crew stood ready with spears and harpoons. 'The peaceful visit ended when the excited navigator ran his harpoon with all his strength down between his legs and into the cartilaginous head of the monster. During the terrific commotion, the whale shark dived, broke the harpoon,

snapped the rope, and disappeared.' Occasionally, as they sped westwards, the explorers ran into schools of whales, huge, snorting creatures that could have splintered the raft with a single blow of their tails; but they showed no hostility. About 600 miles (966 km) south-west of the Galapagos, they were twice visited by giant sea turtles, while sharks followed them most of the time, offering little trouble and becoming excited only when the mariners cleaned fish, and they scented blood. Nonetheless, the explorers never quite trusted them; in one day they pulled aboard and killed nine sharks, each over 6 ft (1.8 m) long, just to dispose of their menacing company.

As pioneer voyages go, however, much of the expedition of the *Kon-Tiki* proved a lyrical experience. Heyerdahl has written feelingly about the exhilarating nights when

I FELT A VIOLENT BLOW

After travelling for more than a hundred days across the vast Pacific aboard the *Kon-Tiki*, Thor Heyerdahl and his companions found themselves being driven towards the jagged coral reef of Raroia at the mercy of the breakers:

'A sea rose straight up under us and we felt the *Kon-Tiki* being lifted up in the air. The great moment had come; we were riding on the wave-back at breathless speed, our ramshackle craft creaking and groaning as she quivered under us. The excitement made one's blood boil. I remember that, having no other inspiration, I waved my arm and bellowed "hurrah!" at the pitch of my lungs...

'But our elation was soon dampened. A new sea rose high up astern of us like a glittering green glass wall; as we sank down it came rolling after us, and in the same second in which I saw it high above me I felt a violent blow and was submerged under floods of water. I felt the suction through my whole body, with such great strength that I had to strain every single muscle in my frame and think of one thing only – hold on, hold on! I think that in such a desperate situation the arms will be torn off before the brain consents to let go, evident as the outcome is. Then I felt that the mountain of water was passing on and relaxing its devilish grip of my body. When the whole mountain had rushed on, with an ear-splitting roaring and crashing, I saw Knut again hanging on beside me, doubled up into a ball. Seen from behind the great sea was almost flat and grey; as it rushed on it swept just over the ridge of the cabin roof which projected from the water, and there hung the three others, pressed against the cabin roof as the water passed over them.

'We were still afloat.'

the ink-black seas, billowing on all sides, and the twinkling stars formed their entire world. Conventional notions of time lost all meaning – they might as well have been travelling in 1947 BC as AD. Sometimes, for a break, two or three of them would take out a rubber float and watch their craft from a distance. 'In moonlight there was an unbelievable atmosphere around the raft. The huge, wet logs fringed with seaweed, the square contour of the sail, the bushy jungle hut with a petrol lamp astern looked like something cut from a fairy tale rather than from reality.'

Food presented no problem whatsoever. Though the explorers had brought provisions of their own, they could also draw for sustenance on the wealth of fish in the seas around. Sharks and dolphins could be speared or hooked at almost any time, while edible barnacles and seaweeds grew all over the balsa logs and were harvested like garden peas. To cap it all, almost every night, a

dozen or so flying fish, often accompanied by baby squid, flopped onto the deck of their own accord after sailing through the air in schools pursued by dolphins or sharks.

Twice on dark nights, a long snakelike fish with huge eyes jumped right into their sleeping bags inside the bamboo cabin, causing great commotion. This turned out to be *Gempylus*, or snake mackerel, a creature thought to live only at the bottom of the ocean because no one had ever seen it alive before. Previously, it was known only through a couple of skeletons which turned up on South American shores. It was a real curiosity, about 3 ft (1 m) long, slender as an eel, with long sharp teeth that could be folded back into the roof of the mouth to make way for its prey.

Man overboard!

The *Kon-Tiki* bore up to the journey superbly, riding the ocean swell and pressing westwards day by day, along the path of the setting sun. Though the green parrot which was the ship's pet fell victim to high seas on the 60th day, it was only towards the end of the journey that they hit bad storms. With sail down and ropes shrieking, the raft rode the wild seas like a duck. But crewman Herman Watzinger, second-in-command, was swept overboard at one point. As the cry of 'man overboard!' went up, he was glimpsed, briefly, struggling behind the stern and making a grab for the steering oar, but a strong wind pushed the raft ahead and he missed. The situation was desperate, for there was no way of turning the raft around or even of stopping to halt the remorseless westward drift. The crew twice threw out a lifebelt but it blew right back on board. They could see Watzinger swimming frantically to keep up with the raft but the distance increased with each gust of wind.

Suddenly, with a line in one hand, fellow crewman Knut Haugland plunged headfirst into the sea and swam towards his struggling companion. Slowly, the two men managed to work their way towards one another. About 90 ft (27 m) behind the raft, they joined hands and the four men on board pulled them back to safety.

At the end of the third month, Polynesian frigate birds

and boobies began to visit their raft, and the explorers saw a rising cumulo-nimbus cloud that hinted at an island, lying hidden beyond the western horizon. Excitedly, they steered for the cloud as best they could and eventually saw a blue haze of land outlined against the sky. But the wind and current kept driving them westwards and would not permit them to steer towards it. Ironically, they had covered 4000 miles (6400 km) of ocean but could not sail the remaining four or so miles in the direction they wanted to go. Anxiously they watched as the little speck of land – the first they had seen for 12 weeks – slid away on their port stern, carrying with it faint aromas of verdant tropical foliage and smoky native huts.

Getting inshore was in fact to prove the hardest problem that Heyerdahl faced. On the 97th day another island loomed up straight ahead and Polynesians in outrigger canoes swarmed out to join them. The explorers, nevertheless, found themselves barred from struggling through to its palm-clad beaches by a strong current and submerged reef. As night engulfed the island, natives onshore lit a great camp fire to help guide them in; but a rising wind caught the

TRAVELLER'S TALE The *Kon-Tiki* journey became the subject of a number of popular books; this one was by Erik Hesselberg, one of the crew members.

raft in its grip and carried it to the open sea. The Polynesian canoeists returned to their vessels and headed back home. With the glare of the fire dwindling, *Kon-Tiki* sped westwards into the heart of the Tuamotu, or Dangerous Archipelago.

Into the Inferno

As dawn broke on the crew's 101st morning at sea, the watchman at the masthead sighted a surf-battered reef that stretched across the whole horizon ahead. This was the notorious 20 mile (32 km) reef of Raroia Atoll and the *Kon-Tiki* was surging directly into it. As the seething inferno loomed closer, the explorers had just three hours to prepare for the worst. While the sail was lowered, everything of value was lashed down in the cabin in watertight containers, and the crew cut off all ropes holding the centreboards in position, pulling them up to get as shallow a draught as possible. Then, with the sharp corals in mind, the explorers put their shoes on for the first time in 100 days and focused their thoughts on one single order: hold on to the raft, whatever happened.

LIVING HISTORY Thor Heyerdahl devoted his life to demonstrating that the oceans need not be thought of as obstacles to ancient travel; instead, they offered open roads.

As the balsa logs hit the reef, avalanches of water bore down on them, snapping the hardwood mast like a match, flattening the hut, ripping up the deck and splintering the steering oar. Grasped by the savage ocean, the explorers were hurled in, hauled out, mauled and hurled in again until, with their strength giving way, they felt a great swell lift *Kon-Tiki* high up onto the crest of the reef and waves of diminishing force push them closer to shore. At last they were able to jump off the debris of the raft and wade towards the safety of a small, uninhabited island. 'Never,' Heyerdahl was to write, 'did any tiny piece of land embody paradise so perfectly to me as this verdant, palm-clad isle with its white and shiny beach facing a crystal-clear lagoon, calm as green glass.'

A week later, they were found by Polynesians from another island who had seen their camp fire and some drift wreckage of their craft. The natives took the explorers to their village where plaited wreaths of flowers were placed around their necks, and a welcome feast began with hula songs around tables loaded with sucking pigs, roast ducks, lobsters, breadfruit and papaya. Celebrations went on for two weeks before a French government schooner arrived to pick them up. Meanwhile, the battered *Kon-Tiki* was towed to Tahiti and eventually transported to the Norwegian Museum of Navigation in Oslo.

Heyerdahl had proved that ancient Peruvians could have made contact with prehistoric Polynesia. But he had not furnished proof that they actually did. For all the publicity that his achievement received, as well as the excitements and ordeals of the trip, academic historians remained unconvinced. A typical comment came from Sir Peter Buck, the leading authority on Polynesia. 'A nice enough adventure,' he said of the voyage, 'but you don't expect anyone to call that a scientific expedition. Now do you?'

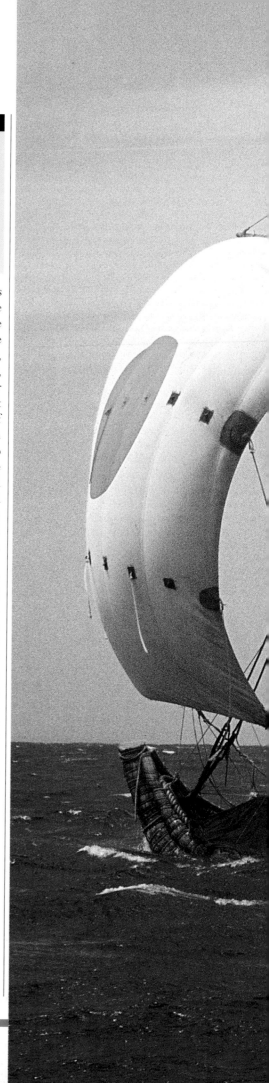

THE *RA* EXPEDITIONS

When the Spanish conquistadores explored the Americas, they found primitive food-gathering peoples occupying the northern and southern extremities of the New World. But across a broad band in the middle lived the much more grand and elaborate civilisations of the Aztecs, Incas and Mayans who boasted pyramids and monumental architecture. Did these cultures arise in isolation? Or did the peoples of the central belt have some contact with the Old World civilisations – notably, with the pyramid-builders of Egypt?

Thor Heyerdahl believed it possible; on wall paintings in Egypt's Valley of the Kings, he had seen reed boats which resembled others on ceramic pots in northern Peru. To find out whether such craft could withstand the rigours of ocean travel, he built a papyrus raft similar to ancient Egyptian vessels. Two hundred and eighty thousand reeds, each about 10 ft (3 m) long, were incorporated into the finished vessel which had a square sail made of heavy Egyptian cloth. The craft was named *Ra*, after the ancient Egyptian sun god, and in 1969 the Norwegian explorer set sail from Morocco in an attempt to cross the Atlantic. After travelling 3100 miles (5000 km), he ran into difficulties during storms. However, the following year in the shorter, more seaworthy *Ra II*, he landed successfully on Barbados after a 57 day voyage.

REED BOATS The inset picture (right) shows helpers hauling the ill-fated papyrus raft *Ra* to the Nile in 1969. Main picture: *Ra II* arrives in Barbados in 1970, proving that transatlantic travel was feasible for the seamen of ancient Egypt.

THE MOUTHS OF HELL

IN THE NAME OF SCIENCE, HAROUN TAZIEFF SPENT A LIFETIME EXPLORING FIERY VOLCANO CRATERS

Throughout history, volcanoes have terrified observers, but the physics and chemistry of eruptions were little understood until the 20th century when a handful of scientists made intrepid crater descents.

Probably the best known 20th-century volcanologist was Haroun Tazieff. Born in Warsaw in 1914, he was educated in Belgium and fought with the Resistance during the Second World War. In 1948, while performing a geological survey in the Belgian Congo (now the Democratic Republic of Congo), he explored the Nyiragongo volcano which rises to 11 400 ft (3470 m) in the Virunga range north of the town of Goma. He discovered a boiling lava lake 650 ft (200 m) below the crater rim, and in subsequent trips to the volcano, took seismographic readings and gathered gas samples from within the glowing cauldron.

Tazieff was drawn to the mountain as if to a magnet – altogether he made 26 expeditions to Nyiragongo between 1958 and 1974.

Tazieff also helped to explore volcanoes all over the world, undersea as well as on land, and in the 1970s made important studies of Mount Erebus in Antarctica. His descriptive powers, revealed in about 20 books on volcanoes, matched his adventurous spirit. In *Craters of Fire* (1952), he reported on the sulphur-choked crater of Kituro, and on how dramatically the levels of the lurid, fiery lake rose and fell, following the weird palpitations of the volcanic abyss. 'I was astonished. Two days previously the red lava had been boiling up to the level of the gigantic lip; now the funnel seemed to be empty. All that incandescent magma had disappeared, drawn back into the depths by the reflux of some mysterious ebb and flow, a sort of breathing.'

BREATHING FIRE Red-hot lava from the Nyiragongo volcano, a magnet for Polish-born geologist Haroun Tazieff, shown here wearing breathing apparatus essential to his survival.

Ringed by the scorching crater walls, Tazieff found himself bombarded that day by projectiles flung up from the base – clots of magma that sped, whistling, through the air, heralded by a dry, clacking sound. It was like being under artillery fire. All around, bombs crashed down, whizzing at his face so that he

A SLEEPING GIANT

Fearsome as it appeared, the Nyiragongo crater which Tazieff explored remained fairly stable for decades. In 1973, equipped with gas masks and fireproof suits, French volcanologists Maurice and Katia Krafft spent an entire week making scientific studies on the shore of its lava lake. Four years later, however, the volcano exploded with awesome ferocity and waves of molten lava heated to 1000°C (1832°F) buried villages in the area around.

had to leap to dodge them. Still, he did not omit to take measurements, plunging the long spike of a steel thermometer into the shimmering screes: at a depth of 6 in (15 cm) the temperature was 220°C (428°F).

On another expedition to measure, photograph and film the eruption of La Sciara near San Vincenzo in Italy, he and his colleagues found themselves caught at night in an avalanche. Amid dazzling red and yellow flows of molten magma, a huge, pale boulder, the size of a village house, crashed past only five paces away from them. When dawn broke on the mountain slopes, they saw a mule coming down unsteadily out of the mists that enveloped the summit. It carried the slumped figure of a rider. 'Something about the man's attitude made us think there was something wrong…In the same moment we all got up and ran to meet him. He literally fell into our arms. It was the film director's right-hand man, General Muratori. Livid, he just managed to gasp out: "Fumes – air!" There was a rattle in his throat.'

It transpired that the general had been overwhelmed by gases at the summit. They tried laying him flat, then sitting him up and offering him tea, but he only struggled more for breath. They decided that they must get him down the mountain as quickly as possible, and six of them carried him off at top speed. However, 200 yd (180 m) farther down General Muratori, having been slowly asphyxiated, died in Tazieff's arms.

FRANCE'S CAVEMAN

MICHEL SIFFRE HAS VENTURED DEEP INTO THE
THE EARTH TO EXPLORE CAVERNS AND STREAMS

Cave-dwellers in prehistoric Europe knew much about the subterranean world. The limestone cliffs of south-west France and north-west Spain, in particular, are riddled with painted caverns that bear witness to human habitation. Realistic images of bulls, horses, bison, reindeer and other animals were sketched in charcoal, iron oxide and red ochre with twigs and feather brushes; in 1940 four boys exploring in the Dordogne stumbled on the caves at Lascaux, with their 17 000-year-old paintings which are now celebrated as the world's finest examples of Stone Age art.

Speleology, the art of exploring caves, is as much a hobby as a science, but it forms a branch of discovery that has exploded in the 20th century. And among the enthusiasts, none is more respected than France's Michel Siffre. He made his name in 1962 when he went underground for two months to investigate a massive subterranean glacier in the Scarasson chasm near Nice. Siffre's descent taught researchers much about physiological reactions to prolonged exposure to darkness and silence. The explorer endured dizziness and depression, as well as profound disorientation with regard to time: when he was brought back to the surface on

September 14, he believed it was August 20. Such experiments in solitary survival were of great interest to physicians trying to assess the effects on humans of long-term isolation in space. Siffre was pursuing his subterranean career during the boom time in aerospatial research; the Scarasson descent was accomplished in the same year that John Glenn was launched from Cape Canaveral to become the first American to orbit the Earth. In February 1972, sponsored by the American space agency NASA, Siffre began a seven-month stint in Midnight Cave in the United States. During sleep, his brain waves and heartbeat were recorded by electrodes; during waking hours, he made scientific observations and undertook an assortment of tests to determine the psychological and physiological effects of the ordeal. When at last, on August 10, he returned to the surface, his vision was impaired and he was

COMING UP Michel Siffre is brought back to the surface, after spending two months in a subterranean cave in south-eastern France, 1962.

in a state of such depression that he was unable to resume his everyday life for some time. Such ordeals take their toll. The feelings of overwhelming depression resulting from long solitary stays underground are not uncommon: they have been known to drive some to suicide.

Siffre recovered from his experiment, and went on to investigate caverns in Central America. In 1975 he led a team into caves in the Poptun region of Guatemala, where they discovered underground streams as well as remains of ancient wall carvings and fragments of Mayan pottery. In later expeditions to the caves of the Peten region, Guatemala's most northerly département, the team found a dozen carved heads from the time of the Olmecs, the ancient American people who evolved the first known Central American civilisation from about 1200 BC.

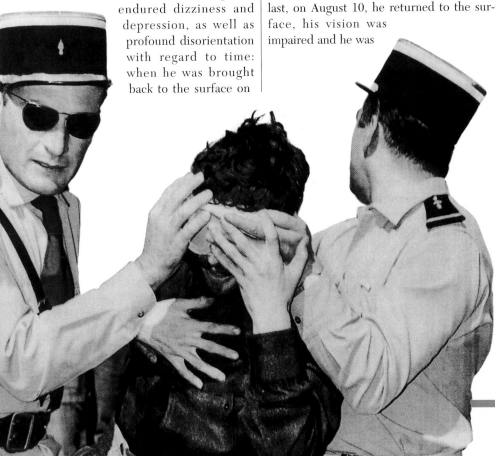

ORDEAL'S END After being hauled to the surface at the end of his 1962 sojourn underground, Michel Siffre had to wear blinkers to protect his eyes from the light.

THE ADVENTURE OF THE *BRENDAN*

COULD AN IRISH MONK HAVE SAILED THE ATLANTIC NEARLY 1000 YEARS BEFORE COLUMBUS?

Not long after leaving the jagged Atlantic shores of the Faroes, rocking in their frail leather craft, explorer Tim Severin and his four companions saw the thin line of a black fin rise above the waves. Then others lifted from the sea. Before long the voyagers detected a pack of six killer whales strung out in classic hunting pattern, line abreast, following the bull, the leader of the group. Spanish fishermen call these creatures *lobo del mar*, the wolf of the sea, because they hunt with the same organised efficiency and because of their ferocious teeth. The stomach of one killer whale,

LEATHER SAILBOAT
The *Brendan* was made of oxhide, using the techniques known to Ireland's mariner monks in the Dark Ages.

Severin had read, yielded no fewer than 13 seals. Would the craft's leather skin cause her to be mistaken for animal prey? The crew watched, helpless, as the killers approached, diving beneath the surface then rising again, puffing spray. The last time the bull rose, he was just 60 ft (18 m) away.

'We heard the full hiss of the creature's nostrils,' Severin wrote, 'and watched the small cloud of mist which drifted on the boat so we could actually smell the animal's stale air. Then the great back dipped. There was a flash of the black-and-white flanks where the water sucked back from the massive body pushing through the sea; and the ripples came across and lapped gently against the leather hull. The killer whale had slid right under the boat, all eight or ten tons of him, curious, intelligent, and completely in control. There was nothing we could do . . . We held our breath, absolutely silent, for what seemed like an age. Whoosh! The great black fin came sliding up out of the water on the opposite side of *Brendan*, the great lungs emptied, and the killer whale began turning ponderously back to his pack.' Severin and his companions also let out their breath. It seemed that they had been inspected and found wanting – they were safe for the time being. But their journey had only just begun.

Severin's craft was called *Brendan* after a 6th-century Irish missionary, Saint Brendan. Latin texts dating back to at least AD 800 described how he and a party of monks had sailed to a land far across the ocean in a boat made of oxhides. If this land was America, Saint Brendan must have reached it almost 1000 years before Christopher Columbus and 400 years before Leif Eriksson led his Vikings to the New World. But was the journey possible in a leather boat? Severin believed it was and, like Thor Heyerdahl before him, determined to test his theory by

20TH-CENTURY ADVENTURER

Oxford-educated Tim Severin is known for other voyages besides the *Brendan* adventure. He also sailed the Pacific on a bamboo raft to test the theory that Asian sailors reached America some 2000 years ago. On his Sinbad voyage, Severin captained an Arab sailing ship from Muscat to China; on his Ulysses voyage, he explored the seascapes of Homer's *Odyssey*; and on the Jason voyage, he steered a replica of a Bronze Age Grecian galley to seek out the land of the Golden Fleece.

building and sailing a suitable vessel himself. Double-masted with oars and rudder, it was constructed according to the exact methods used by the seafaring Irish monks of the Dark Ages. The ashwood frame was covered with a skin of 49 oxhides stitched with hand-rolled flaxen thread. For waterproofing, joints were smeared with fats and greases known in early medieval times: tallow, beeswax, fish oil and wool grease.

The craft set out on May 17, 1976, from Brandon Creek on the west coast of Ireland and first sailed via the Hebrides and Faroes to Iceland where they landed, near Reykjavik, on July 15.

They overwintered there, knowing that the most difficult and dangerous stage of the voyage lay ahead. On May 7, 1977, they set sail again. Heading westwards for Greenland, they met with dark, overcast skies and steady drizzle, where a falling barometer and sullen swell from the south-east warned that worse was on its way.

Before long they were in the grip of strong winds that left them struggling in circles for days without making any progress. Severin and his crew were halfway between Iceland and Greenland, with waves coming upon them as 'great marching hills of water'.

WESTWARD HO! Skipper Tim Severin sets the pace as the *Brendan* heads for America. Left: Severin and his wife Dorothy display a model of their oxhide boat at a press conference held in London prior to setting sail.

Severin describes how, heaped up by the wind, the Atlantic rollers lifted them skywards then tugged them down into troughs where the grey-blue water closed in about them. 'Each time the boat heeled to the pressure of the wind, the leading edge of the leeboard dipped into the sea and, like a ploughshare, carved a great slice of water from the ocean.' The near-freezing sea poured into the bilges and swirled above the level of the floorboards, slowing progress and prompting real fears of sinking. But by pumping out water and stretching a protective apron of oxhide over the hull, they managed to weather the storm. Towards the end of May, they were struggling towards Greenland's coast, where, negotiating perilous ice floes, they turned south. The *Brendan* touched land in America at 8 pm on June 26, 1977, at Peckford Island, Newfoundland. Severin had demonstrated that, with pre-medieval technology of oxhide and ashwood, a voyage to the New World was possible.

AMONG THE ICE FLOES

In June 1977, as the oxhide vessel *Brendan* approached the New World, the crew ran into hazardous pack ice:

'A truly awesome sight loomed up out of the dark just downwind of us – the white and serrated edge of a massive floe, perhaps the dying shard of an iceberg, twice the size of *Brendan*, and glinting with malice. This apparition was rolling and wallowing like some enormous log. Its powerful, squat shape had one great bluff end which was pointing like a battering ram straight at *Brendan*, and it was rocking backward and forward with ponderous certainty to deliver a blow of perhaps a hundred tons or so at the fragile leather...Crack! Thump! The whole boat shook as if she had struck a reef...The next impact was different. This time the ice floe rocked away from *Brendan* as the swell passed beneath us. *Brendan* swung over a broad spur of a wave-cut ledge projecting from the floe. The spur rose under us, caught *Brendan* with a grating sound, and began to lift and tip the boat. "We're going to be flipped over like a fried egg," I thought, as *Brendan* heeled and heeled. Then, with another grating sound of leather on ice, *Brendan* slid sideways off the ice spur and dropped back into the water.'

ROWING THE OCEANS

OARSMEN HAVE ACHIEVED ASTONISHING FEATS IN THE 20TH CENTURY, CROSSING BOTH THE ATLANTIC AND PACIFIC OCEANS ON SOLO VOYAGES

Both Thor Heyerdahl and Tim Severin aimed to prove that the world's oceans were not necessarily barriers to travel in ancient times: to historic seafaring peoples they offered highways that were in many ways safer than long-distance overland routes. The achievements of lone oarsmen in the 20th century have reinforced this notion. Frail as it was, the *Brendan* at least had the benefit of sailpower as well as a five-man crew, but in 1969 a new seafaring record was set when Britain's John Fairfax became the first man to row solo across the Atlantic. He journeyed from Las Palmas in the Canary Islands to Fort Lauderdale in Florida in 180 days. A swifter west-east crossing was made later the same year by Irishman Tom McClean, who set out from St John's, Newfoundland, and arrived at Blacksod Bay, County Mayo, 71 days later.

An even more remarkable feat was achieved in 1983 when another British oarsman, Peter Bird, became the first person to row solo across the South Pacific. He set out from San Francisco on August 23, 1982 and reached Australia 294 days later; the distance was an astonishing 9000 miles (14 480 km).

Bird's story had an unhappy sequel, however. In 1996, while attempting to row across the North Pacific, the 49-year-old adventurer vanished at sea. In June, his capsized boat *Sector II* was found floating adrift on the Pacific waves and his partially illegible logbook, recovered from the vessel, helped to reconstruct his likely fate. The last entries indicate that he had weathered some gales, but was in optimistic mood, with strong south-west winds carrying him forwards, when disaster struck. 'It's good that I am heading in the right direction for once and long may it last.

TRAGIC LOSS Peter Bird photographed in happy mood in Vladivostok in June 1992. Bird disappeared four years later while attempting to row solo across the North Pacific.

Although the gale began … in the south, it's passed to the west behind me, as it were. This has produced the SW winds.'

Several 10 ft (3 m) logs were found in the ocean near the lone oarsman's stricken boat, and it is thought that one of them may have wrecked it by staving in the aft bulkhead as she battled through 30 ft (9 m) waves. It may also have left Bird unconscious, with no chance to put on his survival suit.

LONG HAUL In 1969, Britain's John Fairfax became the first person to row solo across the Atlantic Ocean.

ON GOSSAMER WINGS

AN ALTERNATIVE VERSION OF BLÉRIOT'S FEAT, A MANPOWERED AIRCRAFT FLIES THE CHANNEL

In an age of satellite technology and supersonic flight, it might seem that there is not much left to achieve in the Earth's airways. But a new challenge has arisen. Concerns about environmental pollution have sparked experiments with unorthodox forms of transport that include the fuel-free, manpowered aircraft. Could humans swim through the air as freely as Cousteau's flippered aquanauts glide through the sea? In the prehistory of

---

SOLAR-POWERED FLIGHT

Following his triumph with *Gossamer Albatross*, Dr Paul MacCready devised a new pedal aircraft. The wing surfaces of *Solar Challenger*, as it was called, contained solar cells to generate electricity, and the extra speed meant that it did not need as big a wingspan as its predecessors. In 1981 pilot Stephen Ptacek flew 229 miles (368 km) from Pontoise, north of Paris, to Manston in Kent, southern England, at an average speed of 42.5 mph (68.6 km/h).

---

aviation, many a hapless inventor plunged to his death flapping cumbersome, artificial wings. Modern hang-gliders and microlights do, however, provide something of the exhilaration that the pioneers sought, and true, manpowered flight has also become a reality.

A key stimulus for development was a prize offered in 1960 by British industrialist Henry Kremer for any manpowered aircraft that could fly a figure-of-eight course around two pylons placed half a mile (1 km) apart.

EARLY MISHAP During Allen's first cross-Channel attempt in June 1979, the undercarriage broke.

To keep up with inflation the prize money was regularly updated, but despite dozens of competitors, for years no one could come up with a successful invention. Then in 1977, with the prize standing at £50 000, an American team headed by an aerodynamics engineer, Dr Paul MacCready of California, brought forward their *Gossamer Condor*. Its secret was its one huge wing, built as light as possible. Braced by fine steel cable and covered in Mylar film, the aircraft was made of balsa tubing, corrugated cardboard and foam plastics, and propeller-driven by pedalling as if on a bicycle. MacCready's team won the prize, and to keep interest up Kremer then offered a new reward – this time of £100 000 – for the first manpowered flight across the English Channel.

The see-through flying machine

MacCready's designers set to work again and came up with a refined version of their prize-winning pedal aircraft. *Gossamer Albatross*, as the new creation was called, had a wing and fuselage frame of plastic tubes reinforced with hollow carbon fibre. The computer-designed propellor was also carbon fibre, while the craft's skin was of polyester film so fine that, like a dragonfly's wing, it was virtually transparent. The

aircraft had a wingspan of 93 ft (28 m) – greater than many an airliner – yet even with its pilot it weighed only 215 lb (98 kg).

On June 12, 1979, American racing cyclist Bryan Allen took off from Folkestone on the south coast of England and pedalled through headwinds over the English Channel. Allen was hardly soaring – his average altitude was just 2½ ft (76 cm) above the waves – but he was in the air. The flight took just under three hours and ended with a successful landing at Cap Gris-Nez in the north of France. Once again MacCready's team carried off the prize.

SECOND ATTEMPT The damaged undercarriage of his craft repaired, Allen makes the first manpowered flight across the Channel.

TRANSGLOBE EXPLORER

BRAVING DESERT AND ICE, RANULPH FIENNES CIRCUMNAVIGATED THE WORLD VIA BOTH POLES

When orthodox explorers travel around the world they do so horizontally, that is, following routes more or less parallel to the Equator. Ranulph Fiennes was different; he proposed a transglobe expedition that would take a vertical approach, encompassing the great ice caps of the Arctic and the Antarctic. It was a bold concept, for the only journey ever made that crossed Antarctica, headed by Sir Vivian Fuchs in the late 1950s, had by itself taken two years and cost £1 million. And the only solo crossing of the Arctic had been Wally Herbert's perilous 16 month slog in 1968. Then, of course, there was the rest of the world journey to consider.

Nonetheless, after months of study in geographical libraries, Fiennes believed that the expedition was feasible and sketched a route which more or less adhered to the Greenwich meridian, passing across Africa and the South Atlantic to the Antarctic ice cap, then 'up the other side' via the Pacific to North America and the Arctic. It took him a long time to fix up sponsorship but at last, on September 2, 1979, the Transglobe Expedition set off from London with two Land Rovers, a Range Rover and three trailers.

Desert storms, polar ice

It did not seem to bode well for the explorers when one of the trailer wheels came off in London's Parliament Square. The team persevered, however, driving down through France and Spain and crossing the Mediterranean to Algiers. The first ordeals began as they hit the Sahara. For days the explorers edged south over featureless wastes where dust storms raged and vehicles sank into the soft, loose sand of the wadis. 'The wind stirred sandstorms all night which lashed our tents like driven sleet,' Fiennes wrote. Camel skeletons lay about the trail as they pushed on beyond the Sahara to Timbuktu. Through the swamps and jungles of Mali and the Ivory Coast, they continued to the port of Abidjan where their vessel *Benjamin Bowring* was waiting. Two expedition members were recovering from malaria and a third was still feverish and vomiting intermittently as they left Africa behind them and ventured south across the Equator.

'Sperm whales were seen and flying fish died on the hot decks', Fiennes noted. The

TOP OF THE WORLD   Fiennes on Ellesmere Island in the Canadian Arctic. From here he and his companion, Charlie Burton, would launch their assault on the North Pole.

ship docked at Cape Town on December 8, then turned south for the pack ice.

By January 4, 1980, they had entered coastal waters under the high cliffs of Antarctica. Snow mitts, goggles and parkas now became the order of the day. With temperatures at –50°C (–58°F), Fiennes and two of his party, Oliver Shepard and Charlie Burton, set out for the South Pole. For the 2200 mile (3540 km) journey across the continent, they used motorised toboggans known as skidoos. These offered a boneshaking, zig-zag ride over the interior's ribbed ice hummocks. Fuel supplies were dropped by aircraft, but stocks were limited and detours around ice ridges used up vital reserves. With crevasses offering additional hazards, the trio had to keep their concentration at all times. The weather was deteriorating, and they twice struck camp in total whiteout conditions.

On December 15, however, the three-man team reached the metal dome that marked the American base at the South Pole. The scene was very different from that which had greeted Amundsen and Scott 69 years before. The dome protected eight

THAT SINKING FEELING   Fiennes' Range Rover gets stuck in the sand near Gundan, Niger. The trip was beset with difficulties.

POLES AND PEAKS

MANY CHALLENGING AND INGENIOUS WAYS OF CONQUERING THE WORLD'S MOUNTAINS AND ICE CAPS HAVE BEEN DEVISED BY MODERN ADVENTURERS

A fter the conquest of the North and South Poles in the early part of the century, there remained many more challenges for would-be record-breakers. The first overland crossing of Antarctica was achieved by Dr (later Sir) Vivian Fuchs at the head of the British Commonwealth Trans-Antarctic Expedition of 1955-8. The explorers used aircraft for supply and large yellow track vehicles known as 'Sno-cats', but the going was slow. Tractors often got stuck in the snow, so that dog teams had to be sent ahead to find a safe route for them. Furthermore, Fuchs's party were taking seismic soundings to discover what lay beneath the Antarctic ice cap. Much speedier progress was made by a New Zealand team headed by Sir Edmund Hillary, who started from McMurdo Sound on the other side of the continent. The two parties met at the South Pole in January 1958.

In 1967-9, using dogs, Wally Herbert made the first surface crossing of the frozen Arctic Ocean via the North Pole. But for some bold spirits, the real challenge was to reach farthest north entirely alone and unaided. Between 1984 and 1990, Ranulph Fiennes made several unsuccessful attempts to man-haul to the North Pole unsupported. The feat was finally achieved in April 1994 when Borg Ousland, a Norwegian, reached the spot on skis, after travelling up to 18¹/₂ miles

NEW METHODS Dr Vivian Fuchs and his Commonwealth team crossed Antarctica in 1955-8, using aircraft support and mechanised Sno-cats, which often got stuck (above). Borg Ousland, in contrast, walked to the North Pole alone, without assistance, in 1994.

(30 km) a day for 52 days, pulling a 265 lb (120 kg) sled. He slept in a tent at temperatures down to –40°C (–40°F) and on arrival sent a pre-coded message via satellite – 'Expedition ended. Want pick-up' – to indicate that his record-breaking 620 mile (1000 km) journey was over.

For mountaineers too, the way that a feat is achieved has become a key consideration. In August 1980 Reinhold Messner, a 35-year-old Italian climber, achieved the first solo ascent of Mount Everest, reaching the summit without oxygen equipment. By 1986 Messner had climbed all 14 of the world's peaks over 26 250 ft (8000 m) – and all entirely without oxygen.

prefabricated and centrally heated huts, where a dozen scientists and six or seven administrators lived and worked. The explorers had time to warm up and recuperate before pressing on eight days later.

'Fear sits in your stomach'

From the bottom end of the Earth the trio now travelled north over huge bridged crevasses where, Fiennes wrote, they learnt that sweat comes easily even at subzero tem-

BLIZZARD ZONE McMurdo Sound overlooked by Mount Erebus (above). The Transglobe explorers reached this area in July 1981, having previously attained the South Pole. Inset: Fiennes putting up his tent.

peratures, and 'fear sits in your stomach and creeps down your back'. At a valley leading down to the Scott Glacier, they faced a specially hair-raising descent. But they made good speed on this leg of their journey, sometimes

travelling as much as 100 miles (160 km) a day, and by January 11, 1981, they had crossed Antarctica and reached the Scott Base, in the shadow of Mount Erebus.

Reunited with the main party aboard the *Benjamin Bowring*, the explorers slid out between the ice floes to strains of 'Land of Hope and Glory' from the ship's loudspeakers. The long Pacific crossing was largely

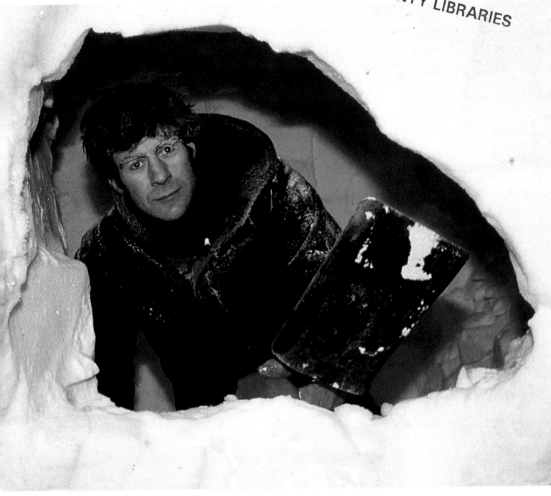

COLD COMFORT Fiennes digging a snow hut. *The New York Times* called his Transglobe endeavour the 'world's last great adventure'.

store hut at Alert; much of their scientific equipment, reserve skidoos, spare parts and rations were destroyed. 'Polar Expedition in Flames', screamed the newspapers back home, and it was speculated that the entire trip must now be called off. Despite all difficulties, however, the two men managed to struggle on to the North Pole, arriving there on April 10, 1982. With the pack ice loosening around them, they then had to follow a tortuous route south through sludge fields. Once, stranded on an ice floe, they were attacked by a polar bear which they only drove off by shooting at it with a parachute illuminating flare. When at last they saw the approaching masts of the *Benjamin Bowring*, their relief was indescribable.

The return was by way of the Greenland Sea and North Sea. On August 29, HRH Prince Charles joined the ship on the River Thames as she made her way back home to Greenwich – almost three years to the day since they had set out.

WORLD TRAVELLER Fiennes' vessel, the 30-year-old *Benjamin Bowring*, photographed at Greenwich. Its volunteer crew came from many countries and backgrounds.

uneventful for the expedition was following well-travelled seaways and it was not until Alaska that they met difficulties again.

Fewer than a dozen expeditions had ever successfully navigated the Northwest Passage in either direction, because of the ice which grips the narrow coastal sea lane for most of the year. The team sent the

AROUND THE UNDERWORLD

Remarkable round-the-world expeditions in the modern age have included the voyage of USS *Triton*. In 1960, captained by Edward L. Beach, this American nuclear submarine became the first vessel to circumnavigate the world under water – a 36 300 mile (58 406 km) journey which the 182 man crew accomplished in 84 days and 19 hours.

Benjamin Bowring back to Vancouver and travelled up the Yukon River in rubber boats. From Tuktoyaktuk they negotiated the Passage aboard a little Boston whaler, passing through channels which were sometimes scarcely wider than the boat's own width. Through the maze of shoals, rock islets and ice-choked sandbars, the whaler picked its

way, sometimes lashed by storm waves, sometimes wreathed in clammy mist or freezing fog. Then came a long trek on snowshoes over the Ellesmere ice cap to a group of four little huts, clinging to the edge of the frozen Arctic Sea. Alert, as the settlement is called, is the northernmost habitation on Earth. From this desolate outpost, muffled up in their sledging gear, Fiennes and Charlie Burton set out on heavily laden skidoos to conquer the North Pole.

Attack by a polar bear

As in the Antarctic, they were supported by food and fuel caches dropped by aircraft. Nonetheless, with thin ice and floes breaking up in abnormally warm conditions, they experienced many moments of alarm. To make matters worse, a fire devastated the explorers'

TIMECHART

1900

Aurel Stein embarks on his first expedition to explore ancient sites near the city of Khotan in western China.

Norway's **Carstens Borchgrevink** investigates Newnes Land and the Ross Ice Shelf in Antarctica.

While extending the telegraph network, Brazilian **Candido Rondon** opens up new territory in Brazil, Bolivia and Paraguay (1900-6).

Mongolian Russian G.T. Tsybikov enters **Tibet's Forbidden City** of Lhasa with a pilgrim caravan.

Italy's **Duke of the Abruzzi** explores the Arctic Ocean (1900-1).

African explorer **Mary Kingsley** dies of typhus at Simonstown near Cape Town.

The first trial flight by a **Zeppelin** balloon is made.

1901

Brazilian aeronaut **Alberto Santos-Dumont** makes his prize-winning balloon flight around the Eiffel Tower in Paris.

Missionary James Chalmers is killed and eaten by **cannibals** on Goaribari island, New Guinea.

French General François Laperrine is appointed **commander of the oases**, peacemaking in the Sahara.

East African Railway is completed.

1902

Robert E. Peary makes his first attempt to reach the North Pole, but is forced back by blizzards after only 82 miles (132 km).

Robert Scott begins his first Antarctic expedition (ends 1904), exploring the giant Ross Ice Shelf.

Danish ethnologist Knud Rasmussen studies **Inuit culture** in Greenland.

Plant-hunter E.H. Wilson brings back the **handkerchief tree** (*Davidia involucrata*) from the mountains of south-western China.

J.M. Bacon flies across the Irish Sea in a balloon.

1903

Sir Francis **Younghusband** launches the British expedition to Lhasa (1903-5).

Plant-hunter **George Forrest** sets out on his first expedition, collecting for Arthur Kilpin Bulley in Yunnan, China.

INTO TIBET Younghusband's troops make their way to Lhasa, Tibet's Forbidden City, in 1903.

Captain **Eugene Lenfant** leads a French party from the Niger basin to the Chad basin.

The first **automobile expedition** travels across the United States, from San Francisco to New York.

The **first successful flights** in heavier-than-air machines are made by the Wright Brothers, Wilbur and Orville, near Kitty Hawk, North Carolina. Their craft was powered by a homemade petrol engine.

ROUGH RIDER Swedish adventurer Sven Hedin, photographed with a prize Kirghiz camel.

1904

Exploring in the Arctic, **Roald Amundsen** discovers that the North Magnetic Pole has moved 30 miles (48 km) from the spot where it had been charted in 1831.

Adventuress **Isabelle Eberhardt** drowns in the Sahara.

1905

Germany's **Wilhelm Filchner** explores in China.

Gertrude Bell makes her first extended trip to the Middle East.

Italian explorer **Pierre Savorgnan de Brazza** dies of dysentery at Dakar.

1906

The Duke of the Abruzzi ascends the **Ruwenzori**, East Africa's 'Mountains of the Moon'.

Robert Peary makes his second attempt on the North Pole, getting to within 174 miles (280 km) of his destination before being forced back.

Fanny Bullock Workman climbs **Pinnacle Peak** in the Himalayas.

The Swedish explorer **Sven Hedin** explores unmapped territory in Tibet.

Percy Fawcett surveys the boundary between Bolivia, Peru and Brazil.

Roald Amundsen completes his navigation of the **Northwest Passage** (begun 1903).

Frederick Cook fraudulently claims the conquest of Mount McKinley, the highest peak in North America.

1907

Aurel Stein explores China's **Caves of the Thousand Buddhas**.

France's **Jacques Bacot** explores the valleys of the Yangtze, Mekong and Irrawaddy rivers.

American **A. Hamilton Rice** begins exploring the Amazon basin.

The Dutch administration begins mapping the **New Guinea** interior.

Italy's Prince Borghese wins the **Peking-Paris** motor race.

PIONEERS Cheering crowds salute Prince Borghese, victor in the Peking-Paris motor race. Background picture: The Wright Brothers at Kitty Hawk, North Carolina, in 1903.

1908

Frederick Cook makes an assault on the North Pole; his claims of conquest are later discredited.

Annie Smith Peck climbs **Huascarán** in the Peruvian Andes, wearing an 'Eskimo suit' borrowed from the Museum of Natural History.

Aurel Stein loses the toes of one foot to frostbite while exploring the **Kun Lun** mountains in central Asia.

1909

Robert Peary and Matthew Henson reputedly reach the **North Pole**, in company with four Inuit: Coqeeh, Ootah, Eginwah and Seegloo.

Ernest Shackleton gets to within 100 miles (160 km) of the **South Pole**; other members of his expedition reach the South Magnetic Pole.

Candido Rondon explores the forests of the **Mato Grosso** in Brazil and discovers the so-called River of Doubt, previously unknown to mapmakers.

Frenchman **Louis Blériot** flies across the English Channel.

1910

Percy Fawcett begins mapping the **Peru-Brazil** border.

William Taylor and Peter Anderson climb the lesser (north) peak of **Mount McKinley** in Alaska.

E.H. Wilson discovers **Regal Lily** (*Lilium regale*) in a remote valley on the Chinese-Tibetan border.

1911

Roald Amundsen and four companions become the first men to reach the **South Pole**.

Hiram Bingham discovers the lost Inca city of **Machu Picchu** in the Andes.

C.P. Rodgers makes the first **transcontinental aircraft flight**, from New York to Pasadena.

A motor car is driven to the summit of **Ben Nevis**, the highest mountain in Britain.

1912

Captain Scott and his party reach the South Pole but die on the return.

Returning to the Machu Picchu region, **Hiram Bingham** clears ruins and finds new Inca sites (1912-15).

German **Wilhelm Filchner** explores the Luitpold Coast in Antarctica.

French **Commandant Tilho** starts mapping the Tibesti range and Ennedi plateau in the Sahara.

Construction of the **first seaplane** by G.H. Curtiss helps ocean exploration.

1913

Hudson Stuck climbs to the summit of Mount McKinley, the highest peak in North America.

Gertrude Bell reaches Hail in central Arabia.

T.E. Lawrence surveys North Sinai with the Palestine Exploration Fund (1913-14).

Australian explorer **Douglas Mawson** survives a lone trek back from an expedition to Antarctica. His two companions – Ninnis and Mertz – die.

1914

Former US President Theodore Roosevelt and explorer Candido Rondon follow the **River of Doubt** to its confluence with the Amazon.

Plant hunter **Reginald Farrer** explores the wilds of Kansu region in northern China.

Ernest Shackleton leads another expedition to **Antarctica**.

1915

British army officer **Percy Sykes** begins travels in Chinese Turkestan, the Tien Shan range, the Pamir mountains and Takla Makan desert.

Canadian **Vihjalmur Stefansson** discovers Borden, Brock, Meighen and Logheed Islands in the Arctic.

EXPEDITION LEADER Ernest Shackleton (right) photographed at the Antarctic base in 1915.

1916

Ernest Shackleton makes his 800 mile (1300 km) **open-boat odyssey** from Antarctica to South Georgia.

T.E. Lawrence explores **Hejaz** while leading Arab guerrillas in Saudi Arabia.

CRASH LANDING Alcock and Brown make a bumpy landing in Ireland, on June 15, 1919.

Charles de Foucauld, a French explorer working among the Tuareg, is murdered by raiding Senusis.

1919

British aviators John Alcock and Arthur Brown, in a Vickers-Vimy aircraft, become the first men to **fly the Atlantic** Ocean, from Newfoundland to Ireland.

Ross and Keith Smith with J.M. Bennett and W.H. Shiers make the **first flight from England to Australia**. It takes 27 days.

1920

George Dyott pioneers Pacific-Amazon air routes.

Rosita Forbes travels across the Libyan desert to the forbidden city of **Kufara**.

François Laperrine dies in an air raid between Algiers and the Sudan.

Plant-hunter **Reginald Farrer** dies of pneumonia while collecting in Burma (now Myanmar).

1921

Lieutenant Colonel C.K. Howard-Bury launches the **first attempt on Everest**; sightings of the 'Abominable Snowman' are claimed.

1922

Tutankhamun's tomb is discovered by Howard Carter in Egypt's Valley of the Kings.

Sir Leonard Woolley begins **excavations at Ur** in Mesopotamia.

Roy Chapman Andrews discovers **dinosaur eggs** in Outer Mongolia.

Norbert Casteret, French pioneer of **cave exploration**, discovers prehistoric wall carvings in the Montespan cave.

1923

Ahmed Hassanein Bey explores unmapped areas of the **north-western Sahara**.

1924

Alexandra David-Néel is the first European woman to enter Lhasa.

Rosita Forbes travels from the Red Sea to the Blue Nile.

Gino Watkins explores between Kangerlugsuak and Prins Christians Sound on the east coast of Greenland.

SUMERIAN TREASURE The gold figure of a he-goat found in the royal cemetery at Ur in Mesopotamia.

Georges Marie Haardt leads **Citroën's 'Black Cruise'** of motor vehicles across the Sahara.

George Mallory and Andrew Irvine die during an attempt on **Mount Everest**.

1925

Colonel **Percy Fawcett** and his two companions vanish in Brazil's Mato Grosso, near the Xingu River.

Albert MacCarthy climbs **Mount Logan** (19 550 ft/5959 m), Canada's highest peak.

Delia Akeley becomes the first woman known to have crossed Africa.

A German research ship, SS *Meteor*, begins an important survey of the **South Atlantic** (continues to 1927).

1926

Richard Byrd and Floyd Bennett are first to **fly over the North Pole**.

Umberto Nobile and Roald Amundsen fly a **dirigible over the North Pole**.

Alan Cobham flies from Croydon to Cape Town and back.

Plant-hunter **Frank Kingdon-Ward** explores Tibet's Tsangpo Gorge.

English Brigadier Ralph Bagnold explores the **Libyan desert** (1926-32) discovering the rock art of prehistoric inhabitants.

Gertrude Bell dies of a drug overdose in Baghdad.

1927

Charles Lindbergh flies the Atlantic solo in *Spirit of St Louis*.

A **manned US balloon** attains a record altitude of 42470 ft (12945 m), but the pilot is dead on his return to Earth.

Charles Kingsford Smith and Charles Ulm **circumnavigate Australia** by aeroplane.

Gino Watkins leads an expedition to Edge Island, **Spitsbergen**.

1928

Herbert 'Bert' Hinkler is the first to fly solo from England to Australia.

DRAMATIC RESCUE An Italian magazine depicts the rescue of Umberto Nobile after his airship crash in 1928.

Charles Kingsford Smith and Charles Ulm make the **first trans-Pacific flight** and the first flights between Australia and New Zealand (there and back).

Pilot Richard Byrd establishes a **permanent Antarctic station** in the Bay of Whales, which he names Little America.

Umberto Nobile crashes his airship over the Arctic; Roald Amundsen dies in a seaplane attempting a rescue.

A Soviet-German team led by **Willi Rickmers** climbs Lenin Peak (23406 ft/7134 m), Russia's highest

PATIENT PLANNING American pilot Richard Byrd (second right) and his team map out their 1926 course over the North Pole.

mountain, situated in the Trans-Altai range.

1929

Richard Byrd and Bernt Balchen **fly over the South Pole**.

Cecil T. Madigan makes the first survey flights over Australia's Simpson Desert.

An Oxford University Expedition to **British Guiana** pioneers the study of the rain-forest canopy.

1930

Amy Johnson becomes the first woman to fly from Britain to Australia.

Freya Stark investigates early Persian sites in the Valley of the Assassins.

France's **Théodore Monod** begins archaeological studies in the western Sahara and Mauritania (continues to 1960).

Dr Alfred Wegener, the German meteorologist who first suggested that all of the continents had once been joined, dies while exploring Greenland.

The **British Arctic Air Route** expedition is launched (1930-1).

The remains of Swedish aeronaut **Solomon Andrée** are discovered on White Island in the Arctic.

1931

Bertram Thomas crosses Arabia's **Empty Quarter** from south to north.

Georges Marie Haardt launches the **'Yellow Cruise'** of motor vehicles across Asia.

1932

Harry St John Philby crosses the Empty Quarter from north to south, following a longer route than that of Bertram Thomas, and discovers the legendary 'ruined city of Wabar' – in reality, two giant meteor craters.

Henri Lhote crosses the Tanezrouft desert in the Sahara.

Amelia Earhardt becomes the first woman to fly solo across the Atlantic.

WORLD BEATER Wiley Post with *Winnie Mae*, the plane in which he made his record-breaking round-the-world flight in 1933.

Plant-hunter **George Forrest** dies during his seventh plant-hunting expedition in Yunnan.

1933

Wiley Post becomes the first person to fly solo around the world.

Jimmy Angel discovers the world's highest waterfall, later named **Angel Falls**, in Venezuela.

Michael J. Leahy discovers **Stone Age villages** in New Guinea's mountain interior.

Bert Hinkler is killed in an air crash in the Italian mountains.

Russian climber **Vitali Abalakov** is the first to ascend Communism Peak (24590 ft/ 7495 m), the highest mountain in the former Soviet Union, situated in the Pamirs.

The wreck of **HMS Bounty** is discovered off Pitcairn Island in the Pacific Ocean.

1934

Ocean explorer **William Beebe** descends to 3028 ft (923 m) in a bathysphere, off Bermuda.

A Soviet balloon *Osoaviakhim* rises 13 miles (21 km) into the stratosphere.

John Rymill launches **British Graham Land Expedition**, which discovers Palmer Peninsula to be part of the Antarctic mainland.

Richard Byrd **overwinters alone** at the Bolling Advanced Weather Station in Antarctica.

Charles Kingsford Smith and P.G. Taylor make the **first west to east crossing** of the Pacific Ocean.

1935

Swiss explorer **Ella Maillart**, with one companion, travels 3500 miles (5600 km) across Asia.

American millionaire Lincoln Ellsworth makes the first **trans-Antarctic flight**, obtaining the first sighting of the Vinson Massif.

Amelia Earhart is first to fly from Hawaii to the American mainland.

JUNGLE CASCADE The Angel Falls, the world's highest cataract, take their name from American airman Jimmy Angel, who reported them in his log book on November 14, 1933. Background: Wilfred Thesiger.

Round-the-world aviator Wiley Post is killed with his friend and passenger comedian Will Rogers in **an air crash over Alaska**.

Charles Kingsford Smith and J.T. Pethybridge disappear near Burma while flying from England to Australia.

1936

Edmund Colson crosses the Simpson Desert in Australia.

Amy Johnson flies from England to Cape Town in South Africa, and then all the way back.

1937

Soviet scientists set up a **drifting ice station** on an Arctic floe.

Amelia Earhart and her navigator Fred Noonan **vanish over the Pacific Ocean**, in the vicinity of Howland Island.

1939

Lincoln Ellsworth surveys much of eastern Antarctica.

1940

Prehistoric cave paintings at **Lascaux** in south-western France are discovered.

1941

Amy Johnson is killed when her plane crashes over the Thames Estuary.

1943

The invention of the **aqualung** by Jacques Cousteau and Emile Gagnan opens an era of undersea exploration.

1946

Wilfred Thesiger begins his travels in Arabia's Empty Quarter.

The **North Magnetic Pole** is observed by aircraft to have moved 250 miles (400 km) north of its charted position.

1947

Thor Heyerdahl sails the Pacific in his balsa raft, *Kon-Tiki*.

1948

Wilfred Thesiger crosses the inland steppes of Arabia and Oman.

Haroun Tazieff explores the crater of the Nyiragongo volcano in the Belgian Congo (now Democratic Republic of Congo).

1950

The Himalayan peak of **Annapurna** is conquered by the French duo, Maurice Herzog and Louis Lachenal.

French explorer **Raymond Maufrais** disappears in the Tumuc-Humac mountains of French Guiana.

Englishman **Sebastian Snow** (a non-swimmer) travels 3500 miles (5600 km) down the Amazon in canoes, balsa-wood rafts and river steamers.

1952

The **Dead Sea Scrolls** are recovered by a French-American team from caves at Qumran in Israel.

French climbers Lionel Terray and Guido Magnone conquer **Cerro FitzRoy** in Patagonia.

Jacques Cousteau explores the Red Sea in his research ship, *Calypso*.

Scientists discover a submarine river, the **Cromwell Current**, flowing under the Pacific, along the Equator.

1953

Edmund Hillary and Tenzing Norgay ascend **Mount Everest**.

SPECTACULAR FIND The Lascaux caves were discovered by four boys on September 12, 1940.

Austrian climber Hermann Buhl climbs the Himalayan peak of **Nanga Parbat** (26 657 ft/8125 m).

1954

Italian climbers Achille Compagnoni and Lino Lacedelli climb **K2**, the world's second highest mountain.

1955

Kangchenjunga (28 208 ft/8598 m), the world's third highest mountain, is climbed by Britons George Band and Joe Brown.

1956

Henry Lhote investigates Saharan rock paintings at **Tassili N'Ajjer**.

US seaplane *Skytrain* is the first aircraft to **land at the South Pole**.

Swedish investigators locate the wreck of the massive 17th-century flagship **Vasa**, in Stockholm Harbour.

1957

Richard Mason and Robin Hanbury-Tenison **cross South America** at its widest point.

International Geophysical Year is celebrated with concentrated research on Antarctica and oceanography.

Under Operation Deepfreeze II, supplies are landed at the South Pole to establish the permanent **Scott-Amundsen base**.

HIMALAYAN SNOWS The 1955 British team that climbed Kangchenjunga, on the Nepal-Sikkim border.

1958

The nuclear submarine USS *Nautilus* travels **under the North Pole**.

Vivian Fuchs's British Commonwealth Trans-Antarctic Expedition completes the **first land crossing of Antarctica**.

US scientists under Edward C. Thiel identify a huge mountain range, the **Dufek Massif**, in Antarctica.

1959

Austrian climber **Toni Egger** dies during an attempt on Cerro Torre in Patagonia; his Italian partner Cesare Maestri survives to make a disputed claim for the conquest of the summit.

Louis Leakey begins excavation for proto-human fossil relics in Tanzania's **Olduvai Gorge**.

A **submarine plateau** is discovered in the Arctic.

1960

Jacques Piccard and Donald Walsh, in USS *Trieste*, descend to the deepest spot on Earth, the **Marianas Trench**.

American diver Peter Throckmorton locates a **Bronze Age wreck** from 1200 BC off Cape Gelidonya, Turkey.

1962

Jacques Cousteau establishes his first undersea habitat, **Conshelf 1**.

French cave explorer **Michel Siffre** spends two months underground, investigating a subterranean glacier

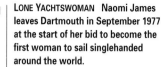

LONE YACHTSWOMAN Naomi James leaves Dartmouth in September 1977 at the start of her bid to become the first woman to sail singlehanded around the world.

in the Scarasson chasm in the South of France.

1964

Robin Hanbury-Tenison crosses South America in a rubber dinghy.

American divers live under water in **Sealab**, off Bermuda, for nine days.

1966

An American team led by Nicholas Clinch is first to climb the **Vinson Massif** in Antarctica.

1967

Lone yachtsman **Sir Francis Chichester** completes his round-the-world voyage in *Gipsy Moth IV*.

1968

Colonel **John Blashford-Snell** descends the Blue Nile in Africa.

American oceanographic ship *Glomar Challenger* begins taking sample cores of the **ocean floor**.

Remains of wrecked ships from the **Spanish Armada** are explored off the south-west coast of Ireland.

1969

Wally Herbert's British **Trans-Arctic Expedition** completes the first surface crossing of the Arctic Ocean via the North Pole.

John Fairfax rows solo across the Atlantic.

Jacques Piccard's research submarine **Ben Franklin** undertakes a 30-day investigation of the Gulf Stream.

1970

Thor Heyerdahl sails *Ra II* across the Atlantic.

A team of **Japanese women climbers** conquer Annapurna III in the Himalayas.

Cesare Maestri conquers Cerro Torre in Patagonia.

1971

The **source of the Amazon** is identified by American Loren McIntyre among the snowbound headwaters of the upper Apurimac.

Florida treasure-seeker Mel Fisher locates the drowned wreck of a Spanish treasure ship, the **Atocha**.

1972

NASA launches the **Landsat** satellite.

Project FAMOUS begins exploring the **Mid-Atlantic Ridge**.

Relics from the wreck of **Batavia** (sunk 1629) are excavated from the ocean floor off Western Australia.

The brothers Villas Boas make contact with the legendary **Kreen Akrore** tribe of South America.

1975

Japan's **Junko Tabei** becomes the first woman to ascend Everest.

Michel Siffre explores caves in the Poptun region of Guatemala, discovering ancient wall carvings and fragments of Mayan pottery.

Hot-air balloon **Condor 1** flies over the Nazca Plains in Peru, demonstrating that ancient peoples of South America may have known the secrets of flight.

1977

The Soviet nuclear icebreaker **Arktika**

reaches the North Pole, becoming the first surface ship to cut through the Arctic ice pack all the way to the Pole.

Tim Severin sails to North America in his leather boat *Brendan.*

1978

Japanese adventurer **Naomi Uemura** becomes the first man to reach the North Pole solo by dog sled.

Dedicated ocean satellite **SEASAT** maps the world's ocean surface, demonstrating differences in elevation that reflect the topography of the ocean floor.

Naomi James becomes the **first woman to sail single-handed** around the world. Her voyage in *Express Crusader,* from and to Dartmouth, Devon, took 272 days.

1979

Gossamer Albatross achieves the first manpowered flight across the English Channel.

1980

Sarawak Chamber, the world's largest cave chamber, is discovered in the Gunung Mulu National Park.

Reinhold Messner climbs Everest solo, without oxygen.

1981

Graeme Dingle and Peter Hillary make the first lengthways **traverse of the Himalayas**, a 3000 mile (5000 km), 10-month trek from Sikkim to Pakistan.

1982

Ranulph Fiennes' **Transglobe Expedition** completes the first circumnavigation of the world via the North and South Poles.

1984

American divers discover a **3400-year-old shipwreck** near the seaport of Kas off the Turkish coast.

1985

Robert Ballard locates the wreck of the *Titanic.*

Lorenzo and Mirella Ricciardi's **African Rainbow Equatorial**

Expedition crosses Africa by boat, in the wake of Livingstone and Stanley.

The **Wahiba Sands Project** is launched by the Royal Geographical Society and the Sultanate of Oman.

1986

American **Will Steger** leads the first overland expedition to the North Pole since 1909 unsupported by aircraft.

Michael Asher and Mariantonietta Peru make the first **west-east crossing of the Sahara by camel**.

Malaysian Heritage and Scientific Expedition find previously unknown flora and fauna in the Endau Rompin area.

The world's **largest underwater lake** is discovered in the Drachenhauchloch cave near Grootfontein, Namibia.

1987

Richard Branson flies the Atlantic in a hot-air balloon.

Exploration begins of the longest known underwater cave, **Nohoch Na Chih**, in Mexico.

GLORIA (Global Long Range Inclined Asdic), a side-scan imaging system towed behind a vessel, is used to investigate the ocean floor.

1988

Will Steger makes a south-to-north crossing of the Greenland ice cap.

Diving off Hawaii, American aquanaut Sylvia Earle reaches a depth of 1250 ft (380 m), to demonstrate open ocean use of the atmospheric diving suit known as a **Jim-suit**.

ICE CUTTER In 1977 the Soviet nuclear icebreaker *Arktika* cut its way through the ice all the way to the North Pole. Background: Junko Tabei climbs Mount Everest in 1975.

1989

Robert Ballard locates the wreck of Hitler's battleship, the **Bismarck.**

A study sponsored by the **National Geographic Society** concludes that Robert Peary got to within 5 miles (8 km) of the North Pole.

Britain's hi-tech research ship *Charles Darwin* completes a three-year round-the-world voyage, collecting data on ocean currents, weather patterns, temperature and salinity.

The world depth record for cavers is set by the French **Groupe Vulcain**

DAUNTING CHALLENGE The south face of Lhotse (27 890 ft/8501 m), on the Nepal-Tibet border, succumbed to a solo ascent by Yugoslav Toni Cesen in 1990.

team, who descend to 5256 ft (1602 m) in the Gouffre Jean Bernard, France.

1990

Will Steger and Jean-Louis Etienne complete the **first unmechanised crossing of Antarctica**, with dogs and sledges, from west to east, via the South Pole.

1993

The previously unknown Stone Age **Liawep** people are discovered in the jungles of Papua New Guinea.

1994

A Franco-British expedition discovers the **source of the Mekong River**, in Tibet.

1996

The **source of the Amazon** is identified as an underground glacier in Apachita Crevice, South Peru.

1998

David Hempleman-Adams completes the **Adventurers' Grand Slam** – the conquest of the highest peaks on each of the seven continents, as well as the North and South Poles.

1999

Bertrand Piccard and Brian Jones are the first to **circumnavigate the globe non-stop in a hot-air balloon**. It took them 19 days, 1 hour and 49 minutes to travel the 26 602 miles (42 810 km) in *Breitling Orbiter 3.*

INDEX

ACKNOWLEDGMENTS

Abbreviations:
T = Top; M = Middle; B = Bottom;
L = Left; R = Right

3 Werner Forman, L; Royal Geographical Society, LM; Mary Evans Picture Library, RM; Popperfoto, R. 6 Science Photo Library, T; Royal Geographical Society, B. 7 Chris Caldicott/Royal Geographical Society. 8 Roger Mear/Royal Geographical Society. 8-9 Corbis-Bettman. 10 State Library of New South Wales, T; Hulton-Getty, B. 11 Culver Pictures Inc, T; Popperfoto, B. 12 NASA/Science Photo Library, T; David Parker/Science Photo Library, B. 13 Rex Features, T; Popperfoto, B. 14 Paul Grover/Frank Spooner pictures/GAMMA. 15 Christine Osborne Pictures, background; Werner Forman Archive, L; Hulton-Getty, LM; Popperfoto, MR, R. 16 Hulton-Getty, T; Richard Packwood/Oxford Scientific Films, B. 17 AKG. 18 Royal Geographical Society, T; Royal Geographical Society, B. 19 Mansell/Time Inc. 20 Roger-Viollet, L; 20-21 Christine Osborne, background. 21 Popperfoto, L; Roger-Viollet, R. 22 Mary Evans Picture Library, T; Popperfoto, B. 23 Topham Picturepoint. 24 Werner Forman Archive, T; Popperfoto, M; Topham Picturepoint, B. 25 Werner Forman Archive, T; Robert Harding Picture Library, B. 26 Roger-Viollet, L; AKG, R. 27 Hutchinson Library. 28 Popperfoto, T; Royal Geographical Society, B. 29 Popperfoto, T; AKG, L; Royal Geographical Society, R. 30 Christine Osborne Pictures, T; Royal Geographical Society, B. 31 Oxford Scientific Films, background; Royal Geographical Society, L; Bruce Coleman, LM; Werner Forman Archive, RM; Werner Forman Archive, R. 32 Royal Geographical Society. 33 Tony Stone/Hulton-Getty. 34 Tony Stone/Hulton-Getty, background; Hulton-Getty, T. 35 Royal Geographical Society. 36 AKG. 37 Robert Harding Picture Library, background; Royal Geographical Society, T, B. 38 Dr Frances Wood/British Library, TL; Robert Harding Picture Library, BR. 39 Robert Harding Picture Library, L; Werner Forman Archive/Stein Collection, British Museum, BR. 40 AGK, TR; Robert Harding Picture Library, B. 41 Hulton-Getty. 42 Hulton-Getty, T. 42-43 Royal Geographical Society,B. 43 Royal Geographical Society, M. 44 Jean-Loup Charmet, TL, TR; Roger-Viollet, B. 45 Jean-Loup Charmet, T; Roger-Viollet, B. 46 Popperfoto, T; Mary Evans Picture Library, M; Roger-Viollet, B. 47 Royal Geographical Society, TR; Bruce Coleman, BL. 48 Royal Botanical Gardens, Kew. 49 Heather Angel, TM, BL; Oxford Scientific Films, BR. 50 Heather Angel. 51 State Library of New South Wales, TR, MR, BL. 52 Darren Jew/Auscape, background; State Library of New South Wales, T. 53 Roger Brown/Auscape, TR; D.Parer

& E.Parer-Cook/Auscape, ML. 54 British Library. 55 Werner Forman Archive, TR; Hulton-Getty, BL; Topham Picturepoint, BR. 56 British Library, T, B. 57 Christine Osborne Pictures, background; Topham Picturepoint, BL. 58 Popperfoto, TR; Roger-Viollet, BL. 59 Royal Geographical Society. 60 Royal Geographical Society. 61 Royal Geographical Society, TL, M; Hulton-Getty, BR. 62 Christine Osborne Pictures, background; Royal Geographical Society, BR. 63 Royal Geographical Society, BL; Topham Picturepoint, BR. 64 Royal Geographical Society, TM; BL. 64-65 Bruce Beehler/NHPA. 66 State Library of New South Wales, TR, BL, BM. 67 Edward Marriott, T, M. 68 Edward Marriott, T, L. 69 John Cleare/Mountain Camera, background; Brown Brothers, L; Mountain Camera, ML; Culver Pictures Inc, MR; Royal Geographical Society, R. 70 Culver Pictures Inc. 71 Kevin Schafer/NHPA. 72 Popperfoto, TR; John Cleare/Mountain Camera, BL. 73 Brown Brothers, T, B. 74-75 Tom Stack & Associates. 75 Brown Brothers, BM. 76 Hulton-Getty, T; Kermit Roosevelt, B. 77 Culver Pictures Inc. 78 Brian Parker/Tom Stack & Associates, T; Library of Congress/Corbis, B. 79 Corbis/Bettman, T; Corbis, B. 80 Royal Geographical Society, TR, B. 81 Roger-Viollet, M; Popperfoto, B. 82 Popperfoto,TR; Mountain Camera, B. 84 Corbis-Bettman/UPI. 85 Corbis-Bettman/UPI, TL; Popperfoto, BR. 86 Hulton-Getty, TM. 86-87 NHPA, TL-R. 87 Adrian Cowell/Topham Picturepoint, BR. 88 Adrian Cowell/Topham Picturepoint, M, BL. 89 Tony Stone/Hulton-Getty, background; Jean-Loup Charmet, L; Hulton-Getty, LM; Roger Mear/Royal Geographical Society, RM; Popperfoto, R. 90 Corbis, TR; Roger-Viollet, B. 91 Mary Evans Picture Library, T; Hulton-Getty, BR. 92 Jean-Loup Charmet, TL. 92-93 Hulton-Getty, B. 93 AKG, TR. 94 Mary Evans Picture Library, M; Royal Geographical Society, B. 95 Mary Evans Picture Library, BR. 96 Popperfoto, T. 96-97 Royal Geographical Society, B. 97 Royal Geographical Society, TL; Popperfoto, M. 98 Hulton-Getty, TR; Popperfoto, BL. 99 Roger Mear/Royal Geographical Society, T; Popperfoto, BR. 100 Corbis-Bettman, TR; Roger-Viollet, M. 101 Corbis-Bettman. 102 AKG, TR; Culver Pictures Inc, BL. 103 Popperfoto, background, BR. 104-5 Popperfoto 106 AKG, T; Culver Pictures Inc, BL; Hulton-Getty, BR. 107 Mary Evans Picture Library, MR; Hulton-Getty, BL. 108 Popperfoto, T; Mary Evans Picture Library, BL. 109 Topham Picturepoint, TR, B. 110 Mountain Camera,T; Tony Stone/Hulton-Getty, B background; Topham Picturepoint, BL. 111 The Mary Rose Trust, Portsmouth, background; Hulton-Getty, L; Culver Pictures Inc, LM; Mary Evans Picture Library, RM; Popperfoto, R. 112 Rex Features, T; Culver Pictures Inc, B.

113 Science Photo Library, M; Hulton-Getty, BR. 114-15 Culver Pictures Inc. 115 Popperfoto, BR. 116 Hulton-Getty, T, B. 117 Hulton-Getty, TR; Popperfoto, B. 118 Popperfoto, T; Hulton-Getty, BL. 119 Mary Evans Picture Library, TR; Culver Pictures Inc, BL. 120 Greg Ochocki/Oxford Scientific Films, TR; Planet Earth Pictures, BL. 121 Popperfoto. 122-3 Kev Deacon/Ardea, B background. 123 Popperfoto, MR. 124 Rex Features, TR; Keystone Press Agency, BL. 125 Hulton-Getty, T, B. 126 Hulton-Getty. 127 Hulton-Getty, T, B. 128 Rex Features, TR; Frank Spooner Pictures, BL. 129 The Mary Rose Trust, Portsmouth, M; Frank Spooner Pictures, B. 130 Sygma, M, B. 131 The Image Bank, background; Culver Pictures, L; Jean-Loup Charmet, LM; Popperfoto, RM; Bruce Coleman, R. 132 Hulton-Getty, R; Culver Pictures Inc, BL. 133 Jean-Loup Charmet, TL; Hulton-Getty, BR. 134 Frank Spooner Pictures, TR; Rex Features, BL. 135 AKG. 136 AKG. 137 Jean-Loup Charmet. 138 AKG. 138-9 Popperfoto, background. 139 AKG, MR. 140 Bruce Coleman, BL; Frank Spooner Pictures, BM. 141 Hulton-Getty, TR, BL. 142 Hulton-Getty. 143 Hulton-Getty, T, B. 144 Popperfoto, background; Rex Features, TR. 145 Popperfoto, TR; Hulton-Getty, B. 146 Royal Geographical Society, T, B. 147 Royal Geographical Society, TR; Popperfoto, BL. 148 Rich Kirchner/NHPA, L; Royal Geographical Society, R. 149 Royal Geographical Society, TL; Rex Features, BR. 150 Hulton-Getty, L; Mary Evans Picture Library, R; Royal Geographical Society, B. 150-1 Science Museum/Science and Society Picture Library, background. 151 Popperfoto, T; Corbis, L; Michael Holford, R. 152 Mary Evans Picture Library, T; Culver Pictures Inc, MR, B. 153 Royal Geographical Society, background; Images Colour Library, TL; Popperfoto, BR. 154 Hulton-Getty, background; Topham/Press Association, TR; Royal Geographical Society, BL. 155 John Cleare/Mountain Camera, background, B; Colin Monteath/Mountain Camera, T.

Front Cover: Corbis, T background; Royal Geographical Society, B background; Roger-Viollet, L; Jean-Loup Charmet, LM; State Library of New South Wales, RM; Popperfoto, R.

Back Cover: Corbis, T background; Royal Geographical Society, B background; Hulton-Getty, TL; Royal Geographical Society, TR; Frank Spooner Pictures, BL; Mary Evans Picture Library, BR.

Endpapers (front and back): John Frost Historical News Archives.

The editors are grateful to the following individuals and publishers for their kind permission to quote passages from the books below:

AA from Journeys of the Great Explorers by Burton, Cavendish and Stonehouse, 1992
A & C Black from Women Climbing by Bill Birkett and Bill Peascod, 1989
George Allen & Unwin from The Kon-Tiki Expedition by Thor Heyerdahl, 1950
Arms and Armour Press from SAS: The Jungle Frontier by Peter Dickens, 1983
Arnold from The Rainbow Bridge by Reginald Farrer, 1921
Barrie & Jenkins from The Rape of Egypt by Peter France, 1991
BBC Books from The Kon-Tiki Man by Christopher Ralling, 1990
Bloomsbury Books from The Great Explorers by Piers Pennington, 1989
Bloomsbury Books from Man Flies by Nancy Winters, 1997
Jonathan Cape Ltd from Arabia Felix by Bertram Thomas, 1932
Jonathan Cape Ltd from Borneo People by Malcolm MacDonald, 1956
Jonathan Cape Ltd from Plant Hunter in Manipur by Frank Kingdon-Ward, 1952
Cassell from My Life as an Explorer by Sven Hedin, 1926
Century Publishing from The Valleys of the Assassins by Freya Stark, 1982
Collins from A Book of Air Journeys by Ludovic Kennedy, 1982
Collins from Mallowan's Memoirs: The Autobiography of Max Mallowan, 1977
Daily Telegraph, Thursday April 30, 1998
Dolphin Press from The Golden Monarch by Michael Carter, 1972
Elder & Co. from Scott's Last Expedition by Smith, 1913
Fontana from Citadels Of Mystery by L. Sprague de Camp and Catherine C. de Camp, 1972
Gale Research Inc. from Explorers and Discoverers of the World edited by Daniel B. Baker, 1993
Guinness Publishing from The Guinness Book of Explorers and Exploration edited by Michele Gavet-Imbert, 1991
Robert Hale from Cousteau by Richard Munson, 1989
Robert Hale from Her Name Titanic by Charles Pellegrino, 1988
Hamish Hamilton from The Amazon by Robin Furneaux, 1969
Hamish Hamilton from Craters of Fire by Haroun Tazieff, 1952
Hamish Hamilton from The Silent World by Jacques Cousteau, 1953
Hamlyn from The Royal Geographical Society History of World Exploration edited by John Keay, 1991
Harper's Monthly Magazine from The Discovery of Machu Picchu, April, 1913
Harrap from Recent Exploration by Charles E. Key, 1946
Rupert Hart-Davis from Bayonets to Lhasa by Peter Fleming, 1962
Heinemann from The River Amazon by Alex Shoumatoff, 1979
Hodder & Stoughton from Francis Chichester by Anita Leslie, 1975

Hodder & Stoughton from The Lost Country by Jasper Becker, 1992
Hodder & Stoughton from To the Ends of the Earth by Ranulph Fiennes, 1983
Hutchinson from The Brendan Voyage by Tim Severin, 1978
London from Explorers All by Sir P. Sykes, 1939
Macmillan Publishers Ltd from Ruins of Desert Cathay by Aurel Stein, 1912
Mitchell Beazley from Great Climbs edited by Chris Bonington, 1994
Mitchell Beazley from The World Atlas of Exploration by Eric Newby, 1975
John Murray Ltd from The South Pole by Roald Amundsen, translated by A.G. Chater, 1912
John Murray Ltd from The Worst Desert on Earth by Charles Blackmore, 1995
National Geographic, Vol 193, No. 2, February 1998
Natural History Magazine, June 1948
Thomas Nelson & Sons Ltd from The Last Secrets by John Buchan, 1923
Orbis from Ballooning by Dick Wirth and Jerry Young, 1980
Oxford University Press from The Myth of the Explorer by Beau Riffenburgh, 1994
Oxford University Press from The Oxford Book of Exploration by Robin Hanbury-Tenison, 1993
Oxford University Press from Unsuitable for Ladies edited by Jane Robinson, 1994
Penguin Books from Across the Top of the World by Wally Herbert, 1969
Penguin Books from The Age of Illusion by Ronald Blythe, 1963
Picador from A Book of Travellers' Tales by Eric Newby, 1984
Picador from The Lost Tribe by Edward Marriott, 1996
Pimlico from The Tribe That Hides from Man by Adrian Cowell, 1995
Quartet Books from Gertrude Bell by H.V.F. Winstone, 1978
Salamander Press from Into the Heart of Borneo by Redmond O'Hanlon, 1984
Sinclair Stevenson from Last Disco in Outer Mongolia by Nick Middleton, 1992
Strand Magazine, February 1904
Swan Hill Press from The Search for Sunken Treasure by Robert F. Marx and Jennifer Marx, 1993
Time-Life Books from The Australian Outback by Ian Moffitt
Weidenfeld & Nicolson from Gobi by John Man, 1997
Weidenfeld & Nicolson from Man Against Nature by Charles Neider, 1995

78-012-3

DAILY EXPRESS

20,833

MONDAY MAY 29 1967

Weather: Sunny spells; showers

Price 4d.

WELL SAILED SIR!

Nasser threat of new Suez ban

TWO Israeli torpedo boats dashed out of Eilath last night towards the Strait of Tiran. Two Jordanian patrol

Armada of cheers greet Chichester

From
CYRIL AYNSLEY, ALASTAIR WILSON
MICHAEL CHARLESTON, ALFRED DRAPER

HOW I DISCOVERED THE SOUTH POLE.

EXCLUSIVE CABLE TO "THE DAILY CHRONICLE."

PTAIN AMUNDSEN'S OWN NARRATIVE.

GE OF CONGRATULATION FROM KING GEORGE.

SUNDAY MIRROR, December 31, 1973   PAGE 2

THE DEAD SAVED OUR LIVES

st the story of
as hushed up.
ere were defiant
o different from
survivor. "The
." Another said:
sus, and how he
and blood among
n fact there has
criticism. Everyone
ill to live.

TUTANKH
MARVELLOUS EGY
From our Cairo Cor

30th November 1922
day Lord Carnarvon and Mr
rd Carter revealed the most
ional archeological discovery
century: the tomb of the
an King Tutankhamen.
bly, it was still intact in
grave robbers and the

The Chicago Daily T

VOLUME LXVIII.—NO. 214.

TUESDAY, SEPTEMBER 7, 1909.—TWENTY-SIX PAGES.

3 a.m.
FLAS

COMMANDER PEARY ALSO REACHES NORTH POLE; D

PEARY VICTOR IN POLAR DASH

EXPLORER WILL WIRE EXCLUSIVE STORY OF ACHIEVEMENT FOR TOMORRO

Peary and the Dramatic Scene He Re-enacted at the North

Returning from North He

FU

F